COCKROACH ON
MY SHOULDER

Richard Newman

David Pack

1945 - 2019

A great friend and a roguish question master

John Cooper

1947 – 2018

A very fine Architect and a good rat catcher

The events which took place in the mid-Seventies in the Middle East are all those from my own experiences.

I have, however, altered timescales around in a few instances to allow the book to be smoothed out, for the ebb and flow of time in real life always provides pockets of monotony which require filling. I hope you will forgive me.

It is essential to say here, before you begin to read my story, that although I laugh and joke at the hilarious events I experienced with my friends, the Qataris, you should know that I laugh *with* them and not *at* them. Qataris, like the English, separated from their politicians are loving, cheerful people, good friends, wanting to succeed, wanting to improve their way of life, wanting the best for their families. Familiar aspirations? I wish them all, good luck in the future and thank them for their goodwill towards me and my family.

I have changed some personal names. They will recognise themselves and I trust they are content with the characterisations portrayed. They are all, every one of them, extremely nice people, hardworking, dedicated to their respective companies and practices. They are also very clever at their jobs. That is why they were in Doha at the time.

When my wife and I look back on our time in the Gulf forty years ago, which is often, we find the excitement of the time undimmed, probably in retrospect, the best time of our lives.

Richard Newman

Contents

Preface

Just forty years separates the equivalent of a frontier town in 1860's America with a sovereign state capable of building air-conditioned football stadia to accommodate the World Cup in 2022. It is a quantum leap, almost inconceivable in 1976, yet, now the sands are covered in concrete and titanium steel, the desert blooms green from artificially created micro-climates and the name of its radio station *Al Jazeera* rebounds daily around the world.

It is like a chemical formula learnt at school. Crude oil + sea water = growth + development, and the Qataris have both in abundance.

What is just as amazing is the speed that this has happened. For years, the British and other Imperial powers held sway over the Arab nations of the Middle East until full independence after the Second World War led to a re-evaluation of what could be achieved with these barren lands.

It was oil of course, a single product, a sole asset, for each of the Gulf states but it was what the world wanted, and they wanted it in spades. Oil has often been a dangerous temptation for a powerful state to invade an oil-rich, less well-armed country and we have seen just such invasions in the intervening years since the end of war in Europe. But, in 1976 the Gulf slumbered in the summer heat, as they drilled for oil at $13.10 a barrel.

To these countries of sand and shattered rock, the wealth created was mind-numbing; it was a time of ludicrous waste and a frantic race to try and catch up with the western nations who were only too interested in helping them spend it. With wealth, comes the ability to buy in expertise, so the sea can be turned into potable water which in turn allows trees to green the land, a colour in this part of the world which had been, previously, as rare as hens' teeth.

But it is the people of this ancient land which provide the most interest, for they do not appear, at first sight, to have changed at all. Sure, they disport themselves with Rolex watches, though they were wearing them in 1975, and they drive around in Mercedes rather than mounting a camel, but their clothing hasn't changed, so a photograph taken a century ago would not have looked much different from today.

It was into this exotic, chaotic and confused world that, in 1975 I stepped down from a plane with my family, to see what pickings there might be on the floor. In those days, there were no mobile phones, no social media, Facebook or Twitter. It meant we all lived in a smaller world where face to face contact was essential for business to thrive. Arab and Jew lived side by side and Islam was known as a peaceful religion, respected as a major force for stability and peace. How can just forty years change all this? While technological advance is a wonderful and necessary gift to us all, perhaps we shouldn't wipe the chalk board completely clean of all we have learned. We need to regain the personal relationships of amity in business and politics, and allow space to come between us and our twenty-four-hour news gathering services?

So, I am looking down from Google's satellite at 30,000 thousand feet on my computer screen trying to isolate the countless new roads which cloud my thoughts; I search for the ancient Suq and a harbour of sea-going dhows and I recall a time when the view was not as muddled as it is now. The Suq, with its smells and sights has gone; our own road is subsumed under a maze of unrecognisable streets. It is progress, I know, but my memories, stirred by the view, take me back to a time when my back didn't creak, and I could swim for an hour without tiring. We are all advancing down a road which we don't know where it will end. As I said, it is progress but just once in a while, it is nice to dwell in the past and remember very good times.

CHAPTER ONE

The Thumb of Qatar

If I had tried it by myself, possibly looking into a mirror as I spoke, it might have sounded like 'Guitar' or 'Catarrh.' But I wasn't alone, in fact I was sitting with two hundred and eighty other travellers. The correct pronunciation arrived at my left ear. It sounded much softer than catarrh, a subtle issue and quite different to any English sound I had heard.

'I beg your pardon?'

This was, after all, nineteen seventy-five and we were still reasonably polite as a nation. The joys of 'wha-?' and 'yer' and 'kay', were yet to come.

'*Ghaht-arrh*, you pronounce it *Ghaht-arrh*.' The bespectacled, diminutive Arab in a gown of immaculate Egyptian cotton smiled up at me apologetically. 'Keep the 'H' deep in your throat. As though you were going to cough. Swing the first sound into the second.'

'*Ghaht-arrh*,' I repeated, aware this was my first Arabic lesson. Jay, my wife, overhearing me, wondered if I was going to be sick and pointed anxiously to a labelled bag in the front of my seat provided for the purposes. 'Arabic class,' was my reply in a rather patronising manner, though I nodded in appreciation to my neighbour at the free lesson. He smiled back, safe in the knowledge he was probably richer than me.

As the vast and brand-new Gulf Air Tri-Star banked left I could see the thumb of Qatar projecting out of the hand of Saudi Arabia. It was as if the Qataris on the left side of the Arabian Gulf (and not the Persian Gulf as we had been taught at school), were cocking a snoop at the Iranians on the right-hand side.

'There's... *Ghaht-arrh*,' I said to my wife. 'And there's Doha, the capital where we are going to live.' This second comment was directed also to my two sons.

'I thought we were going to live in catarrh?'

'No, darling.' I knew she was only winding me up for she had been listening to me quite carefully during my lesson. 'We're almost there.'

Below, the beige, barren, bleak land, criss-crossed with paler tracks which meandered almost aimlessly in all directions, heaved itself like a beached whale out of the turquoise water before disappearing again somewhere in the direction of Saudi Arabia from where we had come.

'*Ghaht-arrh*,' I repeated to my wife, confident now in my pronunciation. Perhaps pronouncing correctly, the name of the country I was going to live in was quite important.

'Thank you.' I said to my friend.

My neighbour had a smile on his face. '*Shu-kran*,'" he replied as he tightened his safety belt. 'Thank you.'

It was my first contact with the people with whom we were to spend the next five years, and though brief, it made me feel that the suddenness with which we had been projected into this new world, was going to be worth it.

The Architectural practice I was working for had decided, in its Partners' wisdom, to get out into the developing world despite the fact we, as British citizens were unable to take more than a pittance out of the country in the way of funds to start up a new business. It was a problem.

While reviewing progress one day on site, a nuclear submarine base in Devonport, the Naval Dockyard of Plymouth, the idea of expanding overseas manifested itself in the form of a Partner calling at my cabin (quite important then?) to see if I would *up-sticks*, family and all, and set up an office in the Middle East. He had warned me he was travelling down from Guildford but did not tell me what it was about. That was strange in itself for we had recently completed the usual monthly site meeting and nothing of a serious nature had reared its head.

'How about Ga-ttarh for starters?' He asked straight away. It sounded like something one should play.

'Where?' came my asinine reply. Anyone knows where Ga-ttarh is...except me that is.

In fact, I did not: have a clue, that is, and in nineteen seventy-five probably not many people outside the Foreign Office or a rough neck knew where it was, or even whether it was a country, and not simply a term for an acute exudation of mucus and white blood cells.

'You will find it quite sunny. Plenty to do, lots of work. Bit of a change from designing nuclear submarine engine cleaning rooms, but all part of life's rich tapestry.'

I was to be reminded of that phrase for the next five years, and in fact, it has stayed with me to the present day. The idea of the country being ' a bit sunny' was one which allowed me to dine out on for many years to come.

'Where would I live? And what are the schools like?' My family consisted of not only a wife, but two sons.

'Details, my dear boy, details we will sort out for you. So, you are up for it then?' the return ball was quick.

'Perhaps it might be an idea if I were to sound out my wife first?' I suggested with a concerned frown. My face, at the news, had just puckered up into what could be described as the underside of a flounder, anxious as I was to keep in with the Partners, but I could just hear Jay saying '… well dear, don't be silly, you've got a nuclear submarine base to finish.' And then, not many seconds later, 'besides, Qatar is a very small peninsular in the Arabian Gulf with a population so small you could get Qatar's residents into Plymouth, four times over. There's no work there. You would need to go to Saudi Arabia for that, and women cannot drive there.'

Outside my site hut, Ark Royal sat (?) in the adjacent dry dock as men swarmed over her decks. She was part of my everyday life now. I would miss her and the hunter-killer submarines on my side of the dock. This offer was right out of the blue and needed careful thought.

You will have gathered already that my wife was, and still is the brains of the family who is often misjudged by me, although to be fair to me as well, this last statement proved she could be wrong…occasionally. When, finally, that evening, I put the point to her that the Partners really did want me to go, she confirmed her wish to be with me, as seamlessly as though it were to be Southend-on-Sea. She would sort the schools out one way or another.

Three weeks later we were in the clouds on a Gulf Air TriStar jet, then only four years from its first roll-out; a new summer suit for me and a variety of frocks for her.

'Do the boys need spades and buckets for all that sand?' I had asked, 'Or will the shops have some?'

When I look back now on those first days with considerable hindsight, I cringe at the naivety of it all, but we were still in our early thirties, our sons ten and eight respectively and a thirst for exploring, what was still a frontier to most people. Besides, the Partners had hinted there could be a Partnership in the future if I kept my nose clean. I wasn't actually sure what that well-worn phrase meant, but I was determined to do my bit for the practice.

My fellow traveller handed over a small pasteboard card. 'Anything, anytime,' Ahmad murmured. '*Insha'Allah.*'

On day one I could report to my Partners that the first essential business contact had been made. Contacts were incredibly important as we urgently needed cash flow to enable the practice in the Gulf to survive. In those long gone days when Harold Wilson's Government was so strapped for sterling we were only able to export £25,000 but even such a paltry sum had taken ages to convince the Government that we would be bringing back ten times that amount each year.

Years later looking back over the balance between our democratic, but essentially, 'tram-lined' Government's way of governing the U.K. against a benign dictatorship into which we had just flown, the democratic way of life did win, but it was a closer call than I had ever believed when in England.

For the present, I was only interested in getting work and seeing some buildings rise out of the sand.

We landed with scarcely a bump, my mind at rest now that the flying over endless waterless desert was over. It had not given me a comfortable feeling, having seen *Lawrence of Arabia* twice, the film, that is, Lawrence had been dead for forty years by this time. As we passed through our cabin to the steps, there being no loading bridge at this fairly basic airport, all four of us peeked in to the first-class cabin where the seats had been installed with gold-coloured leather *thrones*: there was no other way to describe them.

Being restless as always to move on, I was one of the first arriving at the exit point where the steps disappeared into the Arabian night. There was, however, a problem, as it was clear, the tarmac had caught fire. Certainly, the heat from a blaze was stinging my face, so close was it from the plane. It was a shock as the cabin had been air-conditioned to a nice twenty-one degrees. Cocooned, we had all been lulled into that comfortable state of mind so that our sensors had geared down ready for the night. Shoved in the back by my sons, I stepped forward ready to help but could see no fire, not even a flame from a lighter.

Dawning came quickly: there was no fire, solely the heat of the day being given up by the tarmac, one enormous night storage heater. I had come to believe, or at least, psyched myself up that the Gulf weather could be resisted with equanimity. If, at eleven p.m. on an April night it was like this, what on God's planet would it be like tomorrow, or worse, August lunchtime? Of course, it could cloud over, but the possibility of it raining for the next six months would result in about four millimetres of moisture. Oh, and a high of forty and at night-time down to a cool twenty-eight. Besides even when it rained it did not mean the temperature would fall. All this information came, courtesy of the material I had gleaned from the library. It might be early spring in truth, but summer was the next season in line.

An open balcony hanging on the rather tattered Terminal building was crammed with people, from Arab to Indian to Caucasian, the Westerners in short-sleeved shirts, some of the locals in identical outfits as my travelling partner, though quite a few others were much more dirty. The attentive and curious audience, for that is what they were, craned their necks at the residents returning from holiday or a shopping spree. It was evident this was the local entertainment featuring the arriving passengers as they trundled across the tarmac from the plane carrying enormous bundles, mostly wrapped in cloth. Had those come from inside the plane?

We walked into the Customs Hall where ancient, control booths housed the Immigration officers. The sign for Immigration was spelt: *Immygration,* a small point but worth observing on my first day, compounded by a hand-written sign on a door stating *Toylette.* 'I' before 'e' except after 'y' perhaps?

Our four passports were handed over whereupon a smartly dressed Pakistani officer positioned a purple triangular stamp on Page thirty-one, twenty-six, four and seventeen respectively rather than on Page One of the otherwise pristine sheets of paper.

The next stage was to place our suitcases on a table. Around us, we became submerged in total bedlam. People were shouting as they pushed past, the warmth of their sweat making contact with my, already perspiring body. (For God's sake, I was still wearing a vest!). The perspiration poured, nay cascaded, down my face, coming to rest on the lower rims of my glasses (I looked, with my black frames rather like Michael Caine in those days, well, a very little bit), where I stared out on a world half above and half below water level.

'Whisky?' an obviously local bureaucrat demanded.

'Er, no thank you. Not at the moment. Er…*shu-kran*.' I was rather pleased with the ending.

The other sighed loudly, looking to the ceiling for help. 'Have you any whisky with you?"

'Certainly not! This is a Muslim country.'

'Mother-of-God. *Yallah. Yallah*'

The first words were understandable, so I did not need my phrase book. The second I *had* learnt. It meant, roughly translating, p.... off. Repeated once. It was quite a clear message.

Dealt with, examined and passed for Qatari consumption, Jay and the boys tagged on behind me as we started to pick up our bags. With a loud cheer, one of the Partners of the Practice who had flown out earlier to see everything was in order, pushed through the throng on the wrong side of the customs barrier. It did not seem to make any difference as most of Qatar was doing the same thing.

It was good to see John and we managed to hack our way to the cars outside where a vehicle about two hundred metres in length, in pale pink including the wing mirrors, (I have been known to exaggerate at times), was waiting for us.

Here we were received by the car's owner, Daniel, who embraced the family warmly. He pumped my hand up and down as if he were the Prime Minister meeting the special envoy from Pitcairn island, outside that door in Downing Street. He was to be our driver for tonight, Agent's Agent, general factotum, arranger of all things and an Armenian by birth. He snapped his fingers to the porters who loaded up the *Plymouth* with our enormous amount of luggage. I need not have worried, for the width of his boot was about the same length as a Real tennis court and accommodated our stuffed suit-cases with considerable ease.

We cruised along with the hood down looking up at a night sky filled with familiar star patterns, air as warm as a summer's day in Brighton, on our faces. There was a central reservation planted with young Oleander shrubs, each kerb stone painted alternately black and yellow. Between each bush, crouched one or more Arabs in various stages of defecation, or was it just urination? It was difficult to see without staring, and our driver, and even John, seemed oblivious to the events of the mile-long public toilet. I was vaguely reminded of the public Roman loos in terraced stone of long ago. Back in Doha, however, there was this familiar aroma in the air, a mature blend of Oleander and human faeces balanced roughly, thirty to seventy. There was a second strange smell in the air but not that of the carriageway. Daniel, our man, saw me sniffing. 'Tomorrow, the *Shamal* is coming. The sand storm,' he added by means of explanation.

'Wow!' said both our sons at once. They had seen such happenings on television. 'Does that mean we will get lost never to be found again?'

'Probably,' I replied.

'Probably not,' Jay answered firmly.

'Stay in the hotel tomorrow,' Daniel suggested to our intense disappointment. 'It will be difficult to get to the office.'

It was not long before we approached the sweep into what was, in any manner of speaking an impressive hotel. Its west end was close to the boundary fence of the airport.

'Your home for tonight, and now, probably two nights. And I need to get your house checked over,' said John, 'so take time off and get to know the hotel. It is the only entertainment here.' That sounded fun.

While we waited in the foyer of possibly, six hectares of pure white Carrara marble, we became aware of the scrutiny levelled at us by a row of Arabs lounging on leather settees, each one with a loop of ivory worry beads, through which their bony fingers were trawling as if to find some hidden treasure. The hands holding these rosaries were turned up to the ceiling as Adam had been painted by Michelangelo.

Faces though, differed, not just in the sense of fat or thin but of structure. There were a lot of locals defined by their girths, with large and comfortable faces, conscious of the recent wealth pouring into their country. Others, though, had higher cheekbones, more drawn and hollow faces; from a poorer country perhaps? (They turned out to be Yemenis). Well-trimmed Iraqis, urgent in their manner, always holding a leather valise with polished shoes, walked purposefully in four directions. They wore, almost a uniform, of short sleeved shirt in pale blue, grey slacks and shod in black crocodile leather.

The hotel checked us in as professionally and quickly as anywhere in London. Daniel jumped around with registration cards. He decided to fill mine in. I noticed he had filled in the box 'Sex' with YES PLEASE and burst into ludicrous laughter at the absurd joke. Handshakes, promises of meeting soon to speak to our Agent, we found ourselves in two enormous bedrooms with a communicating door, now after midnight, although in Plymouth it would have been only nine in the evening.

Opening a window to look out to sea, the wind began to tug at the curtains and the same smell came back. It was full of dust but something more. Tasting the smell as one would have done to a glass of newly poured wine I was able to savour burning charcoal and the acidity of goat droppings and… something else. This turned out to be cardamon which would become as familiar as the smell of frying bacon back in Plymouth.

The next morning the alarm shrilled… alarmingly. Stirring first, Jay pulled back the three sets of curtains. The sun was out but had a curious ring to it. It was blurred, diffused, as if out of focus through a camera lens, mixing the blue of the sky with yellow dust to colour it green.

Our first day in the Middle East and we were landed with a sand storm!

Cars, however, were going about their business, vans loaded with gear and goods, a few people walking about but they all seemed quite poor. The wind plucked and tugged at the skirts of the Indian labourers attempting to get home after a night shift at some factory or other. Painted kerb stones on the main road were less clearly defined, having broken paviours and pyramids of debris dumped along the gutter line. Thick, black power cables lay across the ground, their cut ends separated into oxidised copper sprays. I had to assume there was no power connected.

Stiff-legged dogs looked hungrily and carefully at each new pile of rubbish they came upon, wary of anyone who edged even remotely in sight; it became evident man did not live in a cosy relationship with these four-footed 'friends' as they did back in England.

Intruding into this, frankly, dismal scene with a flash of panache and eagerness as if it had been a greyhound out for a morning walk, a VCIO tail plane with its familiar Jack appeared around the tall cliff of the hotel, bearing away towards the other end of the runway. As it started its run just two hundred metres from us and at maximum revs, it was extremely loud. (In fact, it managed to produce one hundred and twenty decibels, that is 20 decibels below the threshold of pain, experts argue between 110 and 140,) as it accelerated up the runway. The beautiful plane lifted itself clear, its pilot no doubt pleased to be away from Doha before the storm arrived.

Even as we watched, the sun gave up the ghost as the tempest reached out towards us; an extraordinary roaring sound began to build as air was compressed through the electricity pylons. The volume intensified much like the air raid sirens in the war. The windows rattled aggressively, moaning in their distress, building to a scream, drowning out thought and existence. Apart from this racket, the idea of siting, what was a luxury hotel, and the first for the country, at the end of a runway with the world's noisiest airplane was strange to say the least, the first in a long line of eccentric and outlandish decisions made at the same time that enormous wealth - so much wealth in fact that the Ruler could not even spend the interest he was receiving - was deposited at the door of his tiny country.

While the storm engulfed the country, we had breakfast in a continental style café, the food as bland and as cosmopolitan as any country in the world, anonymous but safe. The approach of the sand storm seen through the plate glass windows made me realise just why we were not going to make it to our new house. The palm trees bent into graceful curves, not the savage arcs which were caused by a tornado but impressive nonetheless. As the sand struck with full force, the landscape disappeared from sight, scouring the roads and driving the litter ahead of it, before dumping the clutter over the boundary walls of the houses into the desert from whence it come.

Behind the glass, in air-cooled comfort we had no idea of the conditions just half an inch on the other side. If one were to be caught out in such a tempest in the future the only thing I could think of would be to sit tight in a car and wait it out.

It was nice to learn there was a bar sited in Room 501, a name to become quite famous as time went by. Room 501 on the fifth floor was, in fact, two bedrooms (500 and 501) knocked together. Inside, alcohol was served only to Westerners: Arabs, or rather Muslims, were strictly prohibited. We learned also that there was a nightclub on the roof where we could spend an evening dancing and dining. So, it wasn't all work and there appeared possibilities for a night out from time to time.

An Egyptian gentleman by the look of him, began to hawk nearby. It was one of those deep, continuous sounds whose owner clearly wanted it to go on forever as he tried to clear the phlegm. Strive as he might, it would not rise to the level the man wished, so he continued, *ad nauseam* to retch. Jay tried to ignore it as she munched through her pitta bread. The noise deepened, becoming gravelly in tone until Jay, with a withering stare silenced the man, removing any further ideas he might have had to continue his morning ablutions. The boys were entranced; mouths open, staring at the man who was committing so many crimes together, that they could not understand why he was not locked up for the next five years.

We left to pass the time in our rooms. The boys tried to watch Arabic television but gave up after the third item covering bi-lateral talks with yet another Middle Eastern country. Later, we found out this was the high point of the day. Television was not to be the great filler of spare half hours, nor, sooner than we thought, would we notice it. In fact, alongside the lack of any newspapers, the loss of English News was no hardship as we began to learn to entertain ourselves with our friends without such modern distractions. It was as if we were transported back in time having to fall back on our own devices. Television can be a great educator, but it is also a huge waster of time, particularly today with 'reality' programmes, cooking competitions and soaps.

The phone rang, surprising me, thinking it was John, but it was the Manager of the British Bank of the Middle East inviting us all to lunch and a swim at his house on Friday. We accepted with considerable enthusiasm, writing down instructions on how to get there by being told it was quite easy as it was '... right next to Jassim's roundabout.' So, that was alright then: all we had to do was to drive to Jassim's roundabout and we would see the house.

To understand why this was a problem one had to realise there were no street names, no door numbers or names and no street direction signs. Being in a half cobweb layout of streets, it was impossible to keep one's bearings as the road was constantly turning away from or into the sun. It only took about half a minute to lose oneself. It was not possible either, to open the window and ask politely the way to the particular roundabout you needed. No-one spoke English except the Qataris and they were in their cocooned cars. To complicate things further, all the houses looked the same from the street, surrounded as they were by lofty identical walls of sprayed render (what was known as Tyrolean in England) on concrete blocks.

Putting the phone down I pulled out the copy of the one and only map of the town, a hand-drawn photo-copy (good old Xerox), and began to study it in detail. It was necessary to learn it by heart, for failure to understand how to get about could only end in us being lost in the middle of our home town: probably starving to death or dehydrating from lack of water within sight of our house. Months later they would find our dried husks lying amongst the other flotsam of this world. Looking at the layout, I realised Doha was a smaller version of Amsterdam, without the canals of course. Concentric roads and their linking radials replaced the water. The cut-off of the web at the sea was imitated in the *Ijsselmeer* of its Dutch counterpart.

Towards evening the phone went again and it was John saying the weather was improving and he would pick us up, hand over our car and then we could dine out in the hotel. He arrived ten minutes later making me realise he had learned how to get about this town with consummate ease in two weeks. If he could do it, so could I.

John arrived in a blue Datsun praising its virtues. Not seeing a single asset to appreciate it was difficult to take in or be enthused as he explained why he had bought this car.

'Goes okay, cheap to service, reliable.' So was a Suffolk Punch. 'But,' he added, with a smirk seeing the despondency settle on my face, 'but the *pièce de résistance* is this.' He patted a lever in the dashboard set horizontally to the wheel.

'What is that for?' I enquired, believing this to be the heater. Heater! Silly.

'This, Richard, is the most reliable air-conditioning unit in any car in the Middle East. It is why most Engineers and Architects drive in them. The air-conditioning is almost instantaneous the moment one swings this lever across. (It was). As soon as you turn it on, out comes ice-cold air. (It did). Not even a Merc. is quicker.' (It wasn't).

I began to see from the safety of the garage, some merit in this single asset as the storm began to abate This had been underlined when I had foolishly stepped outside the lobby to meet John. The heat had been enormous. The sand was still strong enough in its dying gusts to sear my face while the temperature was just slightly on the cooler side of Mercury in summer. (That is the planet, not the metal).

As we ate and planned, I called a waiter over and asked for a Coca Cola, to be told that the hotel and the country only served Pepsi. It was further explained that as Israel produced Coke the Arab countries had switched to the second brand.

Never having been able to tell the difference between them I was happy to keep the peace and oblige the management.

The boys were looking tired and we had to be up early to take on the house. We said goodnight and watched his departure by taxi from behind the safety of the glass wall. Outside, the lamps in the driveway illuminated a road scrubbed clean as a pot-scourer. The trees had returned to their natural, erect positions. No-one was in sight and a feeling of home-sickness tinged my gut for a moment. In two days' time, I would be on my own in a strange, almost wild country, without any knowledge of the language and two hundred Architects back in England dependent upon me finding them work. No pressure then.

CHAPTER TWO

I Become an Alcoholic

The next morning dawned in a brilliant burst of fire, the early sun not yellow as in England but white as one sees in a Bessemer converter pouring molten steel. Already the shadows were hardening into coal, especially inside the palm leaves where the fronds converged together. The sky was an extraordinary palette of colour, no doubt due to the sand and dust still retained in the atmosphere. Pure yellows, ochre's, burnt sienna, raw umber and moody sepia, with touches of purple and mauve, blended together. They stretched out as if they were an Arab version of the Aurora Borealis. Idly I wondered if I could re-start painting as a past-time although trying water colours in the Middle East was fairly pointless. The sun's heat would dry the brush before it had moved half-way across the paper. Point to remember!

Jay and the children remained at the hotel swimming pool as John drove me over to the villa. On the way, however, he took me into town and headed for the Police Station. Arriving, we met Daniel in his enormous Plymouth waiting for us.

'Your exam day, Richard,' Daniel declared with a laugh. 'Just answer the questions one by one. Nothing to worry about, it's very easy.'

Inside the building, streaked with nameless and very foreign brown marks on the plasterwork, was what I could only describe as complete anarchy and chaos, in equal amounts.

The confusion at the airport came nowhere near this disarray of human life. Pure white sound rose and fell in an even sine wave. The noise of several hundred-people shouting at the same time would be alarming if it weren't extremely funny, for everyone was yelling for the same reason. There had to be two dozen languages being spoken, or screamed, and every single one of them was demanding a driving licence.

Daniel turned to me: 'Did you play rugger at school?'

'Yes, I did.'

'Then put your head down and follow me.'

He grabbed me by a shoulder and literally manhandled me through the throng of unwashed bodies, arriving at a battered Formica counter where we were examined by the watchful eye of a policeman.

'Licence, licence, British,' shouted Daniel matching the clamour behind him. 'Mister Richard needs a licence.'

'Okay, okay.' Why did everyone have to repeat themselves? The officer in charge knew Daniel, probably well, and pulled out a tattered book, the Qatar equivalent of the Highway Code. The driving test began. 'What is this Mister Richard?'

'Er, um, a major road ahead?'

'*Zain, Zain.* Very good Sir. And this one?'

'Slow at major road.' And so we continued through the book. Then the last one came up for grabs. There was a slight smile on the policeman's face which I did not like. It was a yellow square with four fine diagonal lines across it.

'Er, um, er, er...'

'Customs post,' whispered Daniel in my ear, more *voce* than *socco.*

Pretending not to hear which was easily possible although the officer in charge of the test was about ten centimetres away, I said with implied knowledge: 'I believe that is a Customs post.' despite never having seen the sign in my life. Good guess.

'Passport please.'

Ah, this was it! For cheating in class I was going to have to surrender my dearest possession. I pulled it out of my pocket wondering if this were the last time it would see the light of day.

Instead, the officer took down the number and expiry date and handed the passport back to me where it was tucked away lovingly in my pocket. There was the characteristic sound one hears in any post office in Britain as the officer stamped a document in the same purple ink I had noticed at the airport. 'You have lady wife?'

'Yes, I have.'

'Bring her here after six in the evening. There will not be such a noise then. Ladies are most welcome.'

This was a kind thought. 'For her licence?'

'Yes please. Tell her about the Customs post. It catches everyone from England.' He clearly enjoyed his joke and

I joined in to keep him happy. Daniel smiled at the man in a knowing way as he took the approved paper.

'Over to the next counter.'

This one was where the details of the document were transferred to a red driving licence exactly like my English version except it was written in Arabic. I had brought along, as advised, a photograph of myself which was stuck into the back cover. Another stamp and I was legally permitted to drive. We were clear to leave. 'I owe you one Daniel.

'I know you do,' he replied but smiled all the same. He had done this many times before as the Agent's agent.

Overnight, the idea of moving into our own house had become much more appealing. We needed to get away from the clamour of this world, if just for a short while each day. John and I drove down a short though rough lane between high, Tyrolean rendered block walls, skirting a dead cat whose mouth had stretched open at the point of death. The single storey property was behind a pair of steel panelled gates opening inwards to channel us into a compound of beaten earth ringed by shrubs. Oleander and hibiscus were blooming and a tree of brilliant flame orange flowers brought shade to one part of the garden. At the bottom of my land was a tall tower with two speakers mounted at the top.

'Ah,' said John, 'that's your local Mosque. That tower calls the faithful to prayer five times a day.' He did not mean the tower would do it, rather, that a man would sing out over the rooftops. John corrected my thoughts by saying it was all done by loud speakers and a tape recorder.

'Amplified, I assume, John?'

'Could be a very weenie-teeny bit,' he confessed, speaking into his shirt as he said it to confuse me.

'What time is the first call then?'

'Ooh, I don't know, before I get up in the morning.' He had been living in the villa for two weeks, so he knew exactly what hour it would wake me, but I did not think it a good idea to challenge one of my Partners on such a trivial event. Besides, I would soon find out.

He explained where everything was, and I was pleased for Jay that the Firm had made sure we would want for nothing.

'Cold and hot water are reversed in the summer. When it is hot the sun heats the cold-water tank on the roof and it becomes the hot water source. Likewise, the hot-water tank power is turned off and becomes your cold water as it is kept under the sink on the cool floor. It's due for the change-over anytime now. You just turn one valve off. Don't forget to pass all of your drinking water through this filter as there is a lot of grit. The water comes from the de-salination plant on the coast so there is no goodness in it. Most people here buy bottled water to drink to get back the minerals they have lost. Then there are the air-conditioning units. One per room is quite sufficient.'

There was a rectangular box half hanging out of the wall into the garden. A grille on the face was pitted with stains as though they had sucked in more than air. I wondered if cockroaches or spiders had attempted to enter the building through these portals (how right I was to be proved) and had been drawn through the vanes of the machines. A hell of a way to die.

'Power does go off from time to time,' John added with another casual nod of his head, a trait which was becoming quite familiar, towards a sub-station which I had seen sitting outside in the lane.

'The engineers come along and put in a new fuse which lasts for something like twenty hours before it burns through. Then, poof, out it goes, and the cycle starts all over again.'

'So, in the height of the summer when the temperature gets to…what…?'

'Forty degrees.'

'Forty degrees. One can be left without any cooling for, four hours?'

'Oh, but the building is specially designed to stay cool. That is why the terrazzo tiles on the floor are there. Do you know, I slept on the floor one night and stayed remarkably cool?' He did not try and alter my figure, so it was probably higher.

Sleeping on a marble chip tile floor did not seem too cosy but I held my peace. In fact, the villa was nice and acceptably large. With high ceilings, the hot air tended to rise and stay there before being removed by old-fashioned paddle fans shoving it towards the air handling units. The coolness of the tiles through my feet could already be felt and we had further shelter with the arched terrace spanning the length of the house as if it were a much smaller version of the cloisters in Fountains Abbey.

As we drove back to the hotel along the main ring road, John explained how the system worked for navigation. I was beginning to understand that all directions were based on the roundabouts which were at every intersection, all named from specific buildings which dominated their junction.

We collected Jay and the boys and drove down through the town, past what was obviously the *Suq*, the market, to the waterfront. The sea stretched out in an amazing range of turquoise, viridian and cerulean shimmers of light with dhows moored head to head. I hadn't realised before just how big these craft were and regular trips to and from India delivered exquisite filigree gold jewellery and fine hardwoods.

Their reflections formed zigzag patterns of highly varnished wood. They flowed towards me as the boats slurped and sucked slightly in the post storm swell. Arab fishermen sat, doing not a lot except to talk and smoke. Some stared idly at our car, but it was no threat to them. No one in authority could possibly be driving such a small, blue vehicle.

'This is the Corniche,' said John. 'Anything of any importance will be built along this road so you need to concentrate on finding interest to put up major structures here. That, for example, will be the Qatar National Bank. Those piles of boxes along the wall are all that remains of a million pound computer that was out of date before it was installed. Another is on its way.'

The half-built building was surrounded by wooden scaffolding, none of it plumbed in level, while workers in white turbans and loincloths swarmed about, with extraordinary dexterity. The whole idea of Health and Safety, insignificant even as it was in England in those days, was as nothing over here. They did not wear any form of helmet or protective shoes and I could see plenty of abandoned wooden shuttering for concrete lying on the ground with rusty nails sticking up towards the sky.

As we climbed out of the car, the sun hit us with a sideways swipe almost as if a fan heater had been placed in the car park. There were some flame trees, quite an apt name, come to think of it, to give shade as we walked towards the entrance to the Shell school which was the only place in the country for children to be educated in English. The Headmistress who had arranged to meet us, showed us round.

'School opens at seven in the morning and ends at twelve, same as the offices. Of course, the men go back to work at four until seven, but we concentrate the learning here and the loss of the two hours in the afternoon will not be felt.'

The boys smiled at each other, delighted with the programme. This was going to be a doddle for them. To me though, the idea of a no-competition policy which she raised, was very disturbing; *everyone's a winner*, the news of which had been delivered in the first breath, as if it were the Holy Grail for children. This was a new idea in the seventies and one day my boys would quite possibly be working here in the Middle East having to win contracts against some of the toughest competition in the world. The boys simply had to learn to be competitive if they were to succeed in life (an idea that over forty years has not changed my viewpoint at all). Each day I would have to undo all the political correctness they had been taught in this school.

After agreeing that the two boys could start the next day, John said he was going back to pack his things. He was off the next day to London having been away from the practice for over two weeks. Jay and I would take our things over to the villa in the afternoon while John would spend the last night in the comfort of the Hotel.

We dropped him at the villa and I drove the three others back to our rooms, gingerly taking the roundabouts with care, not that I was worried about the quality of the roads, more the fact that a number of black and gold Trans-Ams with gold flames painted on the bonnets, would always try to overtake me on the inside lane. As each drove past, the owner could be seen sitting back, left arm draped out of the window to allow the air to dry his palm. You could tell the Qataris at a glance by the way they drove, with no attempt made to slow down when confronted by the arrival of any diminutive Baluchi or Afghani in front of them, having considerable disregard towards their safety. Thus, the road ahead was littered with the sight of scurrying workmen, cotton trousers narrowed at the ankles, ballooning at the tops, in their exertions to get out of the way.

These cars provided a clear signal to pedestrians, the road was for machines and machines alone. However, if you really had to cross the road, then, so be it, and, after all it is God's Will if you make it or not. This included us, of course.

We arrived back at the hotel and re-packed our clothes, checked out and loaded up the Datsun, somehow squeezing the boys into the back. John had, meanwhile returned by taxi to the hotel.

'I am going to need a car as well,' Jay demanded. 'Something small enough to get the boys to school and do the shopping.'

It had already become clear it had become an essential. 'We'll go and find a second-hand job after we have been to the house.'

Having spent a couple of hours with Jay showing her where everything was, we were about to leave for the shops when the house went dark. The silence in the lounge after the roar of the air-conditioning was unexpected, almost shocking, and somehow left us naked. Within two minutes the rooms began to heat up.

'Lie on the floor,' I said with my newfound expertise. 'They'll soon fix the fuse.'

As, ten minutes later it wasn't fixed, we decided it would be cooler in the car, looking at cars. The afternoon was drawing on by now, but it didn't seem to matter. Where ever there was business someone was there to do a deal.

'There's one,' said Jay, seeing a row of cars parked in two rows. The prices, in Riyals only took Jay a second to convert, she being the numerate one in the family. (I was the artistic one if you recall, that is, I was a Chartered Architect).

'Look, a Peugeot 205!'

We got out and walked over to the car, a silver, squat shaped toad or frog. It had two doors and a useful boot. But 'There's no air-conditioning,' I said.

'That won't matter," replied Jay, anxious to get mobile, ready for the school run. 'I'll keep the window open and it won't be for any length of time. Besides, that is why it's cheap I expect.'

Within half an hour we had done a deal, buying the car with our own money.

'Very, very nice,' said the salesman shaking his head negatively across the room. We had learnt quickly that this head shaking meant he thought it was an okay sort of deal, and not one where he did not disapprove of the car. One could interpret that a negative response meant a nodding of the head in the vertical to ground direction. After several weeks of studying faces carefully these rules were found to be generally followed although not always. When the negative response surfaced, the deliverer of the message would look shifty, study the ground in astonishing detail and waggle his shoulders while clutching his hands over his hips. He would add the suffix *'Insha'Allah,' God willing,* of course to cover all eventualities and was, of course, quite true.

The tail end of the wind from the night before combined with the day's increasing heat caused sand devils to funnel up from the sandy floor, each maybe five to seven feet high whereupon they proceeded ahead of us as if they were platoon scouts, following the road, carrying all manner of litter which was dumped in erratic whorls. Over time we would become quite used to these strange sights and skilled at dodging their path.

It was probably not unsurprising that Jay had passed her driving test with full marks, abetted by my expert tuition on the Customs post sign which had made her slightly cocky. Surprisingly, her car's engine had ignited with one turn of the key, though the heat began to build rapidly inside, and the boys were anxious to get some cool air on the move. Jay's face was flushed, well... red.

'I'll follow you,' I said.

She was not sure whether this was a comfort or not but tensely started off to head into the ice cream cones of dust with her window open. She accelerated up the Corniche, the main and most prestigious road in the country, a tiny car when viewed alongside the Mercedes sweeping past either side like the Red Arrows at an Air Show.

I decided to overtake as she was more than capable of finding her way home, relaxing in the cool draft of air on my face. John had been right. The air-conditioning was very efficient. In my rear view mirror the Peugeot trundled along, Jay's arm now resting on the window ledge. She would be alright I surmised, speeding away to the house.

She did not appear five minutes later, as she should have done, though she was close enough to the house to recognise the approaches. I turned and retraced my route back finding her almost immediately. Her face was now definitely red.

'Bloody bonnet,' she exclaimed in front of our sons. 'It just flew up in my face. The catch is loose.' But she managed a smile and drove off again, leaving me to turn in the road where I narrowly missed a water tanker heading out to the 'B' ring road. Some tape sorted the bonnet out in five minutes.

The roads encircling the town were lettered from 'A' forming the inner ring to the outer, 'D' although this last was just a notion on a town plan and contained no buildings. Our house was located on the 'B' ring, one away from the limit at present of any credible development. I did notice, arriving from the opposite direction this time, there was a mountain of rubbish immediately outside our perimeter wall. This backed onto the no-man's-land between 'B' and 'C'. Investigating, by climbing over piles of stone and sand it was clear that the manner in which all refuse was removed was by the simple expedient of throwing it over the wall.

No doubt I would find a place in the garden where one could step up to the top of the wall. (I did). So there was no refuse collection, no post, or newspaper delivery and no milkman. The Rates were probably low! (Non-existent in fact). And water? Well, that was sort of delivered, but not by underground pipe.

We had passed an area where battered petrol tankers were congregating like locusts to a field of wheat, the *Water Suq*. They were of course, water, not fuel, tankers. There was industrial-like activity as the tankers queued to fill up and I realised that this was what John had been talking about early that morning. Each tanker was individual, painted in red, white and green stripes or bands, depending upon the whim and artistic skills of the driver. We had to drive down to this water market, negotiate a rate and let the selected tanker follow the car back to the house. It seemed easy enough but it's considerably different, to say the least, from just letting the hose run in the garden back in Plymouth. That might not be such a good idea here especially as we had to pay for the stuff.

Jay rounded the corner eyeing me critically as I stood atop my rubbish; well… not mine exactly, but the original owner's. 'You ought to plant a flag,' she suggested.

Words such as *rats* and *big as...* floated across my mind. 'Can you imagine the size of rats that will be living in there?' was my response. Jay smiled at me acidly but could not think of anything else to add, the truth being right in her face.

The next morning we both saw John off, taking him to the Airport. He watched me drive with growing confidence. 'You'll be fine,' he said encouragingly. 'Just don't kill anyone here as they work to the biblical law of an *eye for an eye*. Blood money and all that.'

From what he said, he was implying if one of us killed someone, accidentally of course, that the family of the dead person would come looking for me, and then kill me – accidentally of course. Surely not? This was 1975 for goodness sake.

The VCIO packed with Australians going back to the old country for a holiday took off with another roar and scream at a hundred and twenty decibels. The panes of glass in the hotel rattled in protest but failed to drop out. Our last connection with England disappeared into the cloudless sky and we were abruptly alone. The silence following the removal of the four Rolls Royce Conway engines from the scene, magnified by the actual disappearance of the craft into the sky, was as though a boat had sailed hull down away from the island upon which I was then marooned.

I nodded to Jay and we turned back to my Datsun, ignoring the stifling B.O. swirling past our nostrils. The airport was, and would always remain crammed with people, no matter what time of day it was, a constant swirl of white and brown *thawbs* or *dish-dashas'* the Levantine name, more commonly used. The thawb was meant to end just above the ankle but, like modern schoolboys' socks in England, a whole range of heights to the one-piece shift appeared acceptable. There was the mix of raw garlic, unwashed armpit bacteria and the slow drift of half-burnt aviation fuel, redolent of all Arab airports that triggered so many memories where ever my travels took me in the future.

So characteristic of old Hollywood films, was the head dress, known as the *keffiyeh,* often chequered red and white or pure white cloth, dependent upon who was wearing it, folded once into a triangle. The red check originally represented ears of grain or fishing nets from Mesopotamia, I was soon to learn from my Arabic teacher. Everyone wore something on their head just as a flat cap or trilby was once *de rigeur* in England.

The airport was our free entertainment, a theatre, a cinema, a stage on which performers abounded, where those not in work could come and keep cool, use the loo, watch the arrival of Westerners, always good sport, and dream of the time when they too would catch a plane bound for *Mecca* and the annual *Hajj*.

The result was an awful lot of dried phlegm on the ground for the hawking was twice as industrial as compared with that already experienced by Jay's Egyptian friend. I began to think this might be some ritual, rather than idleness, taking an original form of expression. But then, look at football on television any Saturday and what the millionaire players do, hawking three feet in front of and even directly at the camera.

We had left the car parked just across from the main entrance of the terminal having, in those days, the luxury of parking only fifty metres from where it had been left under a corrugated tin lid. It did keep off a lot of the heat and if one had wanted to fry eggs this was the place to do it, also free of charge. An armed policeman sat under a metal roofed sentry box, his rifle pointing to the sky in an attitude which brought a whole new meaning to the word *languorous* or *'standing easy'*. He nodded to Jay as we drove out of the compound and back to the house.

A day later, after a successful indoctrination of the boys into the Shell school we duly arrived at our first Friday, our day off, as it was, for the whole country, and indeed, the whole Arab world which worked on a single day holiday each week and we wanted to make the most of it. Besides, we had an invitation to the bank's lunch and swimming pool.

By now, we had the road map imprinted on our brains and a reasonably good idea of how to get there. We set off along the 'C' ring road heading on an off-set bearing approximately east. This was not a direction I had taken before but before long we came to an enormous roundabout with a lot of weekend traffic navigating itself round in tight circles. Tyres squealed aping an American film in which there is always a car alone in an underground car park. The edges of the tarmac were held together with concrete kerbstones set in concrete, a tough combination for any lorry. However, unaccountably, the kerbs had broken down in many places allowing sand to pour through in miniature copy of the Möhne Dam in Germany during a special day in May 1943.

Beyond the wrecked margins, grit and broken paving slabs littered the desert floor as far as the eye could see. Plastic water bottles, fruit juice cans, plastic sheeting, and discarded advertising signs, receded into the brown haze of the horizon. There was no sign at all of paper or cardboard which the goats had probably devoured. Here and there, a small shrub would struggle as it levered itself up out of the stony waste. It was noticeable how each plant kept its exact distance from its neighbour as the individual root systems challenged each other for the slightest moisture in the ground.

Abruptly, our stream of eastbound cars came to a stop, held up by the imperious arm of a small policeman with a pair of enormous white gloves, quite as big as his head. In front of me the horns quickly began to grunt and groan, snarling at the poor man, who appeared unsure of how long he should leave us waiting. It was too much for the leading Mercedes who felt he did not have to wait at all. Behind the wheel sat a large gentleman in very dark glasses. It was accurate to describe his thawb as extremely tight across his waist. The man eased his car forward towards the man until he was directly behind him. Still the arm was held aloft. The silver car then moved again and nudged the, by now, alarmed traffic controller in the back. As the man was so small the bumper reached up to about his coccyx where it eased him in an easterly direction legs forming a windmill until he was clear of the outer lane. This was the signal for the queue to leap forward as one car, allowing the swirl of oil and petrol fumes to settle over the traffic cop who had so clearly seen sense at the last moment.

I exaggerate, you say? A bit of spin to keep you amused? No, not at all. Many times in the next few months I was to see this event occur, making me wonder why Qatar needed a police force, albeit of overseas origin, willing to go on point duty. It was reliably reported to me that a Sheikh in the past, fed up with being held up, removed an AK47 from the seat beside him (where else do you keep one?) and shot the poor officer in the legs. It did not help, for the policeman fell in the road, thus delaying the traffic even further.

The Bank Manager's house was a riot of oleander, flame trees and bougainvillea with rose bushes and carefully tended lawns on which sprinklers played with total disregard to cost. No doubt, those were my future bank charges going up in spray, I realised with some caution.

But, we had a delightful lunch meeting of about a dozen hardened ex-pats who all made it easy for me and the family to settle in. Promises were made to meet up in the next few days and I allowed the lager (*Oranjeboom,* always Oranjeboom) to slip down with considerable chilling gratification.

A slight issue did arise about half an hour later when the idea of a swim was suggested. There were changing huts by the poolside from which my fellow guests emerged in skins ranging from tawny to deep mahogany. Some of the women had been in the sun so long that they had taken on the hue of Chinese yellow. This is a mixture of mid-brown with sap green and a touch of yellow ochre. It is never a pretty sight to see an otherwise attractive lady with the skin of a pterodactyl.

I appeared last, as always having a problem tying up the strings of my very old costume and, born with the genes of a Norwegian Viking, my skin was as milk-white as any Geisha would have been proud of. Seeing my compatriots thus displayed in their suntans there was only one thing to avert their attention from my pale skin. I slipped back inside the hut on the pretext of forgetting something and stuffed my socks into my trunks. I then draped my towel nonchalantly over a shoulder and sallied forth.

There were equal amounts of stares from the ...*just out of England, are you?* guests, though, equally, the unspoken open-mouths of the men, whose wives gazed admiringly at my...torso.

The water, pale blue and cool under the woven grass awnings, essential to keep the temperature to an enjoyable level, surrounded me like a balm. I had been running on empty for several weeks. Due to the need to get ahead in the detail planning of parts of the submarine base for my successor, apart from organising the family's departure with no breaks at the weekends until now, life now rapidly translated itself into the word *good*.

As I hauled myself out of the water, Willy the Bank Manager came and sat beside the pool edge.

'John asked me to tell you how to register as an alcoholic.'

'Alcoholic? I assumed he was joking about the parties to come.

'No, he was serious. If you want to buy any alcohol in this country you will have to register, declaring yourself fit to drink alcohol, due to your religion not requiring you to abstain from such horrors. You will be allowed six hundred riyals worth of drink each month and if I were you, spend it all, every month. You will need to entertain twice a week at least, and, eight parties a month will just see you through. Beer is lager, that's *Oranjeboom*; whisky is the big drink here, gin and odds and sods. There is some wine, but it doesn't travel very well in this heat as it is apt to be stored on the quayside in temperatures of over forty. The Arabs will try and drink your whisky and, if you are caught selling or giving it to a local you will be sent home…after a prison sentence.'

'So, I guess that means one doesn't.

'One doesn't,' said Willy emphatically, his ample flesh swaying in concurrence.

'Can I claim for my wife as well?'

'Wives don't count here at all. The Qataris put up with English women driving, just, but they have no further rights as we know them. Make sure Jay is covered up when she goes to the Suq as that is where the most illiterate, and thus the most orthodox Arabs are out and abroad.

'I notice your youngest son has very fair hair. You will find he will be stroked on the head a lot as that colour doesn't exist here, but don't worry. These are, in essence, good people and mean no harm.'

Jay was taking it all in. She was trying to make up her mind whether it was more important to cover up or to keep the locals away from her sons. While we had never had a precious attitude to bringing them up there was a need to know more of how this particular part of the world lived and interacted with Westerners before becoming too liberal. I look back on these thoughts forty years on and realise we had nothing to fear from these people. In fact, if anything, we had much less to worry about than being in Britain on a Saturday night.

Eventually, we took our leave regretfully and our thanks were fervent. By the simple gesture of asking us to lunch, the canny banker had been assured that all of our business would be done through him. I left with a promise from the Shell Manager to meet on the morrow to follow up designing some accommodation blocks on *Halul* Island which John had channelled our way. We drove home already confident we would find our way.

CHAPTER THREE

H.E. Protocol

The following morning, I called at the British Embassy to see the Commercial Secretary. David turned out to be a charming and intelligent Diplomat who proceeded to advise me on the protocol of visits to Arab businessmen. Sheikhs were important people but, at the same time they needed the business that I was going to generate, so there was a balance to be wrought. We had to work together to achieve our goals.

'You will be offered coffee made with cardamom when you arrive. Take the offer. You can drink up to three cups, more like large eggcups, but no more. When you have had enough, shake the cup twice.'

He demonstrated with his own large cup of real coffee and managed to spill most of it on a magazine. The coffee ring managed to wipe the smile off Her Majesty's face on the cover of the official booklet. As he was wiping it up, a man walked in without knocking, tall, thinning fair hair with a comfortable air of ease about him, the species which shouted Marlborough and Oxford. He did not appear arrogant in the slightest, but he had the sort of face which clearly said he would not suffer fools gladly. He wore a tie and jacket, refusing to compromise with Arabian weather.

'Richard Newman?' The accent *was* Marlborough.

'Yes,' I confirmed, sure that was my name.

David had leaped up as the door opened. 'Ambassador, may I introduce Richard….' And realised it had all been done for him.

The Ambassador, H.E. as he was known, threw himself into a chair one leg over an arm.

'David explaining how it is all done?'

'Yes, Sir.'

'Remember, never forget this is their country. Don't play the big white chief, don't give them booze and never say, what a nice house you have, if you are invited in.'

'But, surely…'

'Being polite in this instance would mean that the house owner would feel obliged to give you his house to keep.'

There was a fairly long silence. Being quite good at behaving politely, having been brought up alongside Victorian grandparents could now prove problematical and I might have to change one or two standard phrases in my lexicon such as: 'That's a nice Rolex?' Or 'that's a smart suit you have on.' The image of a naked Qatari wandering around the desert unable to tell the time came as a ludicrous idea.

The Ambassador was continuing to talk, not at all dismayed that he was taking over the Consular Services that David had started to list in order of importance. H.E.'s role was not normally to involve himself in day to day business as conducted by the British.

But, his next words were.

'I want you to meet a friend of mine. His name is Ali bin Ali. He's not a Sheikh but he does have the sole Agency for Rothman's cigarettes and over here that makes him a very rich man. You will find that cigarettes in Doha are called *Ali bin Ali's*. I know he has been thinking of building a new Palace but hasn't found the right man yet. And you must meet Commander Hill, retired Royal Navy Commander seconded out here to see if they need a naval base. That's your speciality isn't it?'

In a few seconds, this man had opened up early avenues, giving me contacts which were to become the life blood of any Architect. And a week had not gone by. (Re-reading this I don't think Avenues is quite the right word for any part of Arabia but I'm sure you will understand my drift).

After he left, David went back to the standard format, applying his own knowledge of life with the Arabs until I wondered if I would ever get the protocol right. It was essential if I were to gain the respect of the local Qataris.

As I rose to leave, H.E re-entered. 'Bring your wife over for a film next Friday. We bring in a Betamax in the Diplomatic pouch each week. This is the big highlight of the weekend. My wife will look after your sons. Six o'clock?' What a smashing man he was.

'And...butter's in. Ali bin Ali's. Don't miss out as it will all be gone in a week. By the way, when looking for it, don't forget it comes in a tin.'

I rendezvoused with Jay to collect the boys. She had walked into town, so she could get to know where the main shops were. She looked quite red in the face again from the heat, for it was a long way.

'Bit silly?' I suggested.

'Bloody daft, as it turned out. I kept being hooted at by the locals, all suggesting a lift. And I'm not sure which is the hotter; riding in an un-air-conditioned car or walking on pavements which are red hot. But in balance, in future I think I'll take my car.'

I did not say anything, content in the fact she had probably learnt a useful lesson on how to get on here. Jay was a quick learner, better than me and I, also, would make a number of crass mistakes in learn ing the ropes. There was, and still is, a curious dichotomy between the Arab relationship regarding women with the very considerable respect shown to all females through their religion, as against the leer in the Suq which Jay had experienced from the down-and-outs, the money changers and the stall owners who were, supposedly the strongest of Muslims in their faith. Maybe it was because they knew she was an infidel.

'I might be able to make a bid for a naval base soon,' I said nonchalantly, 'but thought first we would invite Commander Hill and his wife for a drink. I have their address and wondered if you would like to call on them with an invite.'

It was a real problem when someone first arrives in Qatar. How to contact anyone? There was a phone system of sorts although new lines were like gold dust, the application form filling tedious and the end installation not always as logical as one would have hoped. However, there was one handset in the house, but no telephone book. The need to exchange business cards was therefore, crucial. To drive round to someone's house was also difficult when they could not give you an address which could be clearly understood. The conversation might go something like this.

'You know the B Ring Road?'

'Well...yes.' Quite firmly to start with.

'Well, you go along there until you get to a round-about.'

'Well... hang on, there's seventeen round-abouts on the 'B' ring.'

'Well, yes, I suppose there are. It's the one just past that big house with the purple balconies.'

'Well...do you mean the house that has the aerials painted lime green?'

'No. That's the one on the round-about before.'

And so it went on. The three dots after each 'well' would be from someone who had not resided in Doha for six months.

If there were no pauses you were practically a native.

'I'll go and call on them if you can write the note,' said Jay.

'Are you sure you can...'

'Of course. Where's the address.'

After studying the business card supplied by the Ambassador, for a few seconds she looked up. 'It's on the 'C' ring road, not far from us in fact. I head towards the Airport until I find the site for the Bahraini housing scheme. It's on the next corner opposite a filling station.'

'How on earth did you know that?' I queried in amazement as I finished the note handing it to Jay.

'I seem to know my way around this town now.' She took the note and got into her car. 'Back in twenty minutes.'

Needless to say, she was not back in half an hour and after an hour I was beginning to get a smidgen worried when the Peugeot rounded the gatepost.

'I thought it would take a time.'

'Not at all darling. I found it in five minutes, but Jinny is such a sweetie I stayed for tea. He's nice too. They would love to come.'

Behind every great man lies…an even greater wife.

'How on earth did you find them so easily?'

'Easy really. The map of their house is on the back of their card!'

A day later, having left a printer to print some cards for me with a plan of our house location on the back (what a good idea) I went to pay an audience on a Qatari businessman who was known to be pro-British and intelligent. The idea of me wearing a jacket was discarded preferring to wear a smart short-sleeved shirt but with that went the necessity of wearing a tie. No jacket perhaps, but no tie as well was not British and the Arabs still, at the time, expected us to wilt and wither on the vine as we went about our business. The only other essential need was to keep a duster in the car to ensure that shoes were reasonably polished. It only took a moment for them to dull down with the fine dust on the streets. Much of this arose as a result of leaping around piles of dried excrement, (that's human shit by the way), half on and half off the planted areas; surely, they could aim better than this?

I was ushered into a large room where an Arab was rising from his seat in front of a desk. His attire was superb. His thawb was of the finest Egyptian cotton, white as Daz, no, whiter, with a neat black rope circlet, the *Agal* holding it in place. He wore lace-ups incongruously, and a solid gold watch, possibly the same size as one of the Titanic's propeller blades.

'Well…Mr. Richard?' he said studying one of my cards from England. And then: 'My house is your house. Welcome to my poor country.'

I kept quiet on that one, anxious not to take over his nice offices on the first day of work, or his country for that matter. He waved, indicating for me to sit on a large settee of black leather, whereupon without more ado a small boy appeared with a tray of cups and a brass pot. This pot was what Jay was now looking for with its characteristic curving spout and decoration down the handle. The boy, and he really was a boy, poured out an egg cupful, more a tiny porcelain cup with no handle, holding the pale liquid which was deliciously cooling but did not taste of coffee. I learned later it was cardamom as I had been advised by the Commercial Secretary. It was the same scent as I had noticed on my first day from the hotel window. Jassim also took a cup and smiled encouragingly at me.

'You are new to the Gulf, Mister Richard?'

'Yes, Sir. Not even a week yet.' It was not difficult to finish the drink at which point the boy materialised out of a lamp and, lo, verily my cup was full again. In my mind, I began to panic at keeping track of the number of cups we had consumed. I did not have a feel for numbers when under pressure.

'We talked inanities for several minutes, including horses and goats and then I shook my cup as I finished number three. It disappeared in a trice. A slight smile crept across Jassim's face. The first test had obviously been passed.

'I believe you may be interested in doing the designs for some accommodation blocks on *Halul*?' The jungle drums were working well, though the hand of H.E. might have had something to do with it.

'I am hoping so, sir. We have two hundred hungry Architects in England just waiting to get their teeth into something.'

Jassim was clearly impressed with the number of *servants* working for me. At that time, there was no point in being unemotional in my description about the practice.

'I should like to build them. I have a base on the island and we make concrete blocks here in the town. Would you like to see the production line?'

I agreed I would. At the back, the yard opened up to a level concrete floor. A small machine was stamping out hollow concrete blocks in long lines unprotected from the sun. Shrinkage was going to occur if they were not covered up with wet sacks.

'Strong blocks,' he said waving a tasselled fly whisk about from side to side. 'Hmm', came my fascinated reply at seeing how the locals went about making, what was the most prevalent building material in the country. Simply everything was built of blocks, hollow in their cores, into which they could insert reinforcing rods packed with concrete. For housing, they might have been all right, but for Shell's stringent specification needs, they might not reach the tests required.

'I know the manager out there. He always uses my blocks,' said Jassim, amused at my concern, albeit which I thought had been carefully masked from my view.

'They undergo crushing tests over there. They always pass the tests.'

'*Insha'Allah,*' I murmured, one of the four phrases of Arabic learned by heart. Perhaps these tests might be the same as my driving test?

Jassim clapped me on the back. 'Come. I want to show you something.' We went back to his office where he dialled into a large safe behind a picture of the sea-front before the days of the Corniche. It showed Dhows moored end to end along the length of the seafront. He pulled out a squat, glass jar with a lid which he lifted up carefully before withdrawing a piece of stone, white and grey speckle in colour though, otherwise quite ordinary. I could not place it, but that was not surprising not being a geologist.

'Something special, I believe?'

'Well…Mister Richard,' said Jassim proudly. 'Very. It is one of only a few pieces of moon rock in the world outside of the States.'

Now *that* was impressive although there was not a lot one could do with it. He put it back in the jar. 'A date?' he offered.

This was another of those great, early surprises following my arrival where everything was different from what I had expected. The date was quite unlike anything I had eaten out of an *Eat Me* box at Christmas. It was moist, sweet and had a flavour all of its own. The dates we had had access to were invariably small and hard with annoying husks of dried leaf. These were soft without being spongy but huge, twice as big as the ones I had pinched off my grandmother's sideboard. 'That is amazing, I mean…'

Jassim held up his hand. 'Do not trouble yourself, Mister Richard: I don't have to give you all of my date palms. This is nineteen seventy-five in your Christian years after all, but I will send you some. Now, I will speak to Mr Bill on *Halul* and we will get him to speak with you. We shall meet again, very soon.'

I shook hands with this gentle man who had turned to gaze out of his window. 'Before you go, look here, Mister Richard.' He gestured towards the window. 'Look there, what a sight.'

It was a line of camels meandering down the side of the dual carriageway. They were loaded with bright rugs and piled with leather bags, though the shapelessness of their forms gave no hint of what they contained inside.

What an extraordinary blend of his conspicuous pride in showing off the contents of his safe and the unmistakable longing in his eyes for the old days. I had seen a look in his eyes which recalled his youth, the simplicity of the life at the time where everything depended on a good haul of fish out of the Gulf or a goat providing twins to a farmer.

We shook hands again and I walked out with a lot to think about. If this is how business was done in the Middle East, there could be a conflict between the high specifications and controls demanded by our Practice and the need to work with the locals in their own way of life. They believed their concrete blocks were totally satisfactory and had no way of making comparisons with how we did things in the United Kingdom. And, even if they did, why should they spend more money on higher specifications than that which had been successfully used for years?

I made my way down to the Corniche to take in the sea breeze. It was always cooler there but surprisingly few people appeared to take advantage of it. There was no place whereby one could sit out on a bench dedicated to *Bill and Martha – wonderful years here* - and stare out to sea.

The next best thing was to lean against the sea rail where I was able to study the Dhows in better detail. Their high prows swept down to varnished beams and mounds of blue nets rose above the gunwales.

'How do you do, Sir. My name is Fauzi.'

I turned to find a much older man, again in spotless linen but with cracked leather sandals and a red and white checked *keffiyeh,* looming over me. He was very tall despite his age, while the thinness in his frame made him look less significant than he might otherwise have been. As he smiled encouragingly, his jaw dropped alarmingly, in a manner I got to know in time, but knowingly as if he understood that the English on the Corniche were there for a very special reason.

While he talked he stood erect without the need to lean on the rail as I had done. His face was deeply lined, but he did not appear to have had a day's illness in his life. He was a living advertisement for the liberal application of sun, sand and *dates, and, as I found out, cigarettes.*

'*Salaam alaikhum,*' I said, using up two of my sparse, nay meagre vocabulary.

'*Alaikhum salaam,*' he responded automatically. 'You are new, I can see. I can teach you Arabic. I speak good English which was learned at the British Council.'

'That would be nice,' I said warily, 'but I am very busy much of the time.'

'You English work harder even than the Germans and the Koreans, but you can always have time to learn a few words.'

The idea of a few words and to learn how to pronounce them properly sounded good. I had always had a thing about correct pronunciation from the time I learned French in Switzerland and fussy enough to have been accused in the past of speaking French, in France with a Swiss accent. The French naturally assumed I was loaded and lived in Zurich – which I wasn't, loaded that is and didn't, that is, live in Zurich.

'How could we do this?'

'We can meet here, if you like. I will give you ten words to learn each time. After three or four weeks you will be able to greet the Emir on his birthday.'

'I doubt very much if it would be possible to greet the Emir on his birthday. He does not know me.'

Fauzi looked horrified. 'Oh, but you must. Every businessman in the country goes, as well as all his Family and hangers-on.' He looked pleased at that last phrase. 'It is a great day. We all queue up in the *Majlis* in the Royal Palace, shake his hand, wish him long life and go back to work.'

I was given me ten words on a folded piece of paper he had written down already from his wallet. They were in anglicised Arabic, so they could be read directly. The words were useful; their pronunciation not too difficult although one had to work up a wet throat to obtain accuracy in the more guttural sounds.

I remembered the phrase on the plane: '*as though you were going to cough.* It did work.

Extraordinarily, it began to rain. Unfamiliar clouds had built up quickly and the rain arrived soon after. First, dark stains appeared in the dust, half an inch across and spread out as if they were Chinamen in a rice paddy seen from a mountain top. Then they began to get wider until the perimeters touched, overlapped and began to scuttle towards the gutters. It tumbled from the heavens for five minutes and as quickly, retreated until the cloud collapsed, disappearing into the hardening blue sky. Fauzi who had pulled out a black umbrella and allowed me to share a small segment while he continued to ply me with throat actions.

Having mastered these first, vital phrases, I shook the hand of this second gentle man and promised to be there again the next week. Whether I could go on doing this with work already beginning to encroach upon the planned agenda of the day, was yet to be established. Meanwhile, outside the umbrella, the stains had already disappeared, leaving the remains of some discarded orange peel to re-curl in the humid heat.

When I got back to the house my feet took me into the garden. Jay was out and the boys not back from school. I was idly plucking a puff-ball of cotton on a shrub when the noon call to prayer, called the *Dhuhr*, or Zuhr, sounded off, strident, persuasive, demanding, urgent and utterly characteristic of the essence of Arabia.

I had not been so close to the minaret before when the tape recorder was playing, and it made me jump out of my skin. There was no warning of its arrival. One minute there was peace and harmony in our small patch of green, the next, the bees discontinued their nectar farming and zoomed into the air. Startled, I looked up to the loud speakers hanging over the edge of a stone cornice, imagining someone just behind watching to see if I was on my way to the mosque via the back door, but the dark shadows remained unbroken.

There never would be enough *Muezzins* with strong enough voices to make the call five times a day, a tiring climb for what might be an old, if respected man, so the idea of a tape-recorder and amplifier was a good one. Likewise, in England we are running out of vicars, so we have to make do with lay preachers. *Plus ça change.*

The call is undoubtedly one of the most idiosyncratic and unique of the Middle East. The invocation from each minaret can overlay the next by fractions of a second so that the *adhan* as it is known, goes out to the whole town in long drawn out reverberations of sound. The extended notes carry over the houses, calling the faithful to praise Allah, each one slightly out of sync. with its neighbour before dying away one by one in the heat and crackle of the day. Like the smell of cardamom, whenever I hear that sound, it instantly transports me back to Doha almost half a century earlier.

Although I was brought up a Christian, believing, perhaps slightly less than the Archbishop of Canterbury would like, (that the use of the Shepherd's Crook and turning a cheek from time to time was quite sufficient), the idea of devoting oneself to the discipline of Islam does have its strong points. Most Qataris (upwards of 90%) follow the Sunni branch of Islam, being orthodox and traditional Muslims, but there are a small percentage of Shia who lived quite happily with their brothers unlike some other Arabian countries which eventually, caused the Arab Spring to spread like dry rot or new growth, depending upon your view point, along the north coast of Africa.

Islam creates strong bonds in families and a respect for the old, traits difficult to find in Britain today. The established pattern of farming out one's own parents to a nursing home when they become weak and feeble, is just one example, a subject the Qatar Muslim found almost impossible to comprehend.

The boys' noisy return drowned out the ringing in my ears. It had taken them less than a week to accustom themselves to the total change in their circumstances. It was as if they had always lived with a minaret at the bottom of the garden and an air-conditioning wall box to keep them from frying in the midday heat. They now saw it as quite natural to sit under a flame tree to keep cool while racing cockroaches down a dusty path, or to swim in a sea that lapped warm and comfortably around their bodies.

And hot it was getting.

In the few days we had been here it had grown noticeably warmer; at noon, it was about thirty-four Centigrade, about eighty-eight in old money, and it was forecasted to climb to forty-four Centigrade before the summer which, by my rough translation would put us about one hundred and eleven degrees Fahrenheit in the shade. If I were to start building, my site inspections would take me out in the morning sun onto unprotected steel. This would mean a pair of gloves (gloves would you believe?) for the summer months to prevent me being burnt when coming into contact with the steel frames of our new buildings. Too much heat was an issue to remain as a concern in my mind for some time, for I had never been especially good in high temperatures.... well, not good at all and the notion of living in such a sweat had made me ponder long and hard before taking the job. I had not taken into account how the body eventually acclimatises, as the mind eventually accepts it just has to get on with the altered environment.

The telex was clattering away in the room used as an office. The sound was exaggerated by the terrazzo floor and lack of anything soft to absorb the sound. It was from John, assuming the settling in process had begun.

Taking a chair, I cut a tape, advising him of the progress made and letting him know there could be a naval base project to bid for in the future. He would soon be reporting to his Partners at their weekly meeting on that one. Jobs within naval bases we had done many times. A naval base all of itself, and from scratch, was a jewel in the crown to contemplate. It allowed designers to get the interactions working efficiently, uncluttered by centuries of the Royal Navy's organic growth.

My message ended by saying that we were a long way from winning such a job and were up against the Japanese and Koreans and realised I would have to put a great deal of time into the project before being considered. After I re-read the tape I found it far too defeatist and re-wrote it saying that we could win the job if we all put a big effort into selling the Partnership. The response was, of course, positive with the Partners all saying 'we are right behind you, Richard!'

The Ministry of Public Works would need to be my next port of call.

Before this could be achieved there was an even more important job of work to do. As the sun was going down in a fret of humidity and salt-slicked backbone, the Datsun and I took off for a building located on the outskirts of town close to the airport, but slightly hidden and certainly out on a limb. I knew roughly where it was but need not have worried for there were a considerable number of ex-pat cars parked around a large shed, and not a single Qatari inside the compound. It was surrounded by barbed wire with a gate, a sentry and a gun. He glanced at me and waved me through. I was not a Muslim.

'I'm new, need a drink, can you help?' My enquiry addressed the first person inside.

'Come with me, the man replied with a grin. 'This is probably the most important day of the rest of your life.'

Indeed, it was. Inside the tin shed which boasted a single air-conditioning unit, sat rows of shelves rising from the concrete floor: bottles and cases of lager were stacked to the ceiling, I filled in yet another form and added my passport details declaring that I ran a 'company' and was entitled to six hundred riyals worth of booze... sorry, alcoholic beverages, per month. This equated to about £52 (£330.00 in today's money) which could, in those days, buy numerous cases of lager, a considerable quantity of gin and the same of whisky, martini and a number of special liqueurs which I was advised to build up a stock of, as these were still popular in Doha after dinner, a hangover from the British colonial days when we were not as sensitive to local prejudices as we are today.

It was little more than ten minutes later that Richard Newman became a duly paid up member of the D.A.A. (Doha Alcoholics Anonymous) with the dire warning ringing in my head of what would happen to me if any liquor were given away to the locals. It followed the parallel of the American trappers selling hooch to the Indians a century earlier. There were rules about not displaying the stuff outside my house, to unload the cases out of sight and generally to keep the boxes out of the easily offended eye of the Qataris… and locked up.

Thus armed with as much liquor as my allowance would permit, I headed off home. Home! It was already becoming an easy word to say. The car's front wheels lifted lightly from the ground in its own response to the weight it was carrying in the boot, as I drove on up to the house. Jay looked with delight at the Scotch.

'Now we're off to the Suq and we'll stop off at the Water market on the way back. The gauge is low already.'

It was surprising how quickly we had drunk our way through the tank: we were learning how easily it had been to waste water back in England, where we turn on taps without a thought.

We piled into the car and made our way down one of the radiating dual carriageways to the Main Suq, passing the Doha Clock Tower, a rather sparse design but a useful focus for new ex-pats orientation. A parking space materialised as we arrived near the entrance to what turned out to be an enormous, dusty building leading from a maze of narrow earth-beaten paths between the stalls. The road leading to the market was composed of compressed cabbage leaves, carrots and tomato skins rolled by thousands of tyres and feet into a thick brown layer from which issued a smell not dissimilar to rotting comfrey.

We approached the vegetable and fruit market divided from the main Suq by a screen of low stalls. As we walked under a row of tattered awnings, the humidity hit us as if a bucket of water had been thrown into the air. My jeans turned from pale blue to dark in the time it took to get from the car's air-conditioned interior to the first trader. My glasses, in sympathy began to steam up leaving me blind, hands spread out in front of me. For a mad moment, I felt like singing out '*Alms, Alms for the blind*' but I would have been instantly cut down by Jay's sensible approach to everything in life.

As we came up to a stall piled high with really fresh greens, oranges, enormous dates in mountainous heaps, lemons and grapefruits, distorted tomatoes and rude carrots (Sainsbury's would have had difficulty in packaging some of these), I was jostled by the locals also coming out to do their shopping. There were women masked in leather on their faces, their noses hidden in leather peaks, where all you could see was a thin line of sweat around their eyes. Under the black *burka,* the shapeless one-piece dress covering every part of the body, the contained heat must have made it extremely uncomfortable.

There was the, by now, familiar flash of gold on everyone's wrist and ankle, the gold watch almost *de rigeur,* as it was for the men, and many of the older women had henna stains on their palms. They were not averse to offering a piece of their mind to the stall holders and to sniff the fruit before purchasing it. By sniff, of course, I meant that they would slide their leather-covered noses as far as possible into or along the skin of the fruit leaving a faint snail trail of sweat to mark the route it had travelled.

Stacked everywhere were bundles of a green grass-like forage, which turned out to be fodder for the animals and grown on every waste bit of land as well as out in the fields. The word *field* should be taken loosely, for this cultivation was more by luck than the application of modern farming methods, but it did grow easily. To an eye trained to a vegetable patch in England it was most akin to carrot tops.

As we indicated with our hands how many oranges we wanted and sorted out our riyals, the humidity increased with the evening, something it would do every day throughout the summer, so my shirt leaked, allowing sweat to run down my back to come to rest neatly in a meniscus along my leather belt. This was to become so common an occurrence that my belt rotted out every four months or so, along with my watch strap. In the end Jay bought me an expanding gold strap for my watch although not, I would add, for my waist.

Bagged up with fruit and veg. we ventured into the main *Suq* where the daylight softened into a quiet gloom and the flash of whites of eyes became much more prominent. This was a scene unchanged since David Roberts had painted its equivalent a hundred and forty years before. We did not feel threatened but definitely sensed this was a world which did not belong to Westerners. Money changers were at work everywhere with small leather cases, the old suitcase type with a hinged lid; fingers were used extensively, for many of the traders were of other nationalities, just like us. As they worked, they flipped their keffiyehs up over their heads with that casual shift so reminiscent of the Gulf Arab. The action seemed to signify acceptance of a deal while, at the same time, turned the flies away for a short moment in time. These insects, which we became inured to with time, had red heads and evil eyes, intent as they were on vomiting over the lush goods spread before them like a Henry VIII banquet. One skill which remained even after our return to England was the quickly learned ability to snatch a fly from the air, a party trick, no doubt, but at the time a usefully acquired skill.

The boys examined every bright plastic item of nonsense hanging from sisal string. Buckets, pots, frying pans (probably not for bacon) dominated the mass of goods for sale. Intermingled were row upon row of bright, gaudy, tasteless materials for dresses. The colours were so awful that side by side in the Suq the cloth bolts took on a glow of their own, brightening up the dark recesses of the gloomy building. Complex smells rose up to the roof, where no doubt, spiders with legs at least a yard long lived: I had a fancy to separate these aromas one from the other. Compared with those outside the building, these were nice smells, the type you remember from the small wooden boxes your grandmother would often have in a kitchen drawer. All of the spices were here, piled high in galvanised dustbins: cardamom, turmeric, fenugreek and vanilla pods, cinnamon sticks, nutmeg of course and cumin seeds; *ras al hanoute* made up of 35 spices for meat, chillies of every colour: small, dried dangerous ones, where less than half of half an inch would be sufficient for a goat stew for four. The quantities of many spices used in the Middle Eastern dishes are usually far greater than in England with our miniscule glass jars. (Remember, in 1974 we as a nation had not yet got into the swing of cooking as we had by 2021).

So crude was the butchery in the meat market there was not a single recognisable cut; even determining the type of animal was difficult enough. Where the hair was left on which occurred in some cases such as a camel's fetlock or a goat's ear, it enabled us to make a reasonable guess what the beast might have been when it had been alive; mostly the meat was a bloodied mess of gangly flesh where flies hovered above and were expeditiously dispatched simply by swatting them with a hand directly onto the exposed surface of the meat. I could see that this would help the butcher to maintain his meat stock, by weight, for there were many flies and he was accurate in his aim.

We didn't buy anything here and had been told that the only place to buy meat was at Ali bin Ali's supermarket. There was that name again, as evocative as the book *The Arabian Nights* itself. We knew where his shop was as the round-about was named after him, and, as it was on the way home, we decided to see if it was all we had been told.

Ali bin Ali's was built as a single storey, concrete-framed building no different from any other except it was larger than most shops we had seen to date. The construction was standard: sprayed Tyrolean spatter render in light brown on block work – camel brown I presume - and extruded aluminium doors and window frames. On the roundabout itself, facing the main door, a single ox munched away at a trifling amount of grass, whether to advertise his store or perhaps a wandering farmer had stopped off on the way home, we could not determine, but it added a lived in rusticity to the picture. Many a Rembrandt etching would have reflected well in this scene.

Inside the shop, there was a cool terrazzo floor, the space air-conditioned and the tins of food recognisable. It was clean, the first shop to be seen where hygiene appeared to be important. We saw tins of butter stacked up and Jay made an immediate bee-line for it, transferring three tins to her trolley. There was none in the familiar grease-proof paper wrapped blocks.

An ex-pat girl pushed past in the opposite direction saying; 'Meat's in.' before disappearing around a pile of cases with her wire basket. It took us not a minute to navigate our trolley, with its three insecure wheels and a fourth wishing to turn to the left all the time (probably manufactured at Heathrow) to a glass-fronted counter. Brightly lit were slabs upon slabs of Australian beef sirloins. It looked as if they had been hung as long as a badger, dark-brown instead of Tesco red, expensive, delicious. We learnt it was flown in about every two to three weeks but not always on the same day which is why it was so important to keep up-to-date with the camp intelligence.

To this we added charcoal, and orange juice, fresh salads, the butter and the bread. The change, in the form of bank notes, was clean and not crumpled and made us feel that Mr Ali was a man who knew what he was doing. He had, no doubt, calculated that while there were 173,786 Qataris in this tiny country, there were also one hundred and twenty thousand ex-pats, of which a considerable proportion were Westerners, paying no tax and well-paid.

That left only the purchase of water.

The water Suq was merely an assembly of petrol bowsers, well... water tankers in fact, parked indiscriminately on a waste piece of ground. There was no attempt to line the trucks up in a row so that the first to come was the first to fill. The attitude of *Insha'Allah* was evident in every move the water sellers made. For some reason they made no effort to sell, relaxed enough to wait for some needy person to come to them. All the water was from the same source and every tanker would be called out at least once in the evening, so, why the rush? Sensible people. The sons of the owners of these tankers sat cross-legged on the tops of their tankers chatting to each other as they waited for business. It was a close approximation of Mowgli sitting on an elephant's head.

One had to remind oneself constantly, and the boys, for that matter, water was the only thing that made this country possible. Without it there would be sand, and probably not a lot else.

The irony, of course, was that the water came from a desalination plant on the coast fired by oil drilled from the ground. The single resource of the salt water (not even the sand could be used for mortar – it being too smooth and round) combined with the natural reserve of oil and gas directly under the sea floor, allowed oleander and bougainvillea to run riot along the central reservations of all the main roads, so much so that they were being swiped continuously by the slipstream of the trucks.

We negotiated a price for a tanker with much animation of hands and pointing out towards the car, to a dark-skinned man whose baggy trousers were stained with grease. He jumped up into the cab with an agility I could not hope to emulate, and we set off down the road in convoy, my boys singing out to me if they thought he had lost us. Ten minutes later we arrived back at the house where the water man, (or was it waterman?), knew exactly where our tank was in the garden and started up his pump. Soon the gauge showed full and twenty litres of water spilt in the street as he disconnected the hose.

We had booze, we had food and we had water. It was a small step for man but a giant leap for my family.

Very early next morning before it was dawn, leaving Jay still asleep, I drove down to the Fish market close to where the Dhows were moored. Half of Doha was astir but then, these Qataris had, until very recently gone to bed when it was dark and used all of the daylight for work. The sense of timelessness in the room, the way of selling and buying, had not altered one fig in hundreds of years. The fish hall was huge, with raised waist-high marble slabs which ran with fish slime and sea water. These benches were entirely covered in fish, often mountains of them, just like the dates we had seen. When it came to prawns, they came in grey hillocks. Back home these would have been described as langoustines; I could lay them out in rows on a barbeque with a glass of something while they cooked (just ninety seconds) was all one would need to have a meal.

The one fish I had learnt about was the *hamour,* the all-purpose equivalent of cod and what Hans Hass had once called a grouper. It has a long, heavy silver body, often enormous, and was, as we had tried it at the hotel, quite delicious and meaty. One felt by sticking one's teeth into this flesh one was getting real value for money, though it was more expensive than what we were paying in Britain at the time for Cod.

The sounds of the buyers and sellers echoed and clattered along the tiled walls adding to the general cacophony of the gabble of the women continually dismissing the sellers with brief, urgent waves of a hand at anything standing in their way, clearly describing them as a cheap-jack or even a rogue. Tiger prawns shone in the neon light which high-lighted the dark stripes on their backs, and also on those that had been cooked and peeled. We had been advised that the black line down their backs must be withdrawn if we were not to catch *Doha Tummy*, the Middle Eastern equivalent of *Montezuma's Revenge*, or as my sons would so elegantly put it for the French version...*les squittaires.'* These prawns would swim, or was it spring, up the shipping channel, feeding off the sewage outfall and were so abundant that a major fish company had a freezing and packaging company on a nearby pier. It is perhaps necessary to mention that their prawns were hygienically clean and succulent by the time they were ready for freezing.

Of the rest of the fish, there were about sixty varieties of every shape, beautiful pink ones (matching my mother-in-law's scarves), some looking as if they had come off a coral reef they were so coloured and a number of game fish. I recognised Sea Bream and was told another was called, locally, a *Wahoo*, something possibly akin to a Calgary Rodeo. The smell in the air was pure sea air even at that time of the morning so I assumed the place had been properly washed down from the night before, as the fish were so fresh they did not have a chance to smell. I confirmed this by bending down and taking a sniff at an *Hamour* which had not the slightest hint of fishiness about it. It was a place I was to come back to time and time again, particularly when we were planning a dinner party.

The giant prawns tossed in a very hot pan in garlic, lemon, parsley and butter for just a minute or so, would be followed by hamour steaks roasted over the barbeque, where I happily accepted Jay's plea to wear a 'pinny' to prevent the butter bespangling my white shirt. A simple meal hard to beat, but bloody expensive, even for those days. The curse of over-fishing where ever it was in the world was coming closer, if it had not already arrived in this part of the Middle East.

As I came out onto the main street, close by the meat Suq, a local was casually skinning a whole camel which lay in the road as if it were a bundle of wool rugs collected by the W.I. The gleam of the shiny flesh, almost petrol coloured in the sun, made me glad our meat had been purchased at Ali bin Ali's, for this butcher was collecting more than his fair share of the street grit and dust. The boys would not have been amused, for they had quite taken to these strange, attractive animals with their grunts and yowls, the sideways chomping of their jaws and a predilection towards coughing green froth at the world in general. Despite the fact every Arab in the country had one, two, three or more cars, and an open van for delivering anything from a large refrigerator to a case of live chickens, camels were to be seen everywhere in the town as well as out in the desert where perhaps they should be. We had many visits from these delightful creatures for they were often only a stone's throw from the house, whereupon they would bat their eyes proudly, as if to show off their long eye lashes.

We had learnt how to buy food and drink. Now we wanted to be able to find out how to enjoy ourselves and relax as there was no television of any value to occupy our spare time. Many ex-pats, we learned, spent the weekends out in the wilderness. Beyond our house was the desert, the real stuff of sand dunes, stony outcrops and wadis filled with scorpions. We wanted to see for ourselves what this reputably scary and formidable place, devoid of any life which we could recognise, was all about. One problem was, having read so many stories in *Boys Own* annuals, often where the writer had never even seen a sand dune, my preconceptions of the desert did not always accord with the actualité.

It wasn't far away: Just over our boundary wall most of the radial carriageways ended by diving into the sand one hundred yards from the round-about still fully lit with lines of sodium lamp standards to illuminate what was just a very ancient sea of sand. How could I have known then that within twenty-five years the outer 'C' ring would be absorbed behind the 'D' the 'E' and the 'F' roads? It was almost as if the roads were following the sand dunes, trying to keep up with progress.

CHAPTER FOUR

Accident Proneness and Hunter Killers

Commander Hill and his wife Jenny came to dinner. One of the many good things in my life was the fact I have never had to worry about such events, nor would have to in the future. Jay's ability to make a dinner party go well was legendary in England. She was an outstanding cook, never phased to try new foods and new dishes, backed up with bright conversation to cater for the most taciturn of guests. She knew by now that Jack Hill was a very important potential link to the Ministry for Defence; there was a delicate balance between striking up a friendship and ensuring the Commander got the message. This was where the wives had such strengths and I do not write this in a patronising way, for Jay proved herself time and time again in the business world which surrounded her. During the time I had been supervising the contract on site for 'Northlock' the nuclear submarine base in Devonport, Jay had been entertained by the Royal Navy and shown around a Hunter-Killer sub, so she had a working knowledge not only of dockyards generally but understood how deep these boats could go (classified even today) and talk sensibly on SIN's, *Ships Inertial Navigation System*. (Yes, but what's your point?).

Curry and Killer subs were on the menu that night although I could not imagine Qatar needing something quite as sophisticated as that. Killer subs, that is, not curry.

The Commander, dressed in a white short-sleeved shirt but without epaulettes, and dark blue slacks had the indefinable set of his shoulders which said he had spent long hours on the bridge of a destroyer. He was affable, an easy talker as the Navy had trained him to do. His wife was a 'brick,' a well-worn phrase coming to the end of its life but summed up precisely her ability to move things on.

We took some beers onto the veranda overlooking our very own minaret and took in the flame trees now in full bloom. During dinner of local lamb seasoned in a mix of fenugreek, cardamom, cumin and coriander and slow cooked until it had arrived at the point of becoming pink but tender, followed by a fresh lemon syllabub, we managed to slip easily into dockyard vernacular. Jay was becoming used to the fact that work and play had to mix. It was a point learnt quickly, for, with the enormous cost of keeping just one consultant in the Middle East, there was precious little time to play around.

Jack wanted to know just how much our practice had been involved in naval bases and when the jargon switched to the YSM', (Yard Services Manager), PSA' (Property Services Agency) and DOE', (Department of the Environment) and the Royal Navy (the Admiralty) of course, expanding out to cover the practice's own research into stainless steel lined cleaning rooms and Barite concrete shielding, he knew I was not just trying it on. There is something entirely fitting when two people with the same interests can each contribute to the other's understanding of a topic.

Jenny and Jay were chatting away as if they had known each other since the war, and I could see that Jack's wife was as valuable to him as Jay was to me. By the time they left, we had established a very good rapport and arranged that one of my Partners would come out to talk about putting in a fee bid for the naval base.

As Jay washed up, I went into my office and sent off a long telex to Guildford hoping I had not used up too many of my brownie points by assuming a Partner would just jump on a plane and give up his golf for a whole weekend, perhaps on a wasted whim.

In the morning there were two surprise overnight messages. The first was from Shell to say that they wished me to pick up a brief to develop John's proposal for accommodation blocks on *Halul* Island; the other was from Langdon, one of our Partners – he must have been very late to bed as he was three hours behind me – to say he was booked on a Gulf Air flight that next day and would I see he had a good room at the Gulf Hotel. By 'good room, naturally to Langdon, implied a Suite. Langdon was not very well known to me, for he was one of the original senior partners and kept his work confined to the golf course where he was extremely successful at both gaining business and winning golf – though only when it was politic to win. I guessed he would have found it difficult to design a matchbox in those days, but then he didn't have to.

(And perhaps, anyway, that might have been unfair for he created a very successful practice over the years). Conversely there were hundreds of talented designers in the firm who would never make Partner but were happy to design buildings all day long as Associates.

I could just imagine the consternation at Head Office, *'prayers,'* that morning when my telex was read out.

'Richard may be panicking already. We may not have made the right choice sending him out there, but the little buggar says he has got a naval base on his hook. A whole base, not just a couple of buildings. Think there's anything in it?'

'Probably not, Qatar's too small for that, but we can't let him down at this time. He's very new to the job and the investment is high. A few extra bob, seeing if there is anything in it, is worth it.'

Langdon, already at the airport, would have grunted into his pipe, an eternal glowing volcano being a fixture in his life. So fixed was it that when asking a distinguished member of the Royal Family to open one of his buildings a few years earlier, which she had graciously accepted to do, he had stuffed his lit pipe in his pocket on seeing her approach, only to have to dash away while patting himself as smoke curled out from the, by now, well alight jacket.

Langdon was accident prone and stories of him in trouble were legion. My hope was he would not cause a diplomatic incident when he arrived. The Partners did not yet know we had a confirmed commission, small as it was. It was the first fee and would keep me out in Qatar for at least three months.

I sipped my orange juice. With no newspapers to read, no crossword to mull over, I had more time to think about planning out the next few months. Things were happening significantly quicker than one could imagine. On the positive side I only had a single commission; to be fair, and realistic, they were just sophisticated sheds. But, already I was beginning to feel the heartbeat of this small country, which was accelerating down a road of unknown length, in its attempts to break out of the restraints of its desert past.

Jay took the telex from me.

'That's tonight, you realise, and that means today. You had better book a room. Or rather, I will book it on my way back from school. You can tidy the office such as it is. And let Guildford know about the sheds.'

Sheds! *I* was the only one who could call them sheds. They were, surely, accommodation pods for oil operatives on *Halul* Island.

Outside it was going to be another hot day and I thought of Jay taking the boys to school. Going there was always cool enough for her to cope. On the return trip the sky was as brassy as the…the contents of a tin of Brasso, but considerably hotter. I kissed everyone goodbye, remembering that a message sent back from the school a day earlier had pointed out there would be a Sports Day soon although, of course, everyone would be a winner! This was 1975 don't forget, on the brink of absorbing these defeatist ideas so prevalent today. Every child needs the best start in life they can get, and it is unfair, in my opinion, to remove an essential tool as they form their ideas for the future. Those who propose such ideas should go to the Middle East and see how hard the Japanese and Germans work to win contracts for their respective countries. Competition, to them, is a way of life.

Quite unsettled by the approach but dismissing it from my thoughts, I approached Shell's offices in Doha, a fairly mundane three storey block which belied the fact they ran an extremely successful operation in the Gulf. They were, after all, one of the major players in the oil world. Perhaps the simplicity of their offices reflected the reason for their success?

The Engineer who met me was brief, precise, exact, but pleasant enough. He had no time what so ever for those wanting to do things their own way rather than the Shell way, a useful format for us, as they had had years of experience working in the Gulf States. Over American coffee, rather than Cardamom, I was briefed carefully in what they wanted in the way of housing and a detailed schedule of what they sought was handed to me. They had no desire to make the housing anything but workable and efficient and there was no wish to see any architectural element infused into the concrete block walls. The fees were standard RIBA scale so I could not complain at that, but a question arose asking what staffing I had out in Doha. There was a bit of a stumbling about for a few seconds wondering what to say, eventually settling on a compromise. This was agreement that the basic designs would be carried out in the UK with site supervision organised by me.

This, in fact, became the standard routine for all work in the future. We became the supervisors of the work as we attempted to interpret the ever-increasingly extravagant designs coming off the drawing boards. Today, this would have been so easy for the computer-aided designs from

Guildford for they could be sent down the line, where we could have printed off as many copies as we needed, while making the necessary local adjustments to the designs. At the time, we had to judge how many copies we might need and trust they would be accurate. A smudged alteration on a drawing was never a sign of professionalism.

As we were about to finish up, the Shell engineer gave me one piece of advice. 'The Arabs do not understand drawings. Some do not appear to have the ability to read even a three-dimensional work let alone see it in two dimensions. Don't even try to explain a layout to them. Neither do they understand a fee based on a roll of drawings and a specification. They like to pay for blocks and concrete. So, think about a model maker in the future. Qataris understand a model and can see what they are getting. Good luck,' he ended. It proved to be very good advice.

I drove down the Corniche, my left arm thrust straight out with my hand held suspended above the hot tarmac as if I were a local, pleased with life, though uneasy at Langdon's imminent arrival. He had a reputation of being difficult and prickly and I had no desire to have him alter my new-found way of life, and freedom: but, he was one the original Partners, a big cheese as it were, and he might very well insist on altering the tactics or my overall policy. I had just a few hours to come up with a plan which he would accept.

～

'If this is serious, you are going to need more staff out here.'

Langdon and I were sitting in his suite, twelve stories up in the Gulf Hotel looking out over a peacock iridescent sea. A dhow proceeded out of the harbour, more a mini marina these days, as if putting on a display for my Boss. He ignored it completely, focussed as he was on the work in hand. I had been able to tell him about the first job before the coffee had arrived. It was then that the stories about him lived up to the truth.

As the doorbell rang I rose to let the boy in with the tray. Langdon beat me to it, grabbed the tray, misjudged the proximity of the furniture and managed to trip over the glass topped coffee table. He proceeded, in slow motion to spread the order over the floor.

'You want more coffee, mister?'

I shooed him away politely. 'Yes please, but *you* put it on the table next time.' The boy nodded his understanding of the matter as Langdon went into his bathroom to dab himself down.

Langdon had not even apologised. 'I've got a very good man in the London office. Henry is his name and he knows a lot about boats, if not ships. He's at one with water as it were.' Langdon appeared equally at home with water, or rather coffee. I dropped two bath towels on the spreading stain.

'I know him. He and I could get on well.'

'Keep on top of them all as they come out here, Richard. This office could be the start of big things. Keep a tight lid on costs especially, until we get fees flowing. By the way, what's the golf like here?'

'Golf? Well, there are nine browns for the oil men at *Umm Sa'id*, but that's all. It's rumoured Dubai will be putting in a full eighteen greens one day.'

'What are browns?'

'Oil sprayed on rolled sand. They say the smell is pretty bad and the ball travels very quickly, but if you are that keen, I guess I know someone who could get you-'

'No, no,' replied Langdon hastily, more at one with Glen Eagles and the mown spots of Surrey. 'Just thinking of you with business.'

'Well, to date I've not had a game of golf but we have one confirmed project, one possible and two waiting in the wings, so to speak.'

Langdon was going to open his mouth to reply but it collapsed like a dead cod as he saw the worth in what was being offered. 'Good, good.' He turned as there was another knock on the door. I was ahead of him.

'I'll go. Just look at that water out there.'

As surely as a super-tanker is able to dock with a single pilot, our waiter delivered the coffee safely to the table.

'*Shu-kran,*' I said.

Langdon tipped the boy lavishly mindful of the stain on the carpet and closed the door. 'So, you speak Arabic already do you?' he said impressed, looking me in the eye.

'I don't know if I am what you would call fluent, yet,' was my rather cautious reply, 'but I am taking lessons once a week.'

'That's the stuff my boy. Get in with the natives.'

The idea of Jassim being seen as a native in the way that Langdon had imagined, a spear in his hand leading a goat or a camel down the road, was as far apart as Guildford is from Doha.

'And, I think you are going to need a Secretary. I've got one, with a husband who is an Architect.'

'But, what about the costs you mentioned?'

'Yes, yes. We'll sort that out. And you might need your own pool.'

I had explained about the Bank's pool and how useful it was to have as a business tool, 'rather like the golf course in England.'

This was how our practice, which was the fourth largest in the UK at that time, had grown: on people who were prepared to take a risk. I would have to do the same if this office were to grow. Take risks, but calculated risks.

We went through the details of the confirmed job carefully so that Langdon could take it back with him as a clear brief.

'Now,' he changed course abruptly as a dinghy goes about a buoy. 'I need a suit. I hear they make them in a day. And we'll stop off at the site for the naval base on the way.' Never mind that they were in completely opposite directions to each other. There was nothing else to do in Langdon's mind.

We made our way down to the Suq where we parked in the usual place. Langdon strode ahead of me, thrusting money changers and beggars aside in his single, eager yearning to have a new suit. A tailor was found, one of perhaps twenty, chosen for the cleanliness of his shop rather than on any skills he might have had. The owner was sitting cross-legged on a cushion of rough woven yellow and red goats' wool from which he rose with considerable ease. Although he was, maybe seventy there was no sign of arthritis as he bowed to Langdon. We, or rather Langdon, chose a cloth: under some duress I finally came up with the colour 'sand' as a description to give to his wife.

'I'll merge with the desert next time I come out here.' Langdon was getting into the spirit of the whole thing as he knocked over a water hookah which the tailor had been smoking. 'Use a pipe myself,' he said. The man understood nothing but managed to take down a series of measurements.

I glanced at his waist dimension.

'Yes, well, I put on a bit of weight lately. But I'll lose it in the summer.' He was going to need about three summers to get down to my sort of level, but Langdon had already transferred his attention to the hookah which had been set up on the floor again.

'Can I have a go?' he indicated in sign language.

Lord, I thought. He might have to be sent back in the ambulance plane. He commenced sucking gaily on the well chewed plastic end with equanimity. The number of different types of germs would probably please even Porton Down.

'Cool, very cool.' He smiled, and the tailor smiled back. Langdon took another puff. 'Tomorrow? Ten o'clock. Richard, what is the Arabic for tomorrow?'

'*Bukkrah.*'

'Book-rer,' he confirmed seeing the tailor point to his watch. 'And, I'll have some of this lining inside the jacket.'

He had snatched at a swatch indiscriminately and laid it briefly on the suit material. The man seemed to know exactly what was wanted. To me, if he did not die from the germs he would almost certainly be divorced by his wife for the courageous, nay, audacious elements he had put together.

Outside in the car, Langdon chuckled. 'This Arabic thing is not too difficult. I would never have thought I could buy a suit from a man who spoke no English.'

I felt it sensible not to reply until we had viewed the final product when, no doubt, the morrow would bring a possible rethink on the whole thing... er, article.

The Datsun took us down to the proposed site for the naval base and we climbed out in the midday sun's heat. The air shivered in the high temperature, waves bouncing off the sand in almost hysterical manner. I was reminded of David Lean's magical opening shots in *Lawrence of Arabia* when the Arab on his camel was approaching through the heat. The land seemed to split and divide, and then reform for an instant before being carved up again. I could only liken it to the old AGA cooker belonging to my parents when light caught the open plate with the lid off.

I adjusted my floppy hat: Langdon attuned his pipe.

We studied the large site. Langdon passed his professional eye over the junctions between the water and the beach and with the Gulf entrance itself. It was his Practice which had won the nuclear submarine base in Devonport and he had accepted the idea put forward of the expensive lead-panelling to the buildings which had given them their characteristic profile, beloved of Architectural magazines for months.

He patted me on the shoulder. 'I knew it was a good choice to send you out here. Let's go and have a drink.'

It sounded as if he wanted to go to a pub around the corner.

We hadn't even got to base on this job, but he seemed to assume it was in the bag.

'Langdon,' he had told me to drop the Sir, 'the Japanese will be bidding for this one, also the Koreans, let alone the French and the Germans. Then there are the Americans.'

His response was unequivocal. 'The Japanese have no real modern experience of building for war. The Koreans are too tied up with their borders. The French are a bunch of wankers and the Germans, well…'

So that just left the Americans, who, I believe did have quite a lot of know-how, were not wankers as far as I knew and well…it was as good as in the bag.

'Play the same game as them. Don't break the rules, but neither sit back on the line. Never say no, always say yes. We will back you up if you have said something positive that we cannot do. There's always some expert we can call on.'

This was as good as it gets. It gave me considerable encouragement to receive comments such as these. There was nothing we couldn't do was his belief, the same which now lay lightly on my own shoulders. We could take on these massive firms who did not have the problem of issuing small amounts of money to keep a single engineer out in the country.

The next day, after kissing goodbye to Jay who had not seen too much of me in the past twenty-four hours, I drove Langdon down to the Suq on the way to the airport. The tailor received us, shaking his head from side to side in confusing, but positive welcome and Langdon disappeared inside a multi-coloured changing room. A considerable amount of grunting was accompanied by severe lateral movements of the curtain, but he finally emerged, resplendent.

I caught my breath, stumbling to find a few words of support. The *sand* colour of the suit had become, more… orange in daylight, while the lining more… violet (or violent) than purple. The mix of colour reminded me strongly of a Mandrill's bottom.

'Well,' I said at last, 'your wife *is* going to be surprised at how quickly you got a new suit.'

'Rather like it. For Partnership meetings and the like.'

He stroked an appreciative hand down one of the sleeves making me wonder if the arm might come off. But, the suit was well-made. It was just the materials from India that had very little body in them…apart from those colours of course. Perhaps in New Delhi they might be a bit more in tune with the environment? On second thoughts, the material had no 'body' in it.

Langdon was persuaded to change back on the basis he might not want to crease his new suit in the plane. With a nod of agreement, he dived back into his tent, his suit was folded in a bag and the tailor pleased with the cash. At the airport I was quite sorry to see him go. He had invigorated me and shown me how to gain accountability in a manner that brought a new dimension to my new life.

The Gulf Air flight took off on time after much bustling from an incoming 747 from Jeddah. By now I was getting used to the pushing and shoving: one just followed suit. (sorry).

∼

That afternoon Jay and the boys came with me to *Wakkrah*, a small village not far south of Doha. It was made up mostly of small concrete block villas clustered around a curving beach with goat droppings for a pavement and lobster pots bound in bright orange string, stacked up against a grubby wall. Set back from the sea, on a stony ridge was a series of houses each with a low tower rising quite strangely from the roofline. Where the flat roof should have been were four stone columns, one to each corner of the house. In turn these held up a platform of timber poles with woven rushes lashed together in criss-cross patterns. These were some of the last remaining wind tower houses in the country, most having been bull-dozed by the locals in favour of newer, more modern structures of concrete blocks. As the Shell engineer had told me, these people wanted blocks, not wood and paper.

The original idea, and having experienced the beneficial effects since, was that by locating the houses on the rise, the winds from the sea ran up the front face of the walls, passed through the gaps at the tops and out the other side, pulling the heated air from inside. Mediaeval venturi action, commonly known as air-conditioning! Clever people the Arab race *and* they advanced mathematics in the known world as well!

The white-washed walls outside had plaster applied to the stone and, while wet, they had been carved into circular, intricate patterns by removing the surplus from a pattern pricked onto the surface. The doors were in ancient, sand blasted timber having rows of inch-wide headed nails, inserted in neat lines across the timber. Each panel was big enough to contain a Judas Gate with the same rivet decoration. Today, these characteristic buildings, refurbished, allow their canny owners to rent their properties out for double the going rate. At that time, they were disused and falling apart. No-one wanted them, and no-one could see a reason for wanting to live in such a building.

I returned a week later with a sketch book and drew them carefully, realising in a couple of years there would be very little traditional architecture left. Then it would be too late to rescue them for posterity.

The lobster pots were to catch a delicious flat-tailed lobster fished in these waters and was outstanding in its flavour. Cooked in cream and mustard it rivalled the Hamour in its meatiness.

'Why are we here?' Jay asked. 'Besides seeing these houses.'

'If we do have more staff out here, *Wakkrah* is close to Doha, twenty minutes by car but the rents are half those in the town.'

'You're a mean beggar,' she said tartly. 'This is a bit of a hole compared with Doha.'

'Well, just until someone starts finishing those houses on the 'C' Ring road. There's nothing else at the moment.'

'True,' she realised. 'But take on any rents on short term leases only.'

We both gazed out across the untidy village. A single telephone line snaked venomously into the central area, nothing you could call a village green but, possibly, the central rallying point for a Safari Supper in ten years' time.

There was no activity save that a sub-station gate was open; inside two men were installing a new fuse. (Surprise, surprise!). The beach saved the otherwise dismal scene lifted by a turquoise sea, so we suggested to the boys we try out Jay's new purchase. It was an inflatable boat, bright orange on top, blue below, oval in shape, about four feet long, care of the *Suq* where she had seen it hung, gathering dust. Arabs had forty-foot-long power boats; we had an inflatable...four feet long.

Puffing and quite dizzy with the exertion of blowing it up in one hundred point four degrees of heat, we carried the, by now, firm-skinned dinghy down to the shore where we launched it in the water.

Within point five of a second, the wind (wind towers! Hullo!) had picked up the craft, wafted it vertically ten feet into the air and borne it off towards *Umm Sa'id* further down the coast. It was the last we ever saw of our boat, price thirty riyals.

The boys just watched, entranced by their enormous balloon sailing up as close to the sun as Icarus who also fell to earth though probably not into an oil refinery as was likely here. What the guards would make of the boat on their radar as it came in at low level over the dunes was anybody's guess but I fervently hoped there was no evidence to link the offending article with myself. Anyway, Jay bought it, didn't she? Maybe there was a boat store down in *Umm Sa'id* filled with lost inflatable dinghies waiting to be transferred back up to the *Suq* at a later date and sold...'as new.'

Swimming over for the day, now cooler, we drove home ignoring requests for lifts. Anyone without a car might be seeking a ride for reasons other than getting to Doha. And I wanted to get back to remain cool, as in temperature not looks.

In the garden, the heat of the day was lessening into a pleasant temperature. Already, the gauge, quite important to us these days, showing eighty-two Fahrenheit under the flame tree, felt cool to us. We sat on the terrace with our drinks, apportioned now to ensure we always had sufficient stock for clients. Without really trying, Jay had taken on the lovely brown tones that her French blood had given her. She smiled at my glance.

'This could be the start of something good,' she said, sipping her whisky with meaning.

'What about the boys?'

'What *about* the boys?'

'They only have a year here, you know, and then they have to go back to England. To a Boarding School, and-'

'And, you don't like the Shell school policy regarding competition, do you?'

'Frankly, no. Whatever you say to the contrary, you can see competition all around us here. If the boys grow up under such a policy, they will lose out on the best jobs in life. Besides, where ever they go it has to be to Public School, as we don't have an option on that, do we? They will then be put into a competitive environment straight away. House against House.'

Jay knew this was right, but she wanted to hold on to the illusion of the four of us together for a bit longer. It was not an unreasonable wish.

'They'll be out every holiday and I thought you would like your mother to come out with them once in a while.'

If I had gone out of my way to surprise, she could not have been more shocked. Edna, her mother had lived on her own for many years since her early divorce. She spent her life in a close relationship with her many sisters running a book shop in a small country town. The idea of travelling out to these parts of the world she had never heard of, could just not be imagined.

'Mum! But…well…yes…er, she could be the guardian on the plane instead of one of those girls on Gulf Air.' Jay did not like the stewardesses who spent more of their time chatting up the returning Qataris than their other customers in the hope of a gold Rolex for 'being nice'.

'We might need to find an alternative, additional source of whisky, of course.'

'Of course.' It required no further comment by way of explanation.

'It's a very long way.' Jay pondered over the thought as if it was a piece of chewing gum.

'Only seven hours. You could be home the same day. We've done it; we know how long it took. And you could go to see them at their *Exeats*.'

That was a certainty. Apart from the generous UK paid perks from the Practice, there was no income tax to fork out for and thus my income was all net, down to the chilled Mars Bars at Ali bin Ali's. We could afford to let Jay go back when she wanted. She came over and squeezed my hand. 'Another one?'

'Another what?'

'Just another drink. We have a slight surplus to stock at present.'

'Well, okay but not too large. We have a big party coming up soon.'

There had been no time to tell her. 'I want to hold a dinner for all of the team selected for our bid for the naval base; Engineers, Quantity Surveyors, Specialists. There will be about fourteen in all.'

'We need more chairs, cutlery, china, glasses.'

'Okay, okay,' I waved my hands in the air. 'We need to buy it.'

Langdon's ideas had now begun to penetrate my skull. 'At least we have the space.' The living areas were large and the room not unattractive and we would always spill out onto the terrace.

So, we bought the equipment we needed out of our meagre funds. The chairs came from a new furniture store which had opened the day we had arrived in Doha. Just like us, everything was changing, and changing almost by the week, expanding to soak up the enormous oil revenues of the Middle East. It was as if this were a new planet, as far west as America was in the eighteenth century, reflecting a world of hard money, channelled into construction, where possibilities to exploit original ideas and to test them out, could only be dreamed about at home in England. This was going to be one of the most important dinner parties we had ever had, and a lot was at stake.

CHAPTER FIVE

Ships 'N Staff

Two weeks later, having had a successful dinner party with my planned team, came a summons for me to attend a meeting at the Ministry of Public Works. It was a difficult day to go at a moment's notice, as Shell wanted to talk to me about additional work to their accommodation blocks. They understood, however, probably quite used to the Ministries making considerable demands upon them as well.

Jay covered the phone for me, standing in as secretary while I dashed off to the most critical building in Qatar for a Consultant Architect. This was where all of the government work was dished out. Those in charge had enormous power, distributing multi-million-pound contracts at a whim, following the plans set out in the annual budget, a publication almost akin to the Holy Grail. Everyone had a copy and there were a large number of projects which I would have liked to have had a bash at. Half way down on page seventeen was: 'No.143. Qatar Naval Base.'

I was ushered in to see the Minister, a Qatari who normally handed over the day to day running of the projects to an Englishman, a competent engineer who had lived in the country for a considerable time. Today though, a preliminary check was being made by his own boss, as a forerunner to passing on the detail to be handled by his staff. But it was strange, nonetheless, I was told later by the engineer that he was becoming involved,

I smoothed my hair down in a rather self-conscious manner and studied a useful mirror for signs of nervousness. None I could detect, so, onward.

On being summoned into the inner sanctum, the Minister's desk revealed absolutely nothing of his personality. There was not a single item on it, not a sole sheet of paper, not a pen nor a gold inkwell. He had children, I knew, but there were no pictures to brighten his day. It would have been an interesting exercise to have rummaged through his drawers to find one item that was labelled work.

'Mr. Richard. *Salaam alaikhum.*'

'*Alaikhum salaam, Khe fahlik*, Minister?'

'*Zain, Zain, Zain*,' the Qatari smiled reassuringly as he gestured with a beautifully manicured hand to a settee. He called for coffee.

For a few minutes we exchanged civilities, he in immaculate English reminding me of Public Schools and the long vanished BBC News reader of the war, John Snagge. He enquired after the cricket and the heat in England, which was proving to be a scorcher, though, it must be added, not quite like it was here. Summer had almost arrived in Qatar.

When I shook my cup he placed his own down and drew closer across the coffee table.

'Your practice is illustrious for its military work, I understand?' Here it came.

'Illustrious is a too, illustrious word Minister, but thank you for your kindness.' Though, the Royal Navy did have a famous Aircraft Carrier called Illustrious. God! What an asinine start.

'I would like to think that the British Government uses us often as we do a good job for them. We, as a result, have many experienced Architects with a great knowledge of all things military.'

He nodded his head in an appreciative way. 'His Highness, the Emir, may Allah protect him, is very keen to have a Navy in Qatar. A Navy of stature, you understand. One where our patrol ships will fly our flag proudly at their mast heads as they patrol the Gulf. There is much unrest in the Northern Gulf, as I am sure you are aware, and we need to be vigilant at all times on our borders. Borders, Mr. Richard, borders are very, very important to us.'

It was my turn to nod. 'His Highness, Allah bless him has, I am told, a great understanding of the world and international affairs.' (I always became muddled when I tried to spell the word 'syco...sycoph: you know what I mean).

'Whatever we build, it must be of the very best, the finest equipment, the men hand-picked, and the boats- ah-'. He was stumbling over the right words knowing that there would never be anything larger than an M.T.B. for the foreseeable future.

'Ah, the new motor torpedo boats are the fastest anywhere in the Gulf, with engines more powerful than those over the water.'

The implication was, of course, Iran which already had a large navy. 'You could buy the Attack Class, about a hundred and twenty tons mounted with a quick-firing Bofors gun… and two machine guns," It was politic to up the ante where armament was concerned. Qataris liked their guns. 'And twenty-four knots are pretty fast.'

'Quite so.' The Minister's gleamed for a moment as he saw himself behind the Bofors gun sweeping down the channel and taking on the world single-handed. At least, that is what I hoped. 'Would you like to be our designer for our base? In association with Commander Hill who is here. But… I understand you have met him.'

It was a non-sequitur, the last that is. His Intelligence was ahead of mine. Jack must have spoken to him. 'The Commander will write the briefs for you and he and I will be in charge of ordering the ships.'

He rose. There were far more important things for a Qatari Minister to do than chat all day with me. These were busy, busy times.

'I have arranged a meeting with Mr Don to set up your fee arrangements. I regret that it is a time-consuming business collecting fees, as not all Departments have caught up with the modern way of doing things. When you have completed the design, you will need to submit it to His Highness the Emir. Please prepare a separate document for him; perhaps you might have it bound in leather with his name inlaid in gold on it?'

Despite the '...time-consuming business...' quote which smacked of *very* time-consuming business, it made me a very happy man.

'This has been a very great pleasure, Minister. I believe you will be very satisfied with what we can do for you.'

We nodded slightly towards each other, not as much as the Japanese, but an acknowledgement of a transaction in the placing. Twenty years earlier we would each have spat on our hand, which saved paper, at least, if slightly unhygienic. A nod and a handshake were infinitely more preferable.

After the meeting with Don, an ex-pat of many years now almost Arabised, a formality to explain the wonders and mysteries of fee collection, I stepped outside with the precious commissioning letter. This did not give us the right, yet, to go ahead with the full designs, but it did mean that we could draw up the briefs pending the next stages. It brought me into a state of near joy having been in Qatar just four weeks. It did mean, naturally, we would have to satisfy Jack Hill and the Minister of the workability of the designs, but, if so, there was a major commission on my hands.

But we were going to need help.

One needs to realise that a naval base for six or eight motor torpedo boats, although not sounding like a mega-structure as it might have been in England, would, nonetheless enhance our reputation in the Gulf. This would spread rapidly on the news wires to Iraq, Bahrain, the mighty Saudi Arabia, Oman and the U.A.E. and all of these states would prick up their ears to see what we were planning. Defence of their countries was regarded with righteous gravity.

I wanted a pee urgently after the coffee but, of course, over here there were no blocks signposted 'Gentlemen'.... and Ladies of course. While this made no difference to the workmen brought in from Baluchistan, I had a smart tie on and my shoes were still polished, so my pressing need took me quite rapidly towards the Gulf Hotel where the ground floor toilets of western modelling gleamed in their pristine porcelain.

More relaxed, I ordered an orange juice and Danish in the coffee shop and pulled a piece of paper from a pocket to allow me to jot down the actions I deemed most urgent. A Secretary to replace my part-time, unpaid wife; a number two who had to be a good design Architect and one other. Langdon had mentioned a couple. Perhaps they might come?

I put in a call to Guildford and could hear the excitement down the phone and given an official '*well done*'. This was nice, though having done very little to control the route of the contract, most of the work had arisen out of our practice and Commander Hill's fast moves.

'You are going to need another car for yourself; keep the Datsun for your new chap. Housing and fitting out are going to be a priority. Can you manage?'

I could.

The next three weeks merged in a haze of negotiation with a high percentage of my time engaged upon delivering the demands made by new staff rather than put towards securing valuable contracts.

There was a lot of travel to see villas and houses and agree house furnishing packages. An enterprising company provided a complete house package down to salt cellars, pillows and dustbins although, I had to admit to myself the latter article still had very little use here. Jay, of course, was the star as she sifted through a blizzard of documents needed for each new member of staff and checked that each house had whatever it took to settle them in quickly.

My labours took me back to *Wakkrah* and I did a deal on an older villa. Because of its state we managed to take it on a short-term lease. Two Pakistani decorators who had set themselves up in business were interviewed. I told them the whole villa was filthy and they were to wash everything in sight and then paint everything white.

'Everything white Sah. Very good!'

Done, out of mind. Onward!

A few days later, Jay and the boys came with me to the airport, where we climbed up the stairs to that same balcony we had been looking up at, when we stepped down onto Arab soil for the first time. The terrazzo staircase was littered with bits of chapatti and cigarette butts. Darker stains told their own story. We used our elbows to get to the rail and watched the sky until we were able to glimpse the winking navigation lights of the Gulf Air flight.

A long crocodile emerged eventually from the front of the plane composed of travel-weary passengers winding their way to Immigration. I caught sight of Huxley and Rhona before Jay, she diminutive in height as a baby doll, though in retrospect she was still a bit taller than wider, utterly delightful with, as it turned out, a great sense of humour. Huxley proved to be an accommodating man with a cheery, round face and a wish to get on with things. Rhona was, nonetheless pleased to learn they were to be put up in the hotel that night, a stone's throw from the Terminal. We followed their taxi and on arrival briefed the two of them on what the morning would bring when Huxley would need to get his driving licence as quickly as possible. I mentioned the Customs Post sign and Daniel confirmed he would take the two of them to the Transport Licence office while I had a rather more important job to do.

By midnight we were back at the house, the country having two more ex-pats to cope with and me with a staff load which had just risen by two hundred percent, discounting Jay of course. To add to the changes, she chose this time to announce she was going to help out at the Shell school, which gave her some independence and an ability to occupy her active mind. It was also good from my perspective. I was going to be tied up work-wise for a considerable part of the day...and evening and she might have found the long hours difficult to fill.

During the night there came the clatter of the telex down below in the office. It had to be Guildford and I did not bother to get up. If it had been urgent they would have telephoned me. I clambered out of bed the next morning and walked into the office with a mug of tea completely naked. There really was no purpose in wearing anything at all at night, at least in the summer, then remembered my new secretary would be coming in each day so I would have to hide my 'p's" and 'q's" after she began work.

The tape spelt out a whole list of items being sent through the post. Drawings and specifications for *Halul,* the Shell job; confirmation that a leather-bound presentation book for the Emir with plenty of perspectives would be produced after the broad outlines of the new naval base had been drawn up and the designers wished to know his full title; would we like a model maker for six months or so for he could drive a stretched Land Rover out to us at the same time. The cost of the car fuel against an air fare were the same and it would save precious funds if we bought the car in the UK. A Land Rover would be extremely useful as an all-purpose vehicle for everyone to use for the work requiring an off-track vehicle for site surveys. Seeing the desert as we had already done, driving to *Wakkrah*, one could not fail to notice the roads were superb but once the decision had been taken to leave the tarmac, the desert became uncompromisingly sharp and rugged. Studying the Qatar Development Budget there were many possible projects which would require us to cross land where there were no roads at all.

A model maker: well that had to be Harvard. This tangled-haired gentleman, a match for David Essex, who never seemed to shave, yet his beard never grew longer than a stubble, had an ability to build all things in miniature, a skill which ruled me out as a helper in times of pressure. He had a permanent grin on his face wrought by nervousness. Isolated within his miniature worlds for so long, he had retreated from authority happy to remain in his Lilliputian creations of the near-microscopic. His given name was a bit of a mystery and his parents had never enlightened him as to why he was named after an American University.

Our practice, like so many others, had long ago realised that many business clients would nod their heads in acceptance of a drawing yet, on challenge – politely of course- one would find they were quite incapable of reading a plan or section. A model was often the answer and Harvard was a man who could make anything to tiny scale. The idea of him driving through the Saudi desert behind the wheel of a Land Rover was a difficult one to accept for he was a man who often *got lost* in thought as he mused over how he was going to solve a particular problem, let alone the Empty Quarter of the Qatari desert after four thousand miles. This would lead to mugs of tea being knocked over, model varnish being sat on or an apology to the cat for letting it lick up the shellac left to thicken in a saucer. But Harvard was a man who would allow the Qataris to save face, to be able to nod in complete understanding of what we were seeking to build: in fact, it could be Harvard alone who could determine if one of our proposals was to be accepted. He could be described as the most valuable member of the team. It meant more accommodation, though he could stay with us or Huxley perhaps for a month and there would be the new car he had brought with him to use. Not that I would want him to get out too much. The idea of putting him alongside his models in front of some of the high-ranking Ministers of the country was, nonetheless, worrisome. He would need careful briefing on the protocol for each visit. If this was to be a theatrical presentation, then a rehearsal was also needed.

The rest of the telex was also an eye-raiser. It was from the Partnership in general and, at first, I wondered if it was a rebuke for it was a copy of a Minute of a recent Partnership meeting. Fortunately, it was not (a rebuke that is) and in some ways, it was to provide a further stimulus.

What the Partners, in their wisdom had decided was for me to follow up on major projects as they were selected by our research department. A particular division in Head Office would troll through as many magazines and newspapers as they could get hold of on a daily basis, seeking clues on who was planning what. From this they would build up a picture on the likelihood of a project going ahead. In other words, they wanted our sphere of operations to expand to take in Abu Dhabi, Dubai, Oman and Saudi Arabia. Iraq was also on the cards. Once Henry, my new Number Two was in place, the boat builder, more time could be devoted to chasing up clients and projects coming up for consideration. I would already be there, so to speak, ahead of the opposition sitting in England, waiting for a call.

Henry was being held in Guildford while he worked up some broad-brush briefs for the naval base project before he came out and we really needed time to get the operation of the office up and running smoothly. In a very short period, in one of the smallest countries in the world, my life had expanded out of all proportion – it now appeared as if the world was centring on the Middle East. It was, quite simply, my oyster and my workshop - and nothing would be too big to challenge my colleagues back in England.

CHAPTER SIX

Fun and Games

Jay drove me over to the car showroom when it opened at seven. I had received a phone call the day before to say my new car had arrived but if it were not out of the showroom very early the next day some Sheikh would have it and there would not be another shipment for six months.

The Lebanese salesman smiled, as I pushed open the door and saw my new vehicle, another Datsun, waiting for me. This time it was a series 260Z, low-slung, capable of a speed of 127m.p.h. It was really only a two-seater though it had two buckets behind for the boys. Behind, there was a useful boot. Inside, the leatherwork was in black and everything was painted bright red. Anyone could see the car approaching including all those attempting to cross the 'C' Ring Road at rush hour.

'*Yallah*,' he said to me. 'There is already one Sheikh's son sniffing around. There's enough fuel in it to get to the petrol station.'

Leaving before he could change his mind and having filled up the tank, I drove up to the new 'C' Ring where the car could show me its paces. It was exactly what was wanted, small, fast, manoeuvrable and gritty with the Datsun air-conditioning we needed most of all. The large boot would take surveying equipment or a dinner for twenty ordered from the Gulf Hotel if we did not have the time to prepare one ourselves.

I drove on down to the hotel and had an early breakfast waiting for the other two to surface. Huxley joined me in half an hour followed a little later by Rhona. She smiled sheepishly and looked around, her pale face marking her out from the other diners.

'This is quite civilised, isn't it?'

'Ye-es,' I responded. 'But it is not all like this you know. *Wakkrah* is a little more... local, a little... fuller in character.'

'Hmm,' Huxley studied me quizzically, already able to read me like a book. 'Sort of Lawrence of Arabia without the Lawrence?'

Bang on (curious phrase), I could not have agreed more. 'A little earlier than that. Circa eighteen-eighty. Characterful perhaps but no wealth of beams. The villa has been painted and cleaned up entirely, new furniture and fit-out, and in six months you can be the first to choose whatever house becomes available in Doha. And it will be a new one. And...' I paused for effect, 'permission has arrived from the Partners to build a swimming pool. But first we all need to move into our respective houses. As soon as we can find a house big enough to contain the office Henry can then go into yours along with Harold.'

'Quite a merry-go-round,' Rhona clarified, but , as it turned out, was what she was good at.

The issue of keeping Architects out in the Gulf was large, complicated and tedious, for nothing was as it seemed, and nothing was delivered to the house without something vital missing; and most of these goods had been packed in western factories! As a result, it became essential that someone followed up on a day to day basis until the item in demand was installed, connected up and working properly.

Rhona was exactly right for me. She was the type of person who would have walked across India in 1875 with her husband without batting an eyelid. I knew we would get on, even though we had exchanged only a dozen words or so. Like my new car, she had a gritty determination in her which would get the both of them through most troubles. Huxley shared her views.

'Shall we go and see where you are going to live? But we need to go via the Police Station, so you can take your driving licence tests. Don't worry, Daniel our Agent will be there, and he will see you get your passes.'

And so it was. We rendezvoused with Daniel outside the throng of grimy bodies, letting me gaze on, now quite unperturbed by the noise and madcap scramble. Rhona managed to pass her test without help; Huxley misheard an instruction – so he said - but the presiding Police officer told him what to enter in the box. Rhona made a face at her husband, triumphant in passing out above him.

'Not many things that I *am* better at than you, dear,' she murmured, detaching a sweaty arm which had somehow magically attached itself to her bottom.

'You are always better than me darling,' he replied eyeing what was his Datsun now.

'You need to go back to the hotel, then I'll wait for you to collect your bags. You can follow me down to the house. It's not far.'

This was all said with as much light in my voice as possible, as though we were going for a stroll along la Croisette in Cannes. It did have the sand, if not the beautiful people.

Half an hour later we drove off in convoy, Huxley a smidgen more nervous than me on the roads, as he had not driven before on a race track with a bunch of *TransAms'* decorated with red and orange flames scorching across the bonnets. Rhona pointed out interesting things to him as they travelled south, but his hands were clamped in a vice-like grip to the wheel as he stared ahead at the ensuing chaos. I observed carefully that the eyeball in each of his eyes was trained forward without blinking. We learned later that John, back in Guildford, had told him the good old story about an eye for an eye before he left, and he was in mortal fear for his life. It was not to last for long and he quickly adapted to the new way of life as we had. What is overwhelming today is commonplace tomorrow.

Leaving Doha, we drove south along a dual carriageway, leaving housing and randomly placed factories behind us. Although there was a town plan, it was very difficult for the authorities to bring pressure to bear on a people who were seizing every opportunity they could to improve their lives. This included erecting concrete block-making facilities in the middle of nowhere, which tomorrow might well be a housing estate. Piles of stone and broken terrazzo continued to be dumped as far as the eye could see.

The whole terrain down to *Wakkrah* was divided up into irregular plots each contained by two or three high courses of block walls denoting ownership or, at least, possession, perhaps by *force majeure*. Bent and rusted advertising hoardings sagged drunkenly in the desolation as they promoted luxury goods of leather handbags and Chanel perfume. The contrast between the quality of the signs and what they were advertising could not have been further apart.

Two camels munched away at the same large cement paper bag. Their lips moved closer to each other with each chomp of their jaws, but one had to assume their stomachs were impervious to the effects of the hardening of the cement in their intestines. It briefly recalled to mind the scene in 101 *Dalmatians* when Lady and the Tramp were eating spaghetti. There was no sign of their owner, though I had found if one showed inordinate interest in an animal, an Arab gentleman would materialise from his Tardis to examine you from very close quarters.

We eventually made it down to *Wakkrah* and the other two jumped out of their car excitedly. Rhona clapped her hands in glee, evidently finding the beach as her waterfront a definite bonus. The seashore, of course, merged with the sand of the desert making it difficult to see where one ended and the other began. This made it the largest stretch of beach in the world... or the smallest desert.

Walking ahead to the house, I managed to remove the ever-present dead rat which lay supine and drying out on the doorstep, rodent biltong, before it could be noticed. As the others came up behind me Huxley took the proffered key in a rather grand gesture although clearly dismissing any thought of carrying Rhona over the threshold.

The outside of the house looked magnificent I have to agree. It sparkled like a pearl alongside the azure of the gulf waters, pristine white walls and windows. A prickle, however, travelled up my spine, one of those strange sensations which send a vague, indeterminate message to the brain. It was a trifle bizarre that I could not see through the glass of the windows. They were sort of opaque, blanked out, but realised the curtains must have been drawn across after the decorators had finished: one up to them.

My guess was wrong though finished, they had! My instructions had been carried out *to the letter* and all had been painted white. The walls and ceilings of course, virgin white surfaces reflected dazzlingly. The paint had been applied with considerable skill with no runs. Also, to the carpet, the mirrors and the kitchen work surfaces, Formica cupboard doors, mirrors and light switches came next. Power points and light fittings followed inexorably. Incredibly they had missed the curtains but of course had painted the glass windows and frames. They had left the bathroom ceramics but, naturally these would have been left as they were already white. Similarly, the baths...and they hadn't touched the terrazzo floors.

Rhona and Huxley stared transfixed at their new home. I coughed to clear my throat from the inevitable lie forming like a dead frog within my tongue. We walked across the stiff shag pile rug, (the original soft shag pile was de rigeur in those days) to the centre of the lounge. It made Rhona two inches higher; she did not sink down into the tufts of wool as they managed to support her weight with ease.

'A smidgen (good word Huxley) too much white for my taste,' said Huxley.

Rhona's nose began to twitch. 'May I assume you asked for the whole house to be painted white?' she offered helpfully.

What a clever girl. She had it in one. The rule of literalism had, once again, come into play; the art of carrying out an instruction...to the letter.

'I think we had better get back to the hotel while this is sorted out.' And back we drove. At the hotel, Rhona surprised me further. 'Let me deal with the decorators. After all I am working for you now. I'll phone them from the bedroom.'

A few hours later it transcribed that she had got hold of them, ordered them to the hotel and threatened to have them repatriated to Pakistan if the mess was not sorted out. Within quite a short time the house package was replaced, the kitchen cupboards stripped, and the dead rat buried. Events moved on fiercely and vigorously and to their eternal credit the two of them managed to sort the mess out relatively quickly. The painters were charged with the hotel bill.

Taking drinks that evening at my house I suggested we go and see the Estate Agents about a new house for ourselves.

'No.' Rhona was off and away again. 'Let them come to us. After all we are buying, they are selling, and, it will save on your valuable time.' It seemed a fair arrangement.

It did take twenty minutes to explain where we were which she had not bargained for, and I had to step in to do some explaining, but, the next day two Agents arrived, both well dressed (aren't they all) in a Mercedes (nothing changes) and presented themselves to us.

'We have a very, very nice house, Sir. Just behind the American Embassy.'

Ecstasy was not a strong enough word. To be anywhere near the American Embassy was to say simply that *one* had arrived. Elegant roads, well planted, secure, and clean. I opened my mouth to respond...warmly but was interrupted as Rhona exploded.

'Mr Richard doesn't live *behind* anyone! What else have you got?'

I patted her hand frantically. 'I *might,* might consider, wanting to live behind the American Embassy, besides, if I only use the back door then I will be in front of the American Embassy.'

All this was whispered *sotto voce* which made my mouth twist into the shape of a half-opened oyster. Knowing the area, as I did, it was vital we obtained this house.

'Mr Richard might consider it but only if the price is right.' The phrase: 'does he take sugar' came sharply to mind. The volte face was perfectly timed, faultlessly executed to replace her first statement with the second. Between the two there came a gap of the same thickness as a Gillette razor blade...or a single sheet of Basildon Bond notepaper.

By now the two Estate Agents had turned their full attention to the only person who mattered to them. This obvious demon had the power likely to cause them considerable grief unless they agreed to her demands.

'Very, very cheap,' they answered in unison. 'Four bedrooms and a big garden.'

'How cheap is cheap?'

'Ah...er...how about ten thousand five hundred riyals.'

'A week, a month, or a year,' snapped back the request from my brand-new secretary at full throttle.

'A year, dear Lady Rhona.' Rhona smiled. She had no idea whether it was a good price but happy that she was now being addressed in the correct manner.

'Mr Richard will come and see the house and if he likes it he will discuss the price with you.'

Huxley was already thumbing through bulky specifications oblivious to these small day to day traumas Rhona managed to conjure up. His plan, already set in concrete as far as he was concerned, was for us to move into the new house, he and Rhona into our existing one and our new designer, Henry, into *Wakkrah* now it was being sorted out. With a big house for me it could take a pool and the office as a central operation and be close to the American Embassy.

The two Estate Agents literally backed out of the house, hands clasped together as if in prayer, fingertips touching their noses, as they salaamed to the Secretary from *Jahannam* (hell). An exit following an audience with the Pope could not have been more impressive.

When Jay came back from the school later I was able to tell her that there was a good possibility to move once we had received Head Office approval to lay out more funds for another house and its equipment, which was considerably bigger than this one. With its size, we could combine one large lounge for an open-plan office and the fourth bedroom could become a visiting Partners' suite thus removing the horrendous cost of the hotel. Langdon's Suite for two days had cost the equivalent of a month's rent. Upstairs would give us a large apartment and thus a considerable saving could be made.

An idea floated to the surface of my mind, suggesting to my new staff, as they would not be able to drink all of their monthly liquor allowance, the office could take over the balance, and we could begin to stock up with that all important facility for entertaining clients - a cellar. It was inconceivable that a client would come to our office in the evening after work and not take a gin and tonic or a beer on the terrace. One could see how the British in India had developed the taste for quinine in a very short time whether they had malaria or not.

'We'll get the pool, I'm sure,' I told Jay as we dipped crisps into hummus bought locally from a shop which defied description. A sort of 'all-sorts shop' was one label if you could find the label in the first place.

'That'll help the boys with their friends-'

'And we shall find we have a lot of friends we did not know we had, I bet,' Jay replied tartly. 'The only way they can come is if they bring a bottle. And help in its cleaning.'

Various fanciful ideas of running a successful business on the side, selling whisky and gin to ex-patriates at an enormous profit came to mind, but working on the proposed Naval Base, I guessed correctly, would put paid to that idea fairly quickly.

On the paving in front of us, the evening cockroaches had begun to come out of the myriad of cracks. Their bodies gleamed as if covered with Johnson's wax polish. Their enquiring feelers were sensitive to the slightest movement. None of them, however, showed the slightest fear. I crushed one, with a satisfying crunch which exuded a black juice, leaving the body to fester.

'Well, sweep it away,' Jay suggested sweetly.

'No dear. If I leave it there, the others will see it as a no-go area and leave us alone.'

In fact, it didn't. Its brothers and sisters merely walked over the cadaver in their constant search for food. The hummus tub was hoisted higher off the pavings and onto a table. As the legs were made of varnished bamboo, the cockroaches slid back onto the ground so one assumed someone else in the world had experienced the same problem and found a niche market in polished bamboo legs.

'How's school?'

'Good. The children get through a lot of work, as much in the morning as they would have all day in England. And the quality of teaching is so much better. Discipline runs the entire school. Like a public school in many ways.'

I nodded, knowing that the school would not keep my eldest on after his eleventh year but pleased with the discipline. If he were to go it seemed sensible for his brother to go as well, to keep each other company.

'Say, how about we take the others and drive out to the dunes…see the sun go down.'

We arranged to meet on a round-about. Where else? It turned out that the other two wanted to remain in *Wakkrah* until the housing was sorted. My respect for Huxley and Rhona rose enormously for the spirit they showed in those early days. My early assessment of the two was correct; resolving me to do whatever was possible to make them feel at home.

We again drove in convoy, this time, the blind leading the blind as our instructions only consisted of being told that the start of the real desert was south of *Wakkrah* and before we reached *Umm Sa'id*. My rear-view mirror reflected Rhona as she put her two fingers up out of the window in a victory sign. It reminded me to tell them of the situation when a Qatari places his thumb and first two fingers together in a pyramid and raises it slowly in the air.

Umm Sa'id was approached along a road as straight as an arrow. Before the turn-off it began to curve inland and we saw the dunes in the sun, sharp angled, almost sheer in places with a fine spray of red dust spewing off the crests making them seem like waves in a storm breaking on Fistral Beach.

As the land became increasingly desolate, the desert floor became flat, almost levelled as if using a theodolite with some help from God. Small shrubs of a non-descript nature hung in the evening light, becoming monstrously magnified spores as if of an ash tree, but almost nothing else. We could see the tarmac had wandered in and out in tight curves in places; the road engineer had had his training on an F1 circuit. But, there was a reason of course. The dunes moved. A constant and restless sea might be a better description, and there was nothing the locals could do but change the course of the road from time to time.

We drew closer, allowing them to rear up as if they were attempting to block our route, dictating all life, domineering, dominating, the stuff of Hollywood legend and so much larger than we had imagined.

The six of us struggled up the 'easy' slope, about thirty degrees from the horizontal. We chose this route as the shallow slopes were at the backs of the dune and flowed in cohorts as they slipped and slid in the same direction. They were not as daunting from this side. The *difficult* slope fell away almost shear, each grain rolling over its neighbour as they tumbled towards our cars.

In plan, they were shaped like a boomerang, each a thrusting entity on its own, trying to outdo its neighbour in height and sharpness. As we made our first tentative steps upwards, the sand squeaked beneath our feet. Jay naturally mastered the slope first by removing her flip-flops. For every three steps up, we dropped two back down, as the sand collapsed beneath our feet. Finally, exhausted, panting with the effort of appearing fit and not out of puff, we arrived, balanced finely on this razor-sharp crest.

We all stopped, holding our breath, this time not because of the climb but because of the sensational panorama which caused our cars to appear like Dinky toys.

To the west the sun was going down in, a dreadful phrase but accurate, *blaze of glory.* Cadmium reds and oranges, Burnt Sienna's, Raw Umbers mixed on an artist's canvas. There were purples and light mauves blended also into this palette, ready to be exploited. I was reminded of the lurid pictures the Chinese sold on the Hong Kong markets to passing tourists, but this was real.

The dunes flowed away into the distance, utterly silent, unless one bent down close to the surface, where we became aware of the whispering of a million, trillion grains on the move. It was spooky and magical at the same time.

It quietened even the boys who had attempted to race up the slope, too busy to view the skyline until it was stuck in front of their faces. The land was hushed, words quite unnecessary, superfluous even and a single utterance might well have broken the spell. And time was the key word: a land where time had decided to pause for as long as Arabia had been Arabia.

'Wow!' said one boy. 'Crumbs!' said the other. It was difficult to dispute their erudition.

Wherever the sun could not journey, the blackness created in the shadow was intense, not even a shade of grey, as if someone had opened up a seam of coal to the surface. With the disappearance of the sun a few minutes later the coolness settled on our shoulders, toning faces to a deeper tan.

Rhona sat down. 'This is what it's all about, isn't it? Not a flower, nor a tree, no bird song, not even a butterfly, yet it's beautiful.'

She was so right. My idea of the desert had all been learned from Wilfred Thesiger, but his books, while always being a good read, were unable to capture the stillness...and the loneliness. If one had been alone, here, one's mind would have played tricks with the imagination before ten steps had been taken. It was easy to understand that madness could take hold of one's mind if you were on your own, sitting on a dune, for a few days.

The voice-over of any television documentaries on the subject – and there were many - always killed this special enchantment and I made a mental note to write to the BBC in the future, about having a few quiet moments in their next programme.

'The Qataris come out here when they have had enough of the city. You can see why.'

My statement was magnified by the unanticipated and almost abrupt emergence of the stars. Here in the unpolluted atmosphere they shone without a single wink, but so dense, so… so milky, (sorry), almost solid in their look that we wondered if they might fall in on us if we remained too long in one spot. A few minutes later, a meteorite did shoot across the sky to underline the majesty of the moment.

'We must have a Barbeque here one day, towards the late afternoon. We'll bring Henry when he arrives. And, tomorrow we'll get down to some office work, get you set up. I've got one of those new hand-held calculators, all the rage out here.'

No talks, of course, about p.c.s' in 1975, but our typewriters were, at least, electronic. This was directed at Rhona.

'And you, Huxley, you must go to *Halul* as soon as possible. Hitch a lift with Shell transport. Go and see what they are doing. I know the Shell boys are in charge, but it will all come back on us if something goes awry. And you'll learn something about how they construct buildings out here. Remember, it does rain, so those roofs do need to be waterproof.'

The boys were getting restive. As we got into the car a scorpion raced across the ground, luckily in the opposite direction to us. It was small, not like the things one sees in 20th Century Fox studios, but these did give a nasty sting. Open toed sandals were not a good idea for this part of the world at night.

'How about going over to *Dukkan* on Friday? I want to see what is on the other side. It looks out towards Bahrain and Saudi Arabia. Give you an idea of perspective.'

'Only if we have sorted out my office,' said the ever-practical Rhona.

She was right. 'Agreed. Business first. We could meet for lunch and drive over for an afternoon swim. Nowhere is that far away.'

And that is exactly what we did. Rhona and Huxley managed to transfer their things into the Villa, now in reasonable order after the frantic clean-up. They had decided against shag rugs going for reed mats on the terrazzo instead.

We drove over to the other side of the peninsular that Friday, in the familiar convoy. It was about forty miles due west from Doha travelling along a desert road that wandered north-west as it bypassed *wadis* and *jebel* outcrops; otherwise there were very few redeeming features. The desert stretched out alongside the road, flatter than Norfolk, forbidding and slightly threatening despite the sunlight in the height of the day. The heat seared the ground and caused the light to shiver and shatter in ecstasy. For all of us brought up on a diet of *Boys Own* and *Biggles* we had been indoctrinated with stories of men, always men, gasping out their lives on the desert floor and people waving frantically from their wrecked plane to passing aircraft who always failed to see them. And then there were mirages and all those stories to spin the picture further, and Fry's Turkish Delight would get mixed up in there somewhere.

Along the road we saw carefully built piles of stones tapering as they rose, some a foot high, others lower and fatter, just off the sides of the road. Fauzi had told me they were the physical signs of the Bedouin. When they left the road and headed off into the desert, it provided a marker, for relatives and family of where they had gone.

We were thankful for air-conditioning in our sturdy car which poured great gulps of ice-cold air into the back where the boys were engaged in making an interesting looking insect go faster along an arm rest. We were close, though unable to see the ranch where a Sheikh kept a small herd of Oryx, all that was left of the horned deer now almost hunted out of existence. He was a man well ahead of his time in noticing that, if someone were not there to save these magnificent animals, the desert would soon be bare of any wildlife.

Dukkan materialised out of the shimmering light with a fretwork of towers breaking the skyline to the north of the small town and we could see the glitter of the sea well before we arrived. Our two cars turned off the road away from the oil field, down a bumpy track. Signs that civilisation had stretched to this part of the world were the remnants of cigarette packets and discarded bottles of lager. No one was about, not a single human being. Old rubber tyres, empty oil drums and seagull's carcases we did have. Even these were bleached of their colour except, curiously, the beaks of the dead gulls which formed hard orange flashes standing out from their grey, desiccated corpses.

As we climbed out, the temperature difference was immense. We had been driving for an hour cocooned in the car at about 21 degrees. We now experienced forty degrees, that's one hundred and four Fahrenheit, almost exactly double the heat inside my car, and all in the space of five seconds. The blood roared in my ears and sweat slopped down my neck like a sponge full of warm water. Half a minute after that my navel drowned, but by the time we had walked down the slight gradient to the beach we had come to terms with this lunacy: well, sort of. *Dogs*, *mad* and *Englishmen* came to mind in rapid succession to each other.

The land here sloped or rather, collapsed into the sea as if it was a whale's nose or a nuclear submarine's bow plane. The waves, such as they were, smiled droopily as they arrived on the beach and then dropped back, having surrendered to an irresistible force. There was no energy in the water; it had been beaten to death by the heat of the day. A slightest breeze, nay, more like a waft of gossamer, enough to ruffle Jay's hair if she had been two years old again, might otherwise have been described as cooling, though now it was just the same as opening a hot oven door when you have the fan unit working.

Time for a swim.

The British Council had given me a leaflet on wild life in Qatar. This had included a note on those animals in the sea which do not have such a good relationship with man as had been proven on too many occasions in the past. These included the stone fish and the sea snake, the latter currently entering its very own mating season, i.e. seeking territorial rights, at this time of year.

'So boys,' I ended my biology lesson, 'would you please keep away from sea snakes. They have yellow and black stripes running around the body.'

This was backed up with tales of what might happen if they were confronted with one of these three-foot-long striped horrors. It might be quite nasty if one of these encountered a family having a day out, so Jay insisted the boys stay inshore around a small islet lying twenty yards offshore.

The sea was especially good, for there was no impact on the skin just the feel of the pressure of the water. We submerged, "flooding all Kingston valves", to sound for the bottom only ten feet down in crystal clear waters.

Eventually, we emerged from this idyll to lay up a late picnic. Bright brollies were erected and an awning to remove the worst of the sun for it was still too hot to stay out without protection. The boys had swum with white T-shirts on to reflect the sun's rays off their backs while they snorkelled. Rhona emerged from the water, allowing the sea to settle back in its rightful place and Huxley made haste to open cold beers. My youngest son arrived, sniffing food though the eldest was nowhere to be seen. I thought no more of it, merely shouting out that lunch was ready.

It was five minutes later when Jay was just beginning to raise her eyes to the islet once too often that coincided with an extraordinary noise. It was a cocktail consisting of a cow in pain, a water buffalo coughing up phlegm and a sea lion with laryngitis flapping its flippers as it waited for food, a reasonable enough description of the host of baffling sounds assailing our small group's ears. Everything was effortlessly explained when my eldest appeared around the bluff of the island. He was swimming the breast stroke in which he had always excelled, though currently he was ploughing a course through the shallows in what could only be described as Olympian, but not as in *heights*. Each second and a half he expelled these strange sounds. Eventually his feet made contact with the beach, but it just meant they were able to make traction with the sand. He continued to mount the slope with his arms going like circular saws in a Canadian lumber yard.

'Don't forget your feet,' I said rather unkindly.

'Whatever is the matter?' Jay looked witheringly at me, halting her son in mid-step as he headed for the dunes and passed a Pepsi cola into his shaking hand.

'I saw a sea snake, well below me, so I swam on but when I looked down it was coming straight for me. It was moving like a snake, kind of wriggling. And it was yellow and black.'

'Well, it *is* a snake,' said his brother callously, pleased he had not made the encounter himself. He stuffed a pitta bread filled with *hummus* into his mouth and settled back in the shade.

Rhona and Huxley were, by now, quite relaxed with their new boss and had been urged to sit under the awning as soon as possible. We made sure they were covered up.

The sun's heat struck the sand, sneaking in sideways as it attempted to peel the skin, four layers deep from one's thighs without the recipient feeling a thing, well, at the time, at least. It was the morning after those *things* took to the worse. We had learned to take a very large orange pill, Vitamin C, the size of a florin, available in shops to fend off the possibility of sun-stroke; what one might term the 'evening-before pill'.

Jay had now turned even more Moroccan French in hue; my own face was a deep brown except for a vertical fine white line between my eyes where my forehead took exception to the times I forgot my sun glasses, (they are called Ray Bans today I'm led to believe or is it 'shades?').

Jay was idly picking up shells, salmon pink in colour with small razor-sharp crests of chitin curving up in rows on their tops. It is difficult to describe these exquisitely shaped molluscs properly but if you can image a small hedgehog with a Mohican haircut with short but squatter spines, then blown in the wind, and pink of course, well, that's fairly close. Looking around the beach we saw hundreds of different shells. Fine tubes, sand dollars, tapered tops, cowries, spiky clams, multi-coloured Tritons and Fig shells. The collection started on that day and they are with us yet, filling up a drawer in the bathroom cabinet. I had a ridiculous idea once to stick them on the bathroom wall with Polyfilla to give a notion – to visiting guests – of how widely travelled we had been in our youth. Jay then put an end to it by saying they would not be amused with my name-dropping when backing onto a spiny shell, with a bare bottom.

The boys, rightfully covered up with floppy hats and towels draped over their shoulders, had wandered off much farther and returned with a heavy, globular stone with a bland, dull grey exterior. It was, however, almost circular in shape and extremely heavy. I knew what this one was from my earlier research in Guildford.

'Bring me a hammer from the tool kit. And a screw driver. A big one.'

The operating equipment duly arrived but there was also need of a suitable slab to operate upon. The stone was given an almighty bash, but nothing happened as the screwdriver, acting as a chisel merely bounced off. On the third attempt, however, giving it some *welly*, it fell into two neat halves.

Inside, it was hollow but with a purple and mauve lining of hard crystal perhaps half an inch in depth.

'It's a geode, some call them Thunder Eggs. Formed in sedimentary rocks. They can be sawn in two and the faces polished,' I added with some knowledge. Rhona looked on in awe at my inconsequential facts unaware this had been gleaned from books just three months before.

'They must be quite valuable,' said my new secretary, already more of a P.A. than just a typist.

Over-hearing our discussion, the boys rapidly returned to the desert where, in five minutes they had found enough to weigh down my new car. We selected what we thought were the best shapes and they joined the pile of shells.

Jay handed out paper towels and plates with a mandatory salt twist. Our bodies knew exactly when they ran short of sodium for the stiffness in our joints sent a painful reminder of what we might experience with arthritis in thirty years' time. How right I would turn out to be.

The local chicken shop produced quite a plump hen on their spits, if one could ignore the thick, jet black rimes of fat running down the sides of the roasting pans in the shop. With the chilled beer out of the cool box, a well-cooked leg in the other, work seemed a long way off. It was a good start for the new couple, as it was important they were integrated into this completely new way of life as soon as possible so they could then concentrate on the job in hand. There were no illusions that as the work began to build, we would have fewer days like this: besides, the boys would be gone before too long with the exception of the holidays.

When we had sucked the bones and rejected the parson's nose which no-one wanted, we cleaned up the beach, said goodbye to the sea snakes and drove off up a track of gold as the sun disintegrated into horizontal layers between two dunes in front of us.

CHAPTER SEVEN

A Call to The Palace

Four weeks later the office had settled into what could not in any way be described as a relaxing routine, but it was efficient and organised, with Rhona quite clearly at the helm. The two of them had settled in extremely well, with Huxley now handling *Halul* Island and two enquiries for new Palaces for important Qatari families. We had also registered our interest in a huge housing contract to be constructed close to a new Japanese Steel plant at *Umm Sa'id*.

It was then the office received a telephone call from the Emir's powerful advisor and right-hand man, though curiously, not a Qatari, bidding me call at a precise time and date at the Royal Palace. With no idea what it was all about, it was difficult to prepare myself for questions on a specific nature.

I did pull out the jacket to my suit which had hung in a wardrobe since my arrival and put on a tie. Both these seemingly ordinary everyday pieces of clothing were ludicrous to wear in the Gulf as July continued to produce temperatures in silly figures. A jacket would crease in a moment in the humidity trapping the sweat build-up, while the tie became a noose which tightened as the neck girth expanded in the heat. But I had no option as I had no idea who I was going to meet.

As I drove to the Palace the air-conditioning was put to full 'on' to chill myself down as much as possible.

The Royal Emiri Palace was built above a new round-about with a wide sweeping drive flowing up to a massive concrete porte-cochere. It was an unpretentious building to hold someone quite so rich and powerful, for the architecture was pre-modern Doha, or rather, pre-oil revenue Qatar, and did not reflect the new wealth of the country which had come after the Palace had been completed. No doubt someone would rebuild it in due course. (They did, rather well).

My driving licence was demanded at the gate-house by two slightly built soldiers in over-large fatigues and dusty rifles. The first point of sale was not too impressive, but one has to remember these were pre-terrorist days, so the idea of me trying to enter the building with explosives strapped around my waist did not come to their minds as quickly as it might today.

Once inside, I was led along carpets so deep the pile curled over the top of my shoes. No sound escaped the corridors which were wider than the average house. Marble tables lined the way forward, but, unlike Buckingham Palace, there were no flowers to be seen. The atmosphere was cool, almost cold, but the cardamom coffee smelt delicious, the views out to sea magnificent.

I remained in the chair allocated to me for two hours before being summoned: this was a fairly short time when waiting to be admitted to meet an advisor to the Ruler of the country. There appeared to be a strict protocol regarding the time one had to wait for a meeting dependent upon the importance of the subject in hand and of course, how important you were associated with the hierarchy.

There were no tattered copies of Woman's Own or Country Life to keep me occupied nor was there anyone else to talk to. Occasionally, an employee perhaps, a cook definitely at one stage for he was carrying lettuces, would walk by aimlessly, having all the time in the world to contemplate his fate, feet padding quietly on the thick wool as if they had been wearing langlauf skis riding powder snow in Norway. None of them took the slightest interest in me, not even a glance, and for a fleeting second each time, I pondered the possibility that they knew of my fate and were thus unable to make eye contact with me. Deportation or removal of head by a silver sword were two images flitting uneasily on the perimeter of my mind. Eventually a more important looking gentleman, earnest and white long-sleeve shirted arrived.

'You will be meeting with His Royal Highness himself. He has several important questions to ask you. Please answer them as clearly as you can and direct your voice to him rather than the interpreter.' There was a phrase for it, there always is. 'Why me Guv?'

He then gestured for me to follow. He knocked, then ushered me into an enormous room with windows looking out over the Corniche. His Highness was speaking into a walkie-talkie the size of a brick, with its aerial extended fully towards the ceiling. He was facing the sea talking excitedly. His colossal desk did not have a single piece of paper save for a notepad, and a gold pen resided on a stand though more of an ornament and a work of art than to be used to make marks. He kept gesticulating with his arms and hands and, naturally, I looked too.

Hovering in the air about seven hundred metres from the shore was a helicopter. His Highness was obviously in discussion with the pilot for each time the Emir spoke the helicopter moved a few dozen yards in one direction or another.

After five minutes of this the pilot would probably have wished he could fly backwards more easily, for he was having to make minute adjustments to his position each time. Eventually, and after much more excitement, entreaties and beseeching, the great man stood up and shouted loudly: 'Zain!' Only one Zain, you say? So that is what you can do when you are a Ruler. I found that Arabs would not normally deliver a single 'Zain!' It was always in threes.

The Emir, the benevolent Dictator of Qatar, all powerful and very, very rich turned to me, a fairly severe Arab-bearded and thick-set man. He gestured for an interpreter who had arrived by magic carpet, or so it seemed, to come nearer. I was asked to sit, learning later he had just fixed the location of the furthest point out to sea for the new peninsular to be attached to the Corniche, thus creating a grand curving sweep to the seafront. A hotel would be located at its further-most point out in the water. Apparently, a Dutch hydraulic engineering company had the contract to create land out of the coral floor and Americans were designing the hotel so there was nothing for me for the time being.

'Mr Richard,' the interpreter began in thick, overlaid English redolent of a scholarship from the British Council rather than Harvard or Cambridge, 'His Highness would like to know how tall the tower is you are bidding for in Abu Dhabi.'

'Twenty-seven stories Your Highness. But others are also bidding, for other towers, possibly taller ones. We do not have information on the other designs.'

This was the point where the Arabian mentality came into its own. "Could you make your tower taller?'

'Er, no Sire, we cannot.'

'Pray, why not?'

' Well, Sire, we were informed by our Client this was as high as they wished to go.'

(Fuck! I'd really put my foot in it this time).

There was quite a long silence while being studied as if I was a blow-fly on the cloaca of a water buffalo. But, for some reason the Emir liked what had been said. His eyes gleamed.

'So,' continued the interpreter. 'Would it be possible to build a taller tower here in Doha?'

'Yes Sire. The ground bearing rock is strong provided there are no karsts...er holes formed out of the limestone. If we could choose the site careful-'

I was cut off. The Emir opened his mouth and gave forth with his pronouncement. "You may choose your site. But it will be taller, yes?'

'Yes, it will Sire but we will also need to know what the tower is to be for. In other words, how the space in the building will be used.'

This time His Highness looked at me as if I *were* a locust perched on the left testicle of a wart hog. 'That is not the point in question here. You see, Qatar needs a tower, and this tower is to be taller than the one my brothers have planned in Abu Dhabi.'

'Of course, Sire. A tower to outshine all others; a keynote building (I liked that phrase) to place your country on the world map.'

It was glorious stuff to me but very unsure whether I had taken it too far or, contrarily, did not show sufficient enthusiasm. The interpreter had abandoned the translation and was gazing out of one of a long line of windows at the blue sea. The mind of the Emir, an Arab who had had nothing and now could not even spend the interest pouring into his coffers was complicated. The final use of a building was quite secondary to the important effect it would have on its neighbours. I had to remember that, very few years earlier this man, leading his tribe, would have owned virtually nothing of western content. In a few years, he had been transported to a world as alien to him as the moon was to me.

Continuing to make sure my thrust had been felt properly by smiling brightly as if the building design was in the bag, His Royal Highness was starting up again.

'We must find out the height of the tower that wins the competition, and then you will report to me.' There was some firmness in his voice.

'Very well, Sire. I will do my best to find out. We might even win the competition: it is to be known as a Trade Centre, to show off Abu Dhabi's industry and skills.'

The Emir waved aside the comment with his fly whisk as if he were swatting a gnat. He turned to the window smiling at his success, as the orange buoy which the helicopter had now released, bobbed serenely in the turquoise water signifying the start of a grand new plan for the town. One day, he might change the name of Doha to 'Khalifa City', a somewhat grander title than Khalifa Town which already existed in the country and was a poor village in comparison with Doha.

I had completely missed his dismissal of me. No goodbye, no handshake just the swish of the swat through the air and the turn of the head to weightier matters.

I was ushered out, wondering whether it was protocol to have backed all the way to the door as they do in Buck House after being knighted, but the Emir could not see me, gazing as he was out to sea, nor was I going to be knighted.

Two palace guards in red and white *keffiyehs* flipped up over their heads and well-armed, smart and dangerous joined my departure. They flanked me as we walked so closely side by side that I did not think it the right time to ask them where the loo was. It wasn't a pressing matter at the time, but it would be nice to see a Royal urinal. I couldn't help but notice the armed guards lining the walls in the corridors who had not been there before. Was I that much of a risk?

As we walked out to the portico, a Lebanese craftsman was applying sheets of gold leaf to one of the massive door panels. The wind was blowing up from the water and carrying a good proportion of each sheet away into the air. One could just imagine some of this landing in some Qatari's back yard who no doubt would thank Allah for the donation. Verily, a gift from God. That just left frankincense and myrrh.

A staff member ran up to me rather breathlessly and handed me a card. It was an invitation to attend His

Highness's birthday celebrations. So not everything I had said was wrong.

The car had heated up to over a hundred degrees while having my chat with the Ruler. But, the Datsun started without a hiccup allowing me to whack the air-conditioning lever to maximum. Out in the bay bobbed the solitary orange buoy to all the world like just another lobster pot or mooring buoy for one of those fast boats. Had I been the first to witness the new creation for Qatar? The car's black leather seats had returned to an acceptable temperature. My jacket was released from its restricting arms (creased), also my tie (stretched and damp), allowing the blood to re-circulate for the first time in three hours along both my right and left carotid artery.

This had been my first Royal audience with the most influential person in the country without making too much of a hash of it. There might not be any work arising from this meeting, but he now knew my name and that of the practice and my relationship with Abu Dhabi. This could be a double-edged sword, for the Emir might wish to have me on board, to ensure his tower was always taller than others down the peninsula. On the other hand, he might want to keep me well away from his own plans where I could be in touch with Abu Dhabi's Ruler Sheikh Zayed, his 'brother,' as the Emir termed him.

I cursed myself wondering if the meeting, totally unplanned and unexpected, could have been handled differently and realised that whatever had been said, the die was cast. Besides, his invitation was in my pocket.

Rhona had a note for me on my return. 'Henry is coming out next week. We need to move on this house.' She had a check list for me of questions we needed answering. Carefully I hung up my jacket ready for His Highness's birthday. The new suit had been needed after all.

We went down to see the selected villa when it had cooled down in the evening. The two Estate Agents agreed to show me around at four o'clock. It wasn't far, on the same Ring Road as our own address, or rather, location, as it did not have such a thing as an address, but in a brand new development. To call it an Estate was not quite accurate. Estate drums up a picture of neat rows of two storey executive houses all in the same brick with uPVC windows and an evergreen on the lawn no more than five feet high. The one we had come to see was a large house, with front and back raw 'gardens' of broken stone and builders' rubble.

My present garden looked positively Titchmarsh compared with this. On the positive side, the roads were in, and telephone cabling laid. On the negative side there was no sign of electricity. Power was the key in the race to secure these increasingly rare houses, for without it, you could not even move in. However, as we arrived it was confirmed that cabling for electricity was being laid between two lines of silver sand poured the length of the kerbs to *favoured* houses, those I assume that had paid a *premium* to have early power. Too late came the realisation of why the rent was so cheap, as charges for houses were climbing steadily. It had been a wasted journey. The silver sand literally looped backwards and forwards across the road identifying houses for a J.C.B. which was proceeding along the road fifty yards away digging up the brand-new tarmac; but it was quite clear it was not coming to our new house. The markers bypassed

No. 32 Acacia Avenue and moved on to No.36 a far grander house with silver gargoyles on the gate posts.

One of those lightning bolts struck me. They did not come often so it was most welcome now. There was plenty of this silver sand in piles having been used for construction. Having taken a quick shufty at the digger the lines were hastily swept away in the road outside the house we needed while I installed a revised route in clean silver sand which swept precisely and trimly into our property. The Estate Agents nodded enthusiastically as if we were all boys in the dorm having a lark together.

Jay and the boys followed me around the house, studying the two levels of accommodation. On the first floor we had balconies over-looking the other new properties and the 'garden'. We could have a good guest suite, while downstairs on the ground floor the space could be given over to the offices. I use the plural form, for the future meant expansion. There was an area outside the sliding patio doors to the rear which would make a level terrace encircling the proposed swimming pool.

Beyond the rear boundary wall was the desert, flat, and dusty and as evening approached a lonely and unwelcoming place. It was a place where God had not started his work yet – sort of pre-Eden-esque. Better to turn my eyes into the garden, inside the wall which would keep cats and dogs away, if not those clever climbers, rats, as well as the itinerant Bedouin and straying camels having slipped their hobbles.

This containment, common to all houses, defined the Arab in so many ways. It set out the curtilage of his land, enabling him to declare to all and sundry that this was the limit beyond which one did not go unless invited. The Moorish concepts were still retained in these enclosures and I was merely expanding that language by repeating the idea of water as a decoration. We might not create an Alhambra, but we would have our own private world away from the jostle and crowds of this scorched land. In our existing house, which was in a mature quarter, with a mosque at the bottom of the garden, the wall had not seemed so important. Out here where civilisation ended in rat droppings and camel dung, it was essential.

We were interrupted by the arrival of the yellow JCB which had proceeded quickly along its designated route. It cut a channel through the black top directly to the fuse board in a metal shed built into the wall. The Baluch driving his enormous machine which erupted black, oily smoke in some glee, did not even question the sand markings, now slightly scuffed. In fifteen minutes, he had cut the trench and was off down the road to the next. We had arrived just in time. Timing rather than size is everything.

While we were settling terms with the Agents, an Englishman who was a Supervisor for Qatar Power walked along the road with a clipboard. I learnt that he was coming to live in the house across the road. He confirmed that power would be connected in the next week though he warned there could be occasional power cuts. We were, by now, quite used to these and the office would get by so long as we had power over a reasonable length of time. In those days, of course, there were no computers and ancillary equipment, only our dyeline printer which had a need for power, and, most vital of all, the air-conditioning. He shook his head at the trench to our house but, glancing sideways at me and back to his documentation he dismissed any idea that we could have fiddled the lines. Jay smiled sweetly at him and we shook hands as neighbours. She also gleaned from him that the front garden would receive top soil in the next few days and the rubbish, at least would be removed from the back. Probably over someone else's wall into the desert. (This proved correct).

Relocating from a relatively small house in England, this was a palace in the real sense of the word and would form the core of our operations for the country. Jay seemed pleased and Rhona, would, in the next few weeks, settle all the matters concerning the fit-out. Henry might have to be put up in the hotel for a few days as we managed an arrangement of musical chairs. It was now going to happen as we all moved forward one space.

At such times, the use of the word *Insha'Allah* was very helpful. The locals attached the word to almost anything they felt useful to help them connect to their God. They expanded upon this phrase with the ever more helpful sentence: *'Bukkrah, Insha'Allah, Mah'lish'* which more or less translates into: 'Tomorrow, perhaps, God willing.'

We went back to the house to plan what we needed, for as well as a standard fit-out package we would need extra office equipment including one of these new miniature calculators, for I was often acting as a Quantity Surveyor on site needing to make quick calculations for enquiring Qataris. (Doesn't this date my manuscript as much as a history book?). There was no differentiation between an Architect, an Engineer or a Quantity Surveyor in their mind.

The gizmo shop was not far from Ali bin Ali's supermarket, a smorgasbord of cameras, music players and dozens of these calculators, one of which caught my eye instantly. When one looks back now on how those little pieces of equipment have developed to a point where one thinks nothing of beaming Scottie up (well almost); at the time they were quite simply a *must have*. Adding up columns of Riyals and Dirhams and finding percentages of a sum: all this gone overnight along with inky calculations on scraps of paper, the slide rule, SOHCAHTOA and... one's fingers.

The calculator was slim, clear and uncomplicated, powered by a battery the size of a flattened pea and was a fashion accessory to take with me where ever I went. To the younger generation who are reading this it will appear the author is quite simple in the head writing such guff, but today you are not brought up on how magical, technology is. It is merely a tool for everyday use. Then, it was voodoo, black art but still bloody, sorry....very useful. Having seen the thing demonstrated to me I would have paid in chicken's blood or bats' ears if required. Instead, the shop owner was rewarded in riyals.

The main issue was to keep ourselves focussed on the projects we had targeted, to pin down what was coming into the office, responding quickly to our potential clients and politely refusing ideas which would prove non-starters in profit terms, unless there was a political significance to it when the cost could be written off to marketing or public relations.

What was becoming apparent were the sheer numbers of the competition arriving daily from all over the world, and that *did* mean the world. It had now taken up camp on this tiny peninsular and was working almost cheek by jowl with us. Some of the opposition lived just across the road. We had to be guarded in our comment on projects we were involved in with Engineers and Quantity Surveyors we met at parties for a drink, for there was a fine balance in connecting with the correct protocol. The early part of an evening would be taken up with checking out what schemes the opposition were working on. Then, if satisfied, the rest of the evening was to ensure they understood you were simply the best Architectural practice to work with for the new military barracks or whatever one had gleaned over a gin and tonic. A balance was needed for it was never known just when we might find ourselves working alongside one of these companies in concert rather than in opposition.

On my return from the gizmo shop, Rhona had another message for me from a Mr. *Hitoshi Fukida*.

'A Japanese gentleman, he was most insistent on speaking with you today. I told him you would ring as soon as you got back.' (Imagine what could have been done with a mobile phone in those days?).

The Japanese were only in the country for one project: The Steel Rolling Mill at *Umm Said*, already an item in the National Budget. I had been intensely interested at University in Japanese Architecture so perhaps I was ahead of the game, or at least, some of the competition. I knew how low to bow, or not to, so I made ready to ring him straight away. Readers may well be wondering why I should know about this detail, of bowing that is, while ostensibly learning about the wonders of Pagodas...I have no idea, sorry.

'Mr Fukida, my name is Richard Newman. You rang Sir.'

'Ahhh, Mister Nooman. How-er do-you-do. You come see me?'

'I come see you...when?' My Japanese improved even as we talked. I could just see myself bowing to him when we met, not too low to show subservience and not too high showing haughtiness. We agreed to meet in half an hour in his office on the 'B - Ling Load'.

That was interesting, as the offices in that area were quite old-fashioned and were due for demolition in the new plan.

It turned out his office was almost devoid of furniture: a desk, his chair and one other. A coffee table held magazines of Steel plants around the world: stuff to take to bed with you. Mr Fukida bowed, though being on the phone at the time, he was caught between the necessity to be formally polite to me and not to cut off his caller. He was a man straight out of *A Town Like Alice* – early part – his eyes searching and analysing. Dressed in a suit, it was as if he had stepped out of a taxi in London that bore no relationship with the weather or even the country. His face was lined, pale and filled with enormous stress which caused him to dab at his lips with a white handkerchief each time he uttered a word.

'*Moshi, Moshi,*' the Japanese twitched his intense face. A stream of precise instructions issued from his mouth before he replaced the receiver in its cradle.

'Ahhh, Mister Nooman.' This was becoming slightly repetitive. 'We would like to have your Company design our acc...acc...ommodation blocks for us at *Umm Sa'id.*' The words were jerked out of his mouth like a machine gun, guttural and untidy as if he had lost control of speech in any language. The stress hung always on the wrong word and the last syllable.

'How many accommodation blocks, if I may ask, Mr Fukida?'

'Thlee blocks, each two hundred looms.'

'Ahhh, velly good,' I replied. 'What about land? A site?' This was all important as many of the land owning Shaikh's were holding out against the Government for better prices.

'His Highness has said we can have what land we… wequire. The Minis-terlee (tricky one) of Lurks has put a wed line awound a dwarwing. No-one owns the land.'

I was dubious about that but kept my peace. 'Please may I see the contract and the fees proposed? What is the time-scale?'

My Japanese client, a decent, honest man, allowed his face to crinkle further into a prune. 'We have thlee months to be on site.'

'*Zain, Zain, Zain*,' though perhaps I should have just bowed slightly to allow me time to think. This was not the time to commit the office until we knew what was involved.

Christ! We would have to do this one on the hoof, producing an outline to price on and designing the detail as we went. The workers at the Steel Mill would not be Qataris, more likely to be Pakistanis and neighbouring States. The degree of sophistication would be low to us, very high to them. The idea of toilet blocks on each floor rather than individual rooms came to mind; and a refectory rather than a dining room. But, it all came back to the land ownership.

'I would like to drive down to the site. Have a look around and get some detailed maps of the area.'

'Ahhh, good. You come see me when you come back. Then we sign, yes?'

'Yes.'

At the Ministry of Public Works, I found an ex-pat involved with me on another project. He was cautious. 'Umm. The land has indeed been marked on a drawing and approved by His Highness, but I don't think the information has reached the owner. Besides, I understand he does not like the price we are offering. None of these Arabs understand the essence of CPOs' – compulsory purchase orders. May I make the suggestion that you do not place your feet onto the land when you go and see it. Stand on the road side of the blocks. There's really nothing to see unless you like sand.'

He laughed at his feeble joke. I, however, did not laugh. He would also have been acutely aware that only last month one of his local Indian engineers had been shot dead in the north of the peninsular for measuring land with a tape measure. The land deal had not been signed and the owner was not a happy chappy.

'I very much doubt if I will stop the car but I need to see how it relates to the Steel Rolling Mill on the coast.'

'That's about three miles away.' He pulled out a roll of drawings. 'These are copies of the latest land surveys we have. I have not seen them myself yet, but you are welcome to take them. Let me know what you think and stay in touch with me. We have the Japanese on board, but they always bow their heads to say they understand but really they don't.'

'Like the locals?'

'No. Far worse. With the locals, it is usually not so important. Here we are talking about a one thousand two hundred-million-riyal exercise, slightly more than we want to make a mistake with. And the Japanese have a thirty percent investment themselves.'(interesting note: in those days we did not use the term *billion*).

The message was fairly clear. Qatari and Japanese money but, if anything went wrong it would be the Bl-itish who would be at fault, whatever mistakes the two partners made. The lines of stress on my client's face had told me everything would need to be repeated twice and a follow-up letter.

The next day, fatigued with the pace of business and lack of sleep, I drove down to *Umm Sa'id* with Huxley. The principle today would be if we were to come under fire from an AK47 we could return twice the fire power with stones. Joking apart, we had to be very careful and I needed someone with me as a witness to the way we proceeded. I didn't think an Arab would shoot a white man without careful consideration, but all it took was a jumpy finger.

None of this did I tell Jay.

We motored down the *Umm Sa'id* road, past *Wakkrah* where we ran parallel with the coast. Oil tankers appeared at regular intervals smudging the far horizon like small puffs of cloud, reminding me of the vast quantities of the black stuff the world was taking out of the ground. While, perhaps in thirty years' time we may have solved the problem of replacing the internal combustion engine, the planet is, meanwhile, dependent upon oil for so many other things in life – just think of plastics – and that could be the next worry rather than the car itself.

There were no such concerns about oil as we drove south, as Huxley chatted about the future, as he saw it. Fuel was so cheap here that the subject did not feature in our budgets, and as mentioned, there was enough surplus of the stuff for Dubai to make a golf course out of it.

I slowed down as we began to approach *Umm Sa'id*. Huxley got the drawings out and we stopped to spread them over the bonnet. This was fairly daft for the heat threatened to curl the paper up into a tight ball and to bring on an immediate bushfire. Between us we managed to find the site on the map and to determine where that was in relationship to the road running straight as an arrow far into the desert horizon. We drove on for another mile at which point a low concrete block wall, some two blocks high appeared. Its flank wall bounding the road acted as a barrier to the driven sand so all we could see was a row of rectangular prisms locked together but essentially making the point - *Keep Out*.

'Whatever you do, Huxley, don't step over that block-work. Photographs as well might be a bad idea.'

We liked to take hundreds of photos for each project though the reason went back into the mists of time. In the office we would show the developed prints (no digitals in those days to speed things up) to Rhona who would always say, 'well that's nice,' but we could not even tell which picture was which, as each shot had so little in the way of a redeeming feature. As an aid to planning they were of no use.

'Uh, oh!' Huxley screwed up his eyes away from the glare as he studied the map. 'Look at this buggar!'

It *was* a buggar.

We had not been able to study the maps before but, clearly marked, running diagonally across the whole site were three oil pipe-lines lying on the surface of the sand. 'We'll have to work around those or let them into the ground.'

Huxley however, as a purist Architect, was thinking only of the aesthetics of the site.

'Real eyesore.'

'Huxley. This camp is probably going to be the most luxurious building the workers will ever have lived in. A few pipelines will hardly matter.' There was, of course, the need to keep personnel away from such pipes filled with volatile fuel.

'How do you feel about humps?' I asked Huxley. 'Sort of camel humps in the site...to cover the pipes.'

'The site would be split into two,' growled Huxley unsure whether flippancy was in the air. It did not really matter as we had the resources to do whatever was needed to accomplish the job. The one thing we were not short of was cash, but, it was extraordinary that the site, of all the square miles of nothing turned up with three unwanted pipelines.

We drove on slowly, our necks craned to the right as we studied the terrain, both of us keeping a weather eye on sharp shooters, possibly with red and white keffiyehs.

'Buggar... again!' It was me this time. 'Buggar! Buggar! Buggar! I simply don't believe this.'

Our virgin site had thrown up another problem, one we could not cover with sand. Five stone tablets stood up forlornly in the sand, scarred by the wind, no inscriptions but definitely graves.

'Why the hell here of all places?'

'Could we move them?'

'I very much doubt it. And by my judgement, those graves are right in the middle of the housing camp. The fact they are out here might mean they were not Muslims. Any deaths would surely have taken place in the village of *Umm Sa'id* down the road by the sea. The site is close to the sea at this point. Perhaps they were sailors, ship-wrecked in the past?'

This time we took careful photographs on the telephoto lens for proof when we went back to see the Ministry of Public Works, whose sensibly chosen site was fast becoming a bit of a tale. *These* photos would have value. There was a bit of a pantomime as we attempted to shield the camera from hostile eyes, but we managed to get off a couple of clicks in the end.

A decision was made to drive on to the refinery to get our bearings. Inside the main gates, which hung open in those days, we eventually stopped alongside an American engineer who invited us into his air-conditioned cabin for a cup of tea where we explained the reason for being in the vicinity. He knew of the graves. Having heard our tale of woe concerning the pipelines he pulled out a set of drawings in a tight roll from a tube.

'Hate to say this, fellas, but there is a third problem for you, that is, several more problems although all of the same nature.'

Huxley stared back into my face as his eyebrows rose a full two centimetres. He could see 'six hundred looms' going into the sea.

'Sink holes,' the engineer proclaimed, stabbing a finger at the drawing which had considerably more detail on it than those back in Doha. 'They are all over the place.'

'What's a sink hole?' Huxley wanted to know.

'A sink hole, or as you call them, swallow hole, or a karst out here, is a saucer-shaped depression in the desert. When rain passes down into the ground it can form a water course as it dissolves the limestone. If it has collected carbon dioxide on the way down the solvent action causes holes. Sometimes big ones. The ground can collapse above underground caves. That's why we can't use the land.'

'Rain? Here?' Huxley wanted to know more. He loved to learn.

'Biblical rain. Thousands of years ago. There's very good water down there you know, and lots of it.'

'So, pipelines, graves and sink holes. Anything else?'

'No, no. That's all I believe.' He rolled the drawings up. 'You will need to survey the ground very carefully before you build.'

The phrase, 'I should co-co,' oozed into my thoughts. We thanked the man and asked where we could get copies of his drawings. Mr Hitoshi would need to know all the details. His stressed face would crumple like a cigarette paper when given the news which might lead him to committing *hara-kiri*. Mr Hitoshi might call it *seppuku,* but the end result would be exactly the same.

The engineer advised me to call into Head Office of Shell in Doha where he was sure we could buy copies. He provided the drawing numbers which were helpful as there were literally thousands of rolls of paper in the files.

'I'd better handle this one,' I said on the way back. So engrossed were we that we had not noticed the rise in temperature going on outside. We had not been exposed long enough for our air-cooled bodies to notice the alarming change. At *Wakkrah* I dropped Huxley off to collect his car. Climbing out of mine, a physical wall of heat struck out at anything in its path. It stretched the skin on my face as if it had been plastered with a mud pack, seared my eyes despite my shaded lenses and clamped me with a cloak of extremely unpleasant prickles. The heat was actually reflecting off the inside of my lenses into my eyes. Huxley made a run for his house as if it were a downpour and didn't want to get wet, while I very sensibly jumped back into the insulation of the car. We had learned, vaguely, that the weather was going to hot up in the week, but it still took us by surprise: and Jay and the boys were on their way home in an un-air-conditioned car.

'I'll see you at the office,' I yelled out before driving off.

It was close on to midday when the school finally came into sight. The temperature here read 46 degrees or 114.8 Fahrenheit. Jay's car was parked under the shade of a flame tree, but she had got out and was standing talking to a new friend.

'Want to come back with me. Leave the car until later?'

'Boys can go with you, if you like. I've got used to it now.'

There was the spirit which gave India to us on a plate. At that moment, the boys ran out of school. They were tanned, healthy and growing fast. They had made friends and hardly noticed the heat which threatened to melt the special temperature tarmac on the road. Though it was designed to take the extremes of the sun, there was a slight softness about the surface which made me realise this was hot even for Doha.

'*Ma'habbah* Dad. What are you doing here?'

'Want a lift home with me?'

'No thanks. Your car is too small.' It said it all.

'See you back home. We have to finish packing this afternoon.'

I drove back via the new house, clamping my sunhat firmly on my head. A floppy hat to keep the sun off my head had become essential. My hair was very fine (but still there, reader) and at this temperature it would burn through to my scalp. Having experienced a burnt head once already, this was not the time to repeat the practice.

A lorry was delivering piles of what seemed like good quality soil. The fact that in doing it the driver had scraped the front gate, and the side of his lorry, was all in a day's work to him. Grass seed had suddenly become an urgency; a lawn to give cover, and shade to the house with shrubs and trees. Oleander and flame trees to crawl all over the masonry as much as possible would give it a lived in look.

The electrical engineer had already installed himself at the opposite side of the road and another house on the corner was being cleaned ready for occupation. Better still by far, the ends of a black heavy cable snaked up to and into the main fuse board in the garden. It might be nice if the trench had been filled in but this was another department.

Back at the house I tried to plan the next few days over a cold beer. The Dutch lager *Oranjeboom* had become a staple drink albeit permitting myself only one for lunch. There were a lot of ex-pats out here who lived for the next drink and were now wedded to a life out in the Gulf of cheap gin and beer. That was not in my plans for the future.

When Jay arrived back showing a pronounced sweat line along her forehead she parked under our tree and left the doors open. A wall of heat erupted out of the interior, reminding me of the film *Backdraft*, just as if she had opened her oven door, but she never complained...ever. Very annoying at times.

'Pizza and salad, then we'll get the boys things together.' Rhona has already started packing up the office, such as it is.'

At that time, we still did not have a huge amount of filing, only two heavy plan-chests to move which came to pieces anyway, so the whole room was in boxes ready to be moved with just the urgent day-to-day items left out.

That evening after a successful move of everything that was not vital to sustain us in the old (old!!) house we invited a number of friends over for a last barbeque. We had Australian sirloins, each about two inches thick and a Lebanese salad full of olives, tomatoes, feta cheese and crisp lettuce, torn not cut. The whole was tossed in olive oil, fresh coriander and white wine vinegar. It was simple fare but delicious, cooked to order on a fire that was not threatened with rain or a chilly evening to spoil the effect. Though it was a 'goodbye to neighbours' party, we were not moving too far, and they were anxious to remain in close contact as they knew we were – hopefully - going to build a pool sometime soon in the future. What no-one knew in Doha was that Henry had organised, with Partner approval, a set of construction drawings for a pool, and the equipping section of the Practice had already ordered a complete set of pipes and filtration equipment, underwater lights and cleaning gear. It had been shipped a week earlier leaving us to organise the construction. It was the nature of the Partnership: they looked after those that looked after them.

As we sat on the terrace and watched the flames of the barbeque settle down to a flickering glow under a pile of silken grey ash, I turned my mind to the meeting set up for the next day with the Japanese. It had come to my mind that Mr. Hitoshi would do almost anything we suggested as a way of moving the contract forward. His inbuilt politeness was of little value in the Middle East, particularly where half the world was snapping at the other half's heels on a daily basis.

There was a real need for Mr Hitoshi to talk to me before any of the heavy-weight partners in the venture became involved, even if the Japanese were providing most, if not all, of the expertise and cash to the tune of thirty percent of the total capital cost. Qatar itself would be the principal land owner and put in the rest of the cash. We could design anything they asked of us so long as it was remote from the steel rolling mill itself. One area where we had no expertise was in heavy industry which was mainly engineering work – steel tubes and frames, blast furnaces and the like, none of it familiar to our designers back home.

It was Mr Hitoshi's responsibility to sort out the reported issues with the site. Like so many joint ventures which would come along in the next few years, there was a danger of allowing an issue to fall between the two cliffs of joint clients. Often it was left to the practice to sort it out, but the protocol had to follow the line of us first having to ask permission. There was a need to make sure that the Ministry of Public Works took in hand the ownership before a detailed survey of the *Umm Sa'id* site was carried out. As Queen Victoria once said, 'I am not amused,' and neither would I be if the silver foxes arrived to pick over my whitened bones in the sand.

Huxley put it quite well, placing it somewhat in the vernacular: 'Bloody essential if you know what I mean.'

My neighbours lay torpid in their chairs, engaged in the sort of languid conversation where each word falls sideways out of the mouth, and the beneficiary brain has to wait to collect enough syllables to make sense of the sentence. They were lulled by the tremendous heat now dissipating out of the sand. Even the veterans had not experienced temperatures such as this for a number of years, where the bougainvillea leaves crumpled at the corners and the flame trees wilted for lack of moisture. Brown legs, shod in shorts and thin T-shirts, flip-flops kicked off untidily under the chairs were all that anyone wore in the evening unless it was a trip to the Embassy for a Betamax film (remember them?). There was a casualness about the whole scene as if we were a pride of lions after a kill, stomachs sated by piles of flesh, with our tails idly flicking away the flies from the carcase.

A rustle in the dried leaves made me look up. The light from the fire caught the eyes of a rat whose sleek body confirmed there was plenty of food for such rodents, despite the barren desert outside the back door. One glossy coat would mean more baby rats somewhere, but I was too tired even to throw a stone. It had been a hard day, full of concerns if not disappointment. The work from the Japanese was essential if not exciting fodder for our practice, and we needed to ride on their back for a while. Besides, the Partners back in England now had an opportunity to establish links with the Japanese Directors who would have an office in London for sure. There might well be additional office building work from them.

Gradually the conversation turned into yawns, wide, open-mouthed no hand-cover-up sort of yawns, ending a usual day where the pressure never stopped for a moment. Neighbours drifted away wishing us well in our new house and promising to clean the pool in a rota….if we got one!

In the morning, the air-conditioning switched off as the call to prayer started up. There was obviously a battery in the mosque tower to keep the call going at such times. For the two to coincide exactly, was a new event, but the end of the call saw me with my feet resting on the cool terrazzo floor by the side of the bed. My eyes followed the skirting around the room. Though we had not spent a great deal of time here, it was home, and the move would unsettle us for a while until, that too became our only address. It was a useful sized house with no known problems. The new tenants, Huxley and Rhona would not find too many strange issues when they moved in. Not that they would be permitted to arise with Rhona. She was a strong girl mentally and would deal with any problem by meeting it head-on.

An hour later, I entered the offices of the Japanese steel company with some trepidation. They would not want to hear a list of problems with me whining about 'others' issues. We were paid to deal with these. Balanced with this, however, was the need for the client to learn the facts and not some fudged story.

Mr Hitoshi was waiting for me. We shook hands and bowed gravely and got down to work. He was anxious to see what we had learned. His wrinkled face studied my own in anticipation of good news.

'Well, the site is big enough but there are problems.'

'Ploblems, ploblems?' he repeated. 'What sort of ploblems?'

'Well, there are three plob, er, problems.' From which I went on to describe exactly what they were. Mr Hitoshi's eyes began to retreat even further into his face under the heavy lids. The oil on his hair dried. A lank lock dropped over his face where it was anxiously swept back again. Sweat beaded his brow.

'But, don't worry. If you give me permission to talk to the Ministry we will sort the issues out (I thought that phrase might be better than the original one he had struggled with). His face cleared as if by magic. The black hair straightened as if newly wrapped around hair tongs.

'You can do this? Today?'

'Today Sir, if you permit me?'

'Ah-so, *very* good.' In his excitement, he had managed to pronounce the word *very* correctly. He realised it and smiled even further.

My discussions with Hitoshi engaged my mind with a flashback on the stupidity of war. The awful things that had been done in the past in the Second World War between the Japanese and the British, triggered by politicians and not ordinary people. This gentle man had a family, children no doubt, a wife and an extended family. He only wanted to get on with being a success in his life and support his family. It mirrored my own.

We shook hands warmly. 'Leave it to me Mr Hitoshi. By this evening I will have no problems for you.'

It was not the first time I had had to make a promise which might determine the rapidity of my rise within the practice. This was an important client. As we said goodbye, this time he bowed lower than usual, in a sincere appreciation of my help. It made me even more resolute to do whatever was necessary to get this project moving forward.

In the Ministry of Public Works, the Engineer was complacent at first, not understanding the full issues which was causing me to sound alarms. Eventually he woke up to the fact the accommodation blocks could be seriously delayed and thus the steel workers could not start work. He rang the Minister who was in. We walked up the stairs together and entered the large office with its wood panelling from a far off tree of exquisite origin. We exchanged pleasantries after which we pulled out the site drawing. There they were. The graves were from a wrecked ship in the *thirties*. As no-one knew the origin or religion of the dead seamen the records showed that they had been buried according to Islamic law but away from the graveyards of the Qataris. It was agreed we could place a small fence around the graves, agreeing that as no-one had come along calling to visit the graves in fifty years, everyone would be satisfied.

It was an interesting fact that the local Muslims were prepared to tend to what, possibly were infidels' bones, taking care that the alternative Christian God must be looked after as well as their own. And, if you read the Koran, as I have, you will see the respect that Jesus was held by Mohammed.

I warm to such ideas.

The pipe-lines would be dealt with by the simple expediency of digging trenches to drop them out of site. It was explained to me that unless there was a requirement, such as this, there was simply no need to sink the pipes out of sight. Why bother?

'For what reason, Mr Richard? It is only sand. There are no nice apartment blocks looking out on the pipes.' He had a very good point.

The swallow holes were another matter.

'You will have to survey the whole of the site you want to build on, including any roads. The mosque must be placed with great care on the ground. Small holes you can fill with concrete, large ones you will have to design around.'

'What, Minister, should happen if there is a swallow hole we do not know about or are unable to find for whatever reason, and we build upon it?' A reasonable question I felt.

'Then it is the Will of Allah. We cannot go against His great Will and if He decides that is to be the way, then that is what will be.'

It was a very simple way of looking at things, far removed from the cut and thrust of Guildford's design offices where ultra-sound would be used to determine the depth and extent of such holes. I am not sure how we would pit the Standard Specification and Engineering Contract of Works CCCI against Allah's Will but who was I to say? (Can you imagine that happening in Guildford in 2021 say, when the Health and Safety Executive got wind of it?).

I then touched on the last, sensitive subject. Ownership.

'I realise, Minister that your offices have taken on the titles of the land but does the original owner know this, and has he been paid?'

'Sheikh Jabor has agreed the sale of his land. It was worthless anyway, so he has made a good sale.'

'But the money, Minister? Has it been handed over?' My voice had risen a single octave, but it was enough to cause the Minister's eyes-brows to rise.

'*In'shallah.* This Sheikh does not have a bank account. He likes payment in cash. It may not have reached him yet.'

By a series of diplomatic sidesteps and possibly one through the back door, he came to understand that we could not carry out the detailed survey unless Sheikh Jabor was content to see others striding across his land, worthless as it may be. Sweat, despite the air-conditioning, began to trickle down my back again. Outside, the evening call sounded, and the Minister looked at his watch.

'We will see that you are kept in safety on our land, Mr Richard. Do not worry.' He got up and shook hands before leaving his office by a side door. He was one of the faithful after all and he was being called by something far higher up the ladder than the rights or wrongs of a Sheikh. Our Engineer smiled thinly, knowing that we would not go on the site until he had been down there himself. A muttered series of words sounding very much like *flak jacket* and *hard hat came from his mouth* as we left but Mr Hitoshi, at the very least, would be able to sleep tonight.

CHAPTER EIGHT

A Slight Gaffe with a Table

A nd now we were four. Henry arrived on time to the accompaniment of the jostling crowd, the heat – severe even at night, and the, by now, familiar smell of frying sewage on the central reservations wafting through the oleander.

Henry was a tall man, a giant, young but old, young because of his passport age, old because he exuded confidence and maturity. I felt, instantly, that he could take over many of the new projects we were working up leaving me to spend more time with clients.

The shuffled cards involving three house moves back to back, had gone surprisingly well with no hiccoughs as we had had when the other two had arrived. It was like a game of Monopoly moving on with one's properties into newer, better houses. We moved our caravanserai out in the early morning and arrived, a few hours later at our new oasis. Our staff transferred into the vacuum of our vacated space. Henry was to live in *Wakkrah* and Rhona had already transferred her own clothes and possessions without the help of Huxley into our old house.

He was up to his eyes sorting out preliminary contracts for a number of minor projects beginning to build up in the filing cabinet, while keeping Shell, a demanding if professional client, content, pleased to consider giving us more work in the future.

Rhona delighted herself in being in the old quarter of Doha, close to shops and relative sanity, being able to talk to ex-pats across the road and hang the washing out with a reasonable chance it would be there when she returned.

Her new house, our old house, was quite different to the previous property in *Wakkrah*. Admittedly, sometimes it had been difficult to describe our approach road as anything but a refuse dump. Litter was spread by feral dogs tearing the insides from paper rubbish bags and carrying the best bits from the rear of the houses to the front where they lay at night on the warm tarmac chewing mindless things which took their fancy. The wind blew the sand and the workmen dug the roads up so many times it left a lumpy, criss-cross pattern as if it were a giant Scrabble board. *(Research note. Was Scrabble invented by 1975? Yes it was. This is interesting. Scrabble was invented in the 1930's as a way of staving off boredom in the Great Depression).*

It all combined to make the road to the house look rough as ferrets bedding, a situation Rhona was determined to remove. This left Henry in *Wakkrah* on his own, though our model maker, Harvard, would join him when he arrived in the Land Rover. It was my belief Henry would not be fazed by living by himself and most of the time including the evenings – for we always worked until seven, and then moved into the social hours - he would be with us. Rhona had plans to see he was invited over every weekend and Jay had the same idea of home-cooking for a bachelor. She made a mental note to find an explanation as to why all of her boss's staff had a first name beginning with 'H'.

As we drove to the, by now familiar, destination of the hotel for the proverbial rest over before the start of work, I explained to Henry that we were both invited over to a young Sheikh's house in two days' time. This man wanted to meet my Number One, as Henry was to be called from now on. The young Qatari, Shaikh Hamad was one of those English Public School educated Arabs, with an immaculate accent and a fine taste in clothes, a charming manner and an eagerness to impress and seek his fortune. Although there was money in his family, his father was getting on in years with a penchant for holding onto the purse strings a little too tightly. Hence our invitation to see what mutual interests lay between us and how we might develop some of his own ideas as opposed to those of his father.

To Henry, I talked protocol, etiquette and the need to communicate in language this man understood. When it was explained to him that his host had a very fast boat, Italian built, all glossy curves and va-va-voom, he said that he had a good relationship with an Agent in Chichester Harbour who sold such toys. That sounded a good entrée for the evening for Henry had a reputation as a very good boat builder himself, albeit with individual boats and not production lines. It would leave me to get on with Hamad's Agent, a much more difficult man from Bahrain who always wanted to remind me *he* was the Agent and thus it was in his sole remit as to who got the job. That meant, in the future, a backhander or three would be demanded, something the practice would not be willing to accept, though the problem could be put on the back burner for the time being. Henry was also wised up in the manner of eating Arab-style. It was explained we would be sitting cross-legged on pink silk cushions in the Shaikh's *Majlis*, eating with one's right hand and pulling off chunks of yellow lamb fat from a whole carcase.

'I understand the bit about the sitting but why the right-hand? I'm left-handed as you know?'

'Because, dear man, the left hand in Arabia is for wiping your bottom. And, by the way, don't show the soles of your feet. That's just as bad as doing a *Moonie*.' Henry made two mental notes and filed them away for further use.

The next day the five of us had a first serious conference in the main office of our new house. Rhona took Minutes and the men nodded enthusiastically at the plans for the pool. In fact they had to be reminded several times that swimming and building the pool were not the only reasons we were sitting out in the Middle East.

Most of the new equipment and files were boxed and stacked in a corner to be installed after the meeting. Jay was there as the top half of the house belonged to her and she was keen to see we did not encroach too far without her knowledge. Henry's ability at building boats confirmed to me that he would be in charge of the pool project and after all other business was finished, he opened up the drawings. It showed a liberal sized pool and again, I was struck at the

generosity of the Partners. We described to Jay how the whole
office operation would dovetail with her household which
made her a very happy lady. It cannot be overestimated, in
those early days how important such a facility as a pool was,
not only to business but to the well-being of the family and
our growing staff numbers. For business, it was the equivalent
of having one's own golf course in your back garden, a fact
which Langdon had sussed very quickly. Not only business
colleagues but friends as well would be welcome which would
allow Jay to pass an easy afternoon after work. As the school
did not go back in the evenings as we did, she was always
able to gain a couple of hours to relax before the daily trip
to the Suq.

A draft plan for the next three months was agreed,
and the two men got down to sorting out desks, chairs and
filing cabinets though not before Rhona had settled where
her reception desk was to be sited. From the commanding
position she had chosen very quickly, she could see who
was where, challenge itinerants in the road, check the water
tanker's arrival, receive the post – from her husband - whose
job it was to go down to the Post Office each morning to
see what had arrived for us - keep an eye on the cars and
arriving guests and generally direct her forces when and
where needed.

Part of my plan was to meet as many of the local Qataris
as possible, determine whether they had any future plans for
housing, offices or shops or just wanted to talk, from which
a new Palace might arise one day. Normally, we were not in
the business of designing one-off houses which would be
impractical for a practice of our size. Our overheads were

too high to justify applying a fee scale to a standard house. But, some of these palaces were as expensive as a large office block. A potential house owner might also be engaged in large scale business in the Gulf. A house, even in those days might have a capital cost, for the shell alone, of five million dollars and would be constructed of reinforced concrete by an International Contractor,. It was important that Henry understood the political play in summing up where we might have a 'loss leader' house to win an office block.

In the Gulf, the Interior Designer was as powerful a figure as the Architect and had an easier job for the client could see just where his money was being spent on baths chiselled from blocks of Carrara marble, gold leaf covering doors, leather lined walls and alabaster storks, the latter holding up a gilded canopy by their beaks over one's bath. During our years in Doha we witnessed some quite astonishing layouts. Acres of Burmese teak panelling, gold leaf by the square yard, wonderful, fretted plaster cornices like lace, waterfalls in the house, gardens in the house and secret swimming pools for the ladies to swim without being studied by arriving guests, also in the house.

It was to this end that I had accepted the invitation in which we now found ourselves driving towards Shaikh Hamad's house. The night sky in its starlit magnificence had appeared as we found the address, large enough for Qatari standards but not in the best part of town. It was very quiet, but we were expected as the perimeter lights were switched on. I parked the car by the wall and Henry rang the bell on the outer gate. It opened as if by magic to show a pretty garden, one that any greying Miss Marple would have recognised.

Hibiscus was everywhere, and roses, neatly pruned earlier in the year had kept their shapes. The lawn was immaculate; the green stripes showed someone cared for the final effect. It was, in fact, a lawn to die for and I wanted one just like it. Subtle mushroom-shaped lights illuminated a path alongside pools with fountains.

Waiting on the doorstep was Shaikh Hamad, arms held wide to allow the sleeves of his *thawb* to hang like Jesus on the Mount, Sir John Everett Millais perhaps circa 1850. He looked, also, remarkably like Jesus with his tightly clipped beard and groomed hair, though his polished black shoes might have seemed a tad out of place in The New Testament.

'Mr Richard,' he volunteered in his cultured voice. 'Welcome to my home. And you must be Mr Henry?'

Henry gave a small bow in acknowledgment as he towered over our host and we all shook hands. 'I see you are admiring my garden. I was taught how to grow such things in your country, when I was at school. I am quite pleased with it.'

'So you should be Sir.'

'Please, call me Hamad. And Mr Henry, you are liking this country? A bit too hot for me at this time of year. But, unlike you, I can and am going to England for the rest of the summer as soon as my father agrees.' There was tension in the remark.

'I don't mind being here,' Henry said, 'I want to see if I can become crew for one of the yachts out in the basin, er… harbour.'

'I know the word, basin, Mr Henry. A curious second meaning for the word, is it not? Now, please, come inside.

Tonight, as a special tribute to my two friends, as guests of honour, I am putting on a western style dinner party.'

The two of us tried not to show our disappointment for I had extolled the delights of sheep eyes and fatty lamb to Henry on the drive over to the house. But the atmosphere was positive and we felt we were in with more than a chance on any work arising in the future.

We walked into a very large room which had rounded section timber beams crossing the ceiling at intervals some two feet apart. The walls were wallpapered in the very best red flock Indian Restaurant design, with tassels and silken bell-pulls hanging from the curtains of heavy brocade in contrasting colours of red and gold. Chandeliers were suspended in what might otherwise have been a flood of light, but the crystal was covered in dust from the previous Shamal, reducing the light by a factor of eighty percent.

But, it was to the centre of the room our eyes were riveted.

It was quite clear that Hamad had purchased, just for this evening, a table of Italian origin. It was about twenty feet long with a top composed of toughened smoked glass with its edges polished into a comfortable feel to the hands. This rested on a tubular chrome steel frame with legs that swept away like swans' wings. It had Milan stamped all over it with a price tag still attached to the tube frame, of U.S. dollars five thousand five hundred.

The refurbishment had not gone as far as the cumbersome chairs, which were upright, leather upholstered with tasselled embroidery, uncomfortable to relax in, undoubtedly pulled from his Majlis for the occasion. Such chairs were quite all right when one was waiting to present one's petition to the Shaikh as you sat upright, churning your worry beads through pairs of nervous fingers. Here, it might be difficult to slouch after the port and liqueurs.

Hamad was probably enjoying his first western style meal in Qatar and was immensely proud that he understood such things.

It was from this moment on things began to go wrong.

When Hamad clapped his hands, twenty of his retainers, some straight from the desert all dressed in linen thawbs and red chequered keffiyehs which they now began to flip over their heads. That done they stubbed out their cigarettes on the soles of their sandals, some of which could have done with a tin of Cherry Blossom polish. They smiled up at Henry; to them he looked as if he were aloft on a schooner, they being, to a man, diminutive in size. The men nodded at me, for none spoke English. Nonetheless, we half-circumnavigated the table, raising smiles each time as if they were Uncle Jack who we hadn't seen for a long time, repeating the mantra: '*Salaam alaikhum, khe fahlik?*'

Most of the replies were in the '*Zain*' category though a few, more friendly replied with '*al Hamdilla*' which translates into the Italian as, '*non cè male*' (because the table was made in Italy) or, of course in English, 'not so bad'.

We all stood, or slouched, as Hamad also stood to make a long speech in Arabic quite clearly praising myself and Henry who, damn him, proceeded to study my face intently thinking there could possibly be a dead mosquito stuck to my top lip. I followed up by examining his right ear which had a tennis ball stuck to it. Clearly, neither of us felt comfortable when anyone said the slightest nice thing about us despite the fact that here, it was all clothed in the language of mist and fog.

Our host then turned to English. 'Mr Richard, as honoured guest I wish you to take the chair at the top of the table, and Mr Henry, you take the chair at the other end.'

Saying 'righty-oh', Henry disappeared into the vaguely-lit obscurity and gloom in the far distance, almost disappearing from view so far away was he from me.

Meanwhile, moving to my allocated place, I found it was not possible to move my chair without rupturing my spleen so the gentleman next to me quickly pulled the legs away with alacrity. He was quite used to moving camels around the desert and four more legs would make very little difference. This was the signal for the others to do the same; Hamad wisely took a seat one side of me, his Agent not unsurprisingly, on the other. Hamad was clear his Agent was good for contracts but not for chatting up clients. Henry, however, had a local either side of him, to both of whom he smiled as earnestly as he could. He could not match the stained teeth of course or the cracked, worn fingers now patting pockets for cigarettes to fill the conversation gaps.

In the centre of the table was a quite magnificent cut-glass jug of iced water, weighing probably something in the region of five kilos. It would probably not be possible to 'pass the water please' without doing oneself a serious mischief to the groin but it was there as an ornament replacing the usual bunch of daffodils as a nice change. The retainers looked around to see if they would be getting a Pepsi Cola or a 7up and I nodded fiercely to Henry and back to the water. He got the message. No wine here.

Our young Shaikh clapped his hands again. There was a feeling of passing time, of time two hundred years ago as if we were attending the court of some Turkish Sultan, as Eunuchs (possibly) wandered into the room waiting for the message to start serving. Our other guests broke into chatting together and puffed happily (despite the commands from their own boss) on cheap tobacco allowing the ash to fall to the floor despite the brand new ashtrays on the table.

Hamad called for silence again. 'As we have special, honoured guests tonight we shall eat Western style... as in London' He translated for his staff's benefit. At the word London, they all pricked up their ears for London was something akin to Mecca; well perhaps not quite but a big place, somewhere to plan to go in one's lifetime.

'We shall have soup to begin. It is one of England's specialities I believe? Maggie chicken noodle soup?'

I threw back my head in amazement. Time to contribute. 'Indeed Hamad, probably the most popular soup in the whole of Britain. I was brought up on the stuff... er, it.' It was not the time to disagree now. Besides, it was probably true.

'I have done my research,' he ended proudly, tapping the side of his nose with a chuckle.

The soup arrived in brand new soup bowls of white porcelain each proclaiming the price of U.S. dollars three and fifty cents on the rim. Twenty pairs of eyes turned towards us. I had to assume Henry was also under focus though it was difficult to see in the gloom. Then, every other guest looked up towards me waiting for some sort of movement.

An event can now be described, which is true in every detail though few, perhaps, will believe me. At the time it happened it was upsetting but, like any fairy tale it ended up happily.

I, along with Henry and Ahmed had picked up our spoons and began to eat the soup with the nonchalance and ease of a thousand such actions before. We did not make those awful slurping sounds of the Lower Fourth and if the soup rested on our lips we patted it off with our linen serviettes (with manufacturers finish still adhering to the shiny surface) along with further price tags: also three riyals fifty each. The problem was, however, the large number of gentlemen in the room – well, the rest of the staff in fact - had never done such a thing in their lives. Anxiously and with considerable apprehension they watched the four of us, studying our wrist action carefully and the angle of our arms. Attempting an initial spoonful, the first of the intrepid adventurers successfully collected not an unreasonable amount of Maggie chicken noodle soup in the bottom of his spoon. It was, however, in the transference of this to his mouth that the problem arose. His arm rose nicely but alas, his elbow dropped, and at too acute an angle, allowing the preciously collected chicken broth, with noodle pieces, to slide gracefully down his sinewy and tawny arm onto his thawb looking like small white slugs seeking a fresh, lettuce leaf. I was acutely embarrassed for this man who could have shown me more than a thing or two when it came to eating with the right hand. I can also recall my problems using chopsticks for the first time in Hong Kong.

Things began to go rapidly downhill as one after the other failed to eat anything, while we stuffed ourselves with... er...delicious hot soup. (Temperature outside was around the forty-ish mark).

God, however, intervened at precisely the right moment, just as our friends were attempting to pat their mouths. Many had not yet taken any soup but were unaware the two actions were linked. Soup on lips: pat the lips; no soup on lips: don't pat the lips.

God, (thank God), came along knocking on our door. Why not for goodness sake, after all, it appeared as if His only begotten son was sitting at my right hand.

The table had evidently been quickly put together that day, the instructions, no doubt in Italian, not too easy to understand, *effettivamente, impossibile* and purchased just for this occasion.

No matter what the reason, the glass top weighing a very considerable amount, dropped through the tubular frame... and onto our laps, just two and a quarter inches below. (or, to those who have departed Imperial for Metric I would suggest fifty-eight millimetres).

The fall was instantaneous, silent but seemingly evenly distributed around the table, so we could all share in this surprise, although to be fair to me, Henry's end was a nano-second behind.

But this was not even the beginning of the end and God had not ceased to play. Due to this minute disparity in timing it caused the colossal vase in the centre to fall over. Five gallons of ice-cold water began to rush down the table towards me, a tsunami which swept aside anything and everything before it. Not wishing to have this amount of water residing on my crotch while eating Maggie soup, I did what was quite natural to any Architect.

I raised my knees, having calculated carefully the rise and the effort to do so. This turned out to be three inches or 75mm.

Such an effort caused the glass table top to rise up, as if to combat the natural elements, a shield ranged against the torrent. The water curled like a Hawaiian comber inches (millimetres) from my ironed shirt and began to snarl back down towards Henry, who because of the gloom had not quite taken in the second emergency. He was solely concerned that his two neighbours were quite unsure as to the mental frailty of the guests now sitting in the room with them. Eventually he saw the fizz and froth of water approaching and did what was expected.

Being an Architect, he rapidly made his own calculation on the spot (he had to as he was unable to move due to the weight of the glass top).

He lifted his knees 100mm, that's four inches to you. The water began returning down the table again. In the meantime, the retainers, eyes agog, clued in at last to the disaster approaching their boss, and wondering just what it was that made Westerners so…so, stupid, fell in with Hamad's plan because they had been told to be polite…and he was their boss. So, they began to raise and lower their knees in sequence attempting to keep the water in the middle, as the game seemed to presage. Hamad was mortified, as there was a huge loss of face to the son of the family. As the last drop of water flew off the table with centrifugal force across our faces and thereafter onto the shag pile I eased myself with difficulty from the grip of the glass and gave him a big hug.

'I really wanted to eat in the style that you have always eaten. In your Majlis, on the floor, eating with my right hand.'

It was as if the event had never occurred. 'Would it be possible and for Mr Henry as well? And talk of camels...and business?' I added as an afterthought.

He looked up, self-conscious but grateful, clapping his hands for the others to disappear. The last man picked up his keffiyeh with which he had been mopping the table and slid out from below the heavy glass. With a sigh of compressed leather, the smoked glass top settled onto the chairs.

As we walked through to the Majlis, pink silk cushions had already arrived and spread into a circle. The main course, which was not a surprise to us was, in fact the ubiquitous lamb. It arrived on two enormous dishes, a whole carcase to each lay as dead lambs always do with their front legs crossed in death, atop mountains of yellow rice, saffron perhaps, but it turned out it was turmeric. Great gobbets, each about three inches across, of yellow fat balls, hung over the meat secured by tendrils of white sinew. These also prevented the suspended four eyeballs from rolling down towards us as they glared inconsolably and with much shame at our wickedness. Their sockets challenged the two of us to eat one of the specialist morsels before the older men made a grab for them. Decorating it all were a dozen hard-boiled eggs which, viewed in their nakedness, also looked like eye-balls.

Hamad's staff who were, it turned out, mainly family, had now dried off and returned. They grabbed a pile of rice which they began to squeeze into a lump. Tearing off a piece of meat the rice joined it together in their mouths which unfortunately killed any discussion on the price of goats for some time. They began to smile as familiarity returned and stomachs started to fill.

Nothing daunted, I copied exactly the actions of my neighbour, stuffing the mixture down my gullet which by now was ready for any food. Henry was doing the same adding '*Zain! Zain! Zain!*' from time to time like a seasoned Bedou. So he had become fluent within a week.

One had to admit to needing a smidgen more salt: well some salt at all would have been nice, and perhaps some sort of flavouring? Hamad was quiet to begin with, eating mechanically as he overcame the shock of the Damn Dining Disaster. He was probably contemplating glumly to himself that that would make a good title for a film. As we worked our way down the rice pile, more of those eyes came closer. The other guests would push them away rather as children do with Brussels sprouts on Christmas Day. 'Nothing wrong with them mother, but I prefer turkey at this moment in time.'

As they dug deep the eyes appeared to be moving closer to my sector of the huge platter. Soak us, the family seemed to say, and we'll sort you out, truly.

Hamad woke up and gave a sly smile to one of his men who picked up the dish now considerably lighter in weight and indicated to me to have an eye ball. The other eaters had gone quiet pretending not to notice. It was a test...as to how big a fool I could make of myself. The eye was surprisingly heavy, like a golf ball in weight. Knowing I must not let my hand shake which might show any tremor reminded me of the execution of King Charles the First who asked for an extra shirt, so he would not shiver with cold as they chopped his head off and making the gory public think '.... he was afeard'. After all, this was a defining moment, played out on many a T.V. screen in the past.

It, the eye that is, oozed gravy, well, sort of gravy, well, sort of a greyish, thin liquid. Squeezing it into my mouth as if it were a rubber ball, my teeth clamped onto its top. Silly thing to do really as the bloody *thing* exploded producing an additional amount of liquid in my mouth. I was not only reminded of King Charles that evening but the flavour of lamb's eye which was close to that of rancid butter though rather more rancid than butter, well actually, just rancid, no butter at all on reflection.

The ball having apparently defecated in its own juice now deflated leaving me with a rubbery *thing* which I chewed while maintaining a jolly grin on my face. It is, I can assure you, extremely difficult to smile at all when you have just placed what seemed to be a *used diaphragm* into one's mouth.

When the thing had finally slipped down my throat I asked Hamad how much of a delicacy was the eyeball and was it eaten often.

'Heavens be,' he answered, 'we don't eat those if we can help it. They taste of ranci-'

'Rancid butter?' I filled in nicely.

'There's far better meat to eat than an eye-ball. But it is a tradition to leave all of the meat of the head on the plate.'

For staff I presume? *Zain!* Sucker was another term. It had been an experience based upon anecdote and newspaper articles of such ancient memory that one's mind tended to accept the word unpleasantness rather than 'different.' Worse was to come in the future in my work overseas when in Taiwan being invited to eat a plate of boiled sea slugs.

That was a bridge too far. Hamad's men chortled in glee, triumphant at last.

We cleaned down the platter with the use of pitta bread to leave it almost clean enough to put back on the mantle. The Pepsi cola was fizzy, generating a considerable quantity of gas which when mixed with two tons of lamb required both of us to depart the house soon after the end of the meal. Henry rose carefully as we eased ourselves up from the cushions.

As we left, Hamad came up to me and placed his arm around my shoulders in a friendly gesture.

'Thank you, my friend.'

I knew why he was thanking me and it was not necessary to reply. There was no need to remind him further of the night the table lost its top. We both received a hug from Hamad's family, with Arab chortles to send us on our way. No face was lost and we had established more friends in one evening than we could have done in a week.

We returned home to the weighty matter of building our own swimming pool... after going to the loo.

～

In amongst the long hours which ran from very early morning spanning well into the social hours, we still managed to find some spare time to fill. With no T.V. of any worth, or radio, cinema not yet arrived, the summer heat satisfied itself placing a very real influence on the order of the day. There was a growing need to have a central rendezvous point for our rapidly increasing family, staff and friends. Henry set to, negotiating with a local building firm to excavate the pool and to build it to our design. He, himself would install the pipe-work and monitor the construction. We found a small company that specialised in lining pools in glass fibre and trusted they knew what they were doing. Huxley was able to see a couple of the pool shells they had recently lined and gave his approval to take on one of them. In fact it was as good as any we had seen anywhere else in the world.

Despite the heat and one's fears about poor workmanship, the digger had a hole in four days, cutting through the broken creamy limestone. The spoil was removed by the simple practicality of dropping it over the rear wall where someone in ten years' time could use it for a nice rockery. The stone was almost white in the bright sunshine and had the smell of long-lost water holes, which of course it was, for the liquid had been trapped inside for thousands of years. The excavated hole looked large and even larger when a concrete-mix truck arrived and laid the foundation over Henry's blue pipes, followed by the inevitable hollow block walls which carried reinforcing rods at intervals. Within a week we had the shell of a very decent sized pool. The word began to get around the town that we were building a pool and we began to receive telephone calls on a regular basis, reminding Jay of how they had met at so-and so's party.

We had been warned this might well happen and one of our fears was that we would not have sufficient alcohol to hand around. We had long ago accepted life as we had known it, was gone, to be replaced with a far more intrusive lifestyle. We did, nonetheless, need friends and colleagues alike to know that we would not always be cleaning the pool or handing out drinks. A turn with the water vacuum cleaner or supplying a case of beer would go a long way to being re-invited.

By this first summer we had made a number of good friends, ones that would remain on our return to England. All of us had the same aim in mind, namely to make a success of being in the Middle East, a once in a lifetime chance, so we worked and played together whether in competition or alongside on the same team. We were, as it were, in the same boat for better or for worse.

Talking of boats, Henry's next task, now the pool was beginning to rise out of the ground, was to organise the shipment of some *Minisails,* a rigid plastic one-seater sailing dinghy, easily rigged, responsive and fun. To rig the boat required only the need to step the mast within a box set in the deck: there were no shrouds or stays and the single sail was ready for action in two minutes by sliding the sleeve over the mast. Jay was anxious the boys learn the art of sailing before they left Doha and so put our name down for a boat along with quite a number of other ex-pats. They arrived as part order of a shipment in an extremely large pantechnicon and Henry went down to organise their delivery to our house from where they were collected by the individuals. These little craft soon became a familiar sight around the bay of the Corniche and out on our weekend island. They could be lifted onto the top of a car with ease and two straps were all that was needed to hold it and the mast in place. So from nothing the practice had two cooling outlets for our staff and I felt reasonably certain this would soften the long hours in the office or on site.

Before the glass-fibre pool liner arrived, we had had an unusual problem to deal with. Our youngest came into the house one day saying there were two rats in the pool. He was right. Two, sleek dark coloured rats with whiskers waving angrily at their prison walls were attempting to get out but the sides were sheer and smooth. How they had got in, in the first place, we had no idea, but we had to get them out before the lining was installed. Huxley had the original (?) idea of bashing them on the head with a long piece of timber left over from the construction. Holding it like a lance at a joust he thrust the wood at a rat who, not exactly pleased, sprang aside and sank its teeth viciously into the timber, joined a moment later by its companion who decided to back up its colleague in the attack.

'Watch out!' said Jay. 'They will be climbing up the pole and get out.' She was as perceptive as our children had been. The clever animals realised they had a route out of their custody, and, no doubt were also extremely thirsty. It became a case of *carpe diem* or at least, for them, absolutely more carpe than diem. They began to climb along the timber at the same rate as it began to dawn on Huxley he had two maddened animals with rather long teeth climbing towards his unprotected hand.

'Don't drop it,' Jay added helpfully. 'We can get them out this way.'

'Perhaps,' he replied with a tinge of hoarfrost in his voice, 'you might like to show me how to do it.'

'Just wait till they are half way up, past the *no turning back point*, as it were, then run like f***, well, perhaps hell, for the wall and chuck the whole thing over together. You know, Huxley, when a plane takes off and there is a point when-'

'I know,' he replied with some breathlessness, 'the point of no return.' His breath *was* laboured. 'I know, I know, I know!'

But, it actually worked. By the time Huxley had reached the wall the rats had realised they were going to be freed, although they did not cotton on, this meant an all-expenses paid flight to the desert that ended their ride to their rubbish.

No-one had gone '*errkk*' when they saw the rats. We were getting used to Doha.

At last the pool had a light blue lining, framing underwater lights, and a paved surround. Jay had bought several red, black and yellow brollies with white tassels to keep the flies away. They might have looked slightly incongruous standing up above the broken stone of the rest of the garden, but some additional hard landscaping would soon put this right. The paving surround to the pool, about five feet wide had proved to have a secondary use being an excellent area for our Muslim workmen to pray. They lined up with their bright rugs quite unabashed and fulfilled their prayers at the end of both their day, and ours.

Came the time when we needed to fill it. We drove down to the water Suq and began to negotiate with the drivers who found it incomprehensible that we wanted forty tankers, and at a discount. They put their heads together, glancing occasionally over to where the earnest Englishmen were waiting patiently for them to make up their minds what it was all about. Then, an idea came to me. I cleared a space in the dust and drew a picture of a pool with me diving in. Huge excitement followed as they understood it was a swimming pool.

We did not get much of a discount as each water tanker was an individual business but we had calculated the cost at the full rate, so Jay had some money left over to buy bamboo framed tables and plastic glasses. The boys kept lookout from the top of the boundary wall, which had become their favourite den, as the convoy hove in sight. The column was almost as long as the one Monty had before El Alamein and it was a scene which would have been very familiar to Rommel as the dust from the desert rose over the line of lorries. Their drivers popped their heads out of the windows while they gesticulated wildly in the general direction of our battle-front/house.

There was a considerable amount of jabber issuing from the tanker men who were enjoying the change to the tedium of their normal work. All of them were able to discharge the contents of their tankers straight into the pool with their long hoses which reached easily around the side of the house; we had five pipes at a time by angling their vehicles across the road.

Slowly the water level crept up the blue walls with the sun beginning to send shimmering, sparkling highlights up the side of the house. We were delighted to be almost blinded by the reflections. Miraculously, a dragonfly appeared from the desert and hovered around as if demanding a water lily or two next time it returned. Where it had come from we had no idea, but we received visits quite often in the heat of the day.

At last, by the evening we declared the pool full and open at the same time where upon a number jumped in fully clothed. It was a strange sight, for the pool, light blue and iridescent provided a marked contrast with the surrounding countryside of the dull browns and yellow ochres of the desert.

It was quickly decided that every guest using the pool would have to, by way of payment, remove two buckets of remaining hard core to the opposite side of the perimeter wall, a reasonable trade-off for everyone.

That night in bed, extremely satisfied with the results of our work, especially our lads, a dream bubbled up around me in which I found myself watching the moon sitting in the sky like a silver football. An enormous pair of telescopic poles criss-crossed the orb as they waved backwards and forwards just as Spielberg's torches in the forest in ET. Unable to fathom out the symbolism of it all there seemed to be no relationship between the moon and the long poles, it only became clear when on waking a moment later I found a cockroach on my shoulder, a very big, dark brown cockroach that is, climbing around the moon-lit curve of my shoulder. The feeler must have been pricking my eye, it was so close.

I leapt up. No. No. Wrong phrase. *Levitated* is the right one. I levitated horizontally upwards possibly as much as fifty millimetres (two inches) before flicking the innocent creature to the floor. I then attacked it with a shoe smacking it into the terrazzo as Bond did to his Black Widow in *Dr. No.* You might well smile, nastily, but there were one or two unpleasantness's on this peninsular, such as scorpions and it could well have been one of them.

The nights were often trying, especially in August when the temperatures at night remained high and showed few signs at dawn of falling to a level where one could sit with an early morning cup of tea and feel cool air on one's shoulders.

The air-conditioning units ran continuously at full blast and made it difficult to get to sleep. Their noise was strident, and continuous, in addition to the insistent and quite uncomfortable pressure on the ear drums. Exhausted each night, one fell into a sort of stupor, lying on top of the bed cover in the same state of deshabillé as the day one was born. On waking, there was the sensation of humid air lying on one's chest; you could almost weigh it, so full of water was the atmosphere. Then the sweat would start up on your face, from where it trickled down to the cavity in your chest. (Mine was concave in those days: now, for some inexplicable reason, it is convex!)

Turning, to relieve the pillow of its worst dampness, your armpits would signify that they were fully awake (and full), and then the groin... well, it wasn't worth describing. There is a presumption that we did get used to it, looking back over the years, but we still looked forward to Doha's winter when we had to reverse the water tank heating again and put a fan heater in the lounge. It is why terrazzo tiling is chosen as an ideal material for floors in the summer as it never warms up: in the winter, however, it's a stroppy material as it takes as much heat out of the system as is put in. Thinking about all this one evening with our house and pool established, my staff working well and in close co-ordination, my wife with a useful and interesting job there came the realisation that we had been here six months.

It was then a letter arrived.

CHAPTER NINE

Howdy Partner

Huxley returned from the Post Office one morning looking up at the sky in which the sun had disappeared behind a cloud. This was sufficiently a rare event to stop and stare. He had the usual pile of letters, post marked United Kingdom which he handed to Rhona who, just as she had in Guildford, date stamped them and placed them in neat piles. She had left one letter to be opened, which was strange, for there were no secrets in the office between the two of us. It did, though, bear the underlined phrase, *Personal and Private Attention*: It was from the Partnership.

It was not usual for them to send me a letter, most if not all business was done by telephone or telex, so this one was important. Rhona looked at me strangely as she slit it open under my instruction. She was in charge of the office and was obviously querying why someone would want to keep something from her. She was going to have a word with the relevant Partner at some time in the future.

Passing the single sheet to me I read the contents and handed it back to her silently, aware the lads were watching me as well, allowing them to wait for a moment or two as they do in those ridiculous television competitions.

Unable to contain herself, Rhona broke the silence.

'Congratulations,' she said. And to the others: 'Richard is a Partner now, so you had better learn how to say Sir.'

My hand was pumped up and down. Perhaps there was no physical difference on my face but deep down inside it felt as if a large lump of my favourite sugar fudge had been inserted into my stomach. The practice was the fourth largest in Britain for goodness sake: it made me feel very proud.

Enough. It was time to get on with my work asking everyone to '*keep mum*' until Jay had been told at lunchtime. On reflection, I don't suppose my boys would understand the italicised comment above in today's social media climate.

A couple of hours later the telex began to clatter; it was from *the Partners to the new Partner* and asked me to go as soon as possible to Abu Dhabi and Dubai to follow up some leads which they listed below. As there was no reason why that could not be straight away we drew up an itinerary. Rhona booked me on the local Gulf Air flights for the next day while, that night just the two of us celebrated alone around our pool watching the new nightly event, almost akin to the Aurora Borealis, of the evening light reflecting off the water.

In the half-light of early morning, I was at the airport to board a twenty-year-old BAC I-II flight to Dubai. This little plane was the workhorse of the fleet, jumping around the Gulf States as efficiently as a bus. There were few bags for the hold and almost everyone was dressed and equipped like me. A sharp shirt, a valise and a passport.

There was, nonetheless, one surprise early on in the day.

A Convention was being held in Dubai for Hawkers, not the itinerants' type, nor those that spat well, but bird hawks, raptors, those that fly around when you take their hoods off.

It was an undeniably strange situation, finding myself sitting next to a Qatari with a hawk on his arm. Its hood had been removed, presumably so the bird could note who was getting on the plane. As we took off, the bird tried to fly, causing a feather to float up into the cabin. The bird looked at me with a rather nasty expression in its red eyes as it sought to blame me for its predicament, but its owner smiled and allowed me to tickle its crest. The bird was in a beautiful condition with its plumage shining as if made of silk: the hawk's master was as proud of his possession as another would be with his new Mercedes. He told me these birds sold for very high prices. By high, he meant one million riyals (£195,000 in 1976) at an auction! So quite valuable then?

The BAC I-II is a plane that has a steep climb on take-off. Another first for me was the experience of seeing a considerable amount of goat droppings roll from the front of the aircraft to the single lavatory at the back, as the floor dropped abruptly during our climb up and over the bay. It was not uncommon for a Shaikh, using his position to commandeer a flight to transport his animals to an uncle perhaps, or just to save on the overland journey, to a favourable market. It explained the strange smell on board and the plane had probably brought the goat or goats in from Abu Dhabi from whence it had come. (compare the situation then to Qatar Airways today, one of the prestigious airlines of the world).

With the experience of the past months, it was so much easier to interpret the land which lay five thousand feet below me. The desert, the layout of the small towns and villages as they came into view one by one was so much more comprehensible. It was not just sand and rock with no habitation as it had seemed on my arrival. Today I could make out the plumes of oil smoke from burning off of spare gas, the desalination plant chundering out millions of gallons of water and the subtle pressures of housing nibbling, like the rats in my garden, at the edges of the desert where it surrounded Doha in a semi-circle. There were hundreds of snail trails in the sand, low block walls and lines of posts which showed where new roads might run in the future, straight as rulers, and, of course, the ubiquitous roundabouts.

A number of walled Palaces sat alone and lonely having no rhyme or reason to be where they were. We flew over *Umm Sa'id* and there was the housing site, a sea of sand and rock planned for the steel workers; and there were even the pipelines waving like a rough sea across the desolate tracts. Beyond, the dust and glare blotted out the real, hard desert with its rime of salt crust and rocky Jebel thrust up in deep shadow. Lines of sand dunes, crest upon crest all flowed like Palaeolithic arrow heads on a cave roof, to the north-west, an enormous unyielding ocean so desolate and empty one could only imagine what it was like to be down there. Everything pointed and flowed towards Saudi Arabia.

It was across this wasteland that Harvard would be arriving in the next month having driven along this single road on his own. Heaven help him if the car broke down. I made a mental note to remind the Guildford office to tell him to pack as much water on board as he could and to let us know when he approached the Empty Quarter.

Dubai sparkled in the sun as we banked for the final approach just ten minutes later. Below were the creek and a line of wind towers on a ridge far bigger in scale and grandeur than ours in *Wakkrah*. The water was limpid, a pale turquoise milk with dhows and a hotchpotch of fishing craft of all sizes, seemingly travelling in every direction at once. Out in the bay were row upon row of large cargo ships, moored up to anchors in lines waiting patiently to unload.

The boom in the oil price had led to this enormous expansion in material goods. Showing up at the mast heads were the colourful Japanese and South Korean flags alongside those of the United States and France. At one particular moment in time it had been calculated that one eighth of the world's cement output was headed for this part of the world. We, as a nation were building the new port and were involved in a number of important infrastructure projects dwarfing those in the United Kingdom. It gave me a very good idea of the colossal scale of the investments which were being made every hour of every day by simply pumping oil. It was a fact, the tankers out there were so large, that the crews rode around the decks on bicycles.

Immigration was a light formality, arriving as I did from a neighbouring friendly Arab State, without receiving even a stare as another stamp was being placed, this time on page seventeen. (Also purple for some reason. Maybe it was a pan-Arab ink deal made by Staples or WH Smiths?). It was an

even call between the officer being too lazy to check my book
and just having an off-day. A taxi rolled to a smooth – ish
halt in front of me as he reacted to the wave of my hand and
we drove off, just ten minutes from braking to a halt on the
tarmac apron.

It was not far into town from the airport, with the road
no busier or more developed than Doha, so that from my
house on the 'C' ring road, to the Dubai creek it had taken
less than an hour. But, the streets were cleaner and the palm
trees taller. Long strands of oleander waved in the breeze of
the passing trucks which scattered broken bracts of purple
and orange onto the tarmac. The taxi took me past the site
of an English pub with a Watney Red Barrel sign hanging
up outside, for all the world like a village inn. Having been
away from all that, for months, it made me nostalgic for
home. Dubai was a world apart from Qatar, which again was
a quantum leap from the way Saudi Arabia directed itself in
strict obedience to all the tenets of Islam.

Part of the United Arab Emirates, Dubai had a very clever
and intelligent Head of State, Sheikh Rashid. Four years
before my arrival, he had helped create the Federation of the
seven Emirates, a colossal feat in itself. Having a Customs
Free Port, Dubai was like one of those magnificent Arab
horses chomping at the bit to get under way, everywhere one
turned one's head the possibilities for the future arose, but
knowing it had to wait while its people came to terms with
progress.

A room was waiting for me at the brand new Intercontinental hotel which rose majestically, if totally out of place,
above the creek. There was no doubt it was the tallest and

most modern tower in the city with tinted glass windows and pent house suites. But, it also sent a message: a message that Dubai was on the move and going there quickly.

The room had been paid for the day because there was a telephone, food and drink, an easy address for potential clients to find me, as well as being the most prominent and thus most easily found building in the city. By four o'clock in the afternoon, working through the hottest part of the day but in air-cooled splendour, meeting a number of hastily pre-arranged contacts, the pulse of this thrusting new country began to beat inside me. Sheikh Rashid knew where he was going, and he wanted, amongst a million other things, four football stadia. With the recent advent of *Astroturf,* it was possible to create a sports field in the desert.

Football was as big in the Gulf as anywhere in the world. It was rumoured that Qatar was going to host the next Pan-Arab games which would be announced shortly. Dubai also, would you believe, wanted an ice skating rink within a bigger complex of a children's' play-ground. They didn't even have a real hospital, one of any worth that is, and the airport was struggling to handle the volume of flights which needed to be handled – let alone the air cargo - yet here were entrepreneurs in smart suits talking seriously of building an ice rink in the desert where daytime temperatures soared to forty-five degrees.

Out of my hotel window, the stately wind towers, elegant and in better repair than those at *Wakkrah,* sat on the skyline with their raised roofs scooping up the wind and cooling the fishermen who lived inside them. Below at water level, the ocean-going dhows from India nudged their way into their berths, four and five deep out from the quayside. A grizzled sailor sat nonchalantly on his lavatory which was formed from a crude wooden seat cantilevered out from the side of his craft, depositing his previous meal ten feet below. Fish, large fish and well fed, swam up hungrily in shoals nuzzling at the new supply of food. Fish were on a roundabout: swim, caught, cooked, eaten, excreted, swim…. where they were eventually eaten by their own children. Pale blue nets and wicker baskets were piled in heaps on every deck as the blistering heat of a midday sun rebounded towards the sky.

The rigging of each boat appeared entangled, as if it were granny's ball of wool after a kitten has played with it, but at a command, a crew member would find the correct halyard and give it a heave alongside his mates: miraculously it all shook itself free before setting sail for the mouth of the creek. The canvas would rise into the sky, the effort augmented by words chanted in unison which had probably prevailed for centuries, certainly since Moses had floated around in his basket.

If one disregarded the line of white Mercedes in front of the view, the scene from my window was mediaeval, an unchanged world of fish and smuggled gold, money changing hands at a rapid rate and women in *burkas* waiting impatiently in random lines (not what I would call a queue) for the food to be weighed so they could prepare the evening meal. What a revolution to the present time where everything, quite literally everything, in their lives was to change irreversibly in the next few years.

Outrageous amounts of money flowed from deep in the ground. It was everywhere, reflected in the cars' windscreens and the polished coffee shop glass of the Intercontinental Hotel. Soon, the creek would give up its dhows and its fishermen as they found it easier to rent out their houses to the new businessmen who would never argue about the cost of accommodation.

It was sad, for my practice was one of those in the van of the tumult, involved in this one-way change to their way of life.

One point had become quite clear from my single day in Dubai. My office could not cope with the potential volume of work being generated here in this watery creek. This would require another Architect to be based in Dubai, meaning a spreading of the Head Office's wings even further.

To underpin this suggestion, I recorded forty-one tower cranes around me; some were so close, the crane operators could be seen eating their stuffed pitta bread sandwiches. If we only picked up one per cent of the work, it would keep our practice in expensive holidays for years to come.

At four, a taxi driver drove me by request to Abu Dhabi before my return to Doha. It seemed a good idea to have a quick look at this other mushrooming city which was also a major player in the United Arab Emirates. As if this had not been enough excitement for one day, the driver now demonstrated he was one of those men who believed everything was controlled through Allah's Will: this included the more than reasonable assumption he was going to die on the hundred and nineteen-kilometre road which flew like a javelin, and thus, as straight, between the two cities. There are many stories told of this stretch of tarmac, one of the most dangerous in the world. There is a similar road between

Cairo and Alexandria with a comparable reputation. (The road flies up to the north until it reaches the village of Zamya Abd El-Qadar almost on the sea where it turns ninety degrees to the east. I bet this catches a few late night drivers out!).

The black top was edged either side by the red sand. It was as if a giant millipede was legging it on a bolt of vermilion silk. So long and straight that boredom had to be tightly reined in if one were ever to have a hope of arriving safely at one's destination. It took only a moment to take one's eye off the featureless road at the wrong moment, to meet a very fast car coming in the opposite direction... and on the wrong side of the road. The numbers of cars and trucks travelling at maximum speed that had collided head on with another were too many to be counted by me on the trip. The wrecks were literally everywhere; torn, twisted pieces of steel often unrecognisable as vehicles. The guide book today, suggests politely that it takes one and a half hours to drive between the two. My driver was dreaming of a black Trans Am with flames painted on the bonnet rather than the clapped-out Toyota he currently owned. Thus, it was very desirable for him to accomplish the trip in about forty minutes. Providing an unwelcome distraction (to me), he had managed to string along his rear window, eight tasselled camels which swung in rhythm to the vibrations set up by the car; several others managed to block fifty percent of his front view. Beside him, he had the customary box of Kleenex tissues without which the Arab world would come to a halt; fags, matches, half-eaten dates and a dozen dusty music tapes one of which played incessant and incomprehensible quarter tones as we drove. To this must be added more dust which lay like a grey carpet over everything. My request to have the music turned down, just a morsel, was met with the usual shrug of the shoulders and a perfunctory tap on the radio casing, to no avail.

At pre-Mach One, as the buffeting increased, I gazed out of the window where the desert floor was covered, almost literally in juice cans and bottles, a carpet of aluminium some twelve feet back from the kerb to parallel the road, thrown from speeding cars intent on reaching their destination. Any enterprising Indian could have come along here and picked up tons of the containers and recycled them in Mumbai...and cleaned up the desert at the same time free of charge.

It was getting dark, though an orange glow in the general direction of Abu Dhabi already lit up the horizon. As we rounded a Jebel which reared itself out of the road, we encountered two triangles each glowing red and moving together on the low horizon. We closed upon the strange red objects whereupon they began to come into focus but now in the middle of the road. The driver eventually accepted that something similar to a flying saucer was tracking us on this remote part of the road. Close Encounters became very close. He slowed, coming down from warp speed to something approaching manageable.

'Camels Sah,' came the voice of the driver as smoke leaked from several orifices in his face. 'Two camels.'

Camels? Surely not. They didn't have red eyes?

But they did have red reflective triangles strapped to their backsides. The camels, unfettered by halters, enjoyed the warmth of the tarmac as it gave up the heat of the day. Hitting a camel weighing fourteen hundred pounds at ninety miles an hour would leave very little in the way of a car...

or a human being for that matter within this warm land; and not much camel either. It now explained why there were so many rusting hulks on the sides of this road, the frames distorted beyond any recognition as cars. Many were collisions with other cars, but a number had to be from high speed contact with these animals who had always roamed the desert. (roaming the desert is a bit of a romantic cliché, but roaming is the right word).

God willing, Abu Dhabi hove into view, a skyline of plate glass, aluminium frames and tower cranes. Obviously, the formation of the Federation had been a good move for these Gulf Tribes although how they had all agreed on who would be the Ruler and who might lose face by being the Deputy Ruler was anybody's guess.

My driver agreed to my request to give me a quick tour of the city, which was as chaotic in its way as Dubai, though there were signs of town-planning in progress. The characteristic short trunked palms occupied the central reservations; show rooms shone with chrome and bright white paint; flags fluttered, but the side streets were filled with the all too familiar piles of rubbish. It was as if the two worlds of order and chaos existed necessarily side by side, the one, essential to show off the modern city, the other to remind us of how it was, even if for a very short time.

Abu Dhabi did not have a creek, but it had the sea itself. The creek in Dubai brought an Arabian character to the city despite its modern buildings. Here, the atmosphere might have been like a seaside resort in England, but the comparison ended at the Corniche itself for behind the sea-front rail and the pavement were towering blocks which reared up almost out of the dual carriageway itself. Not a lot of candyfloss and nary a sign of a pin-ball machine.

Many signs were in English. This was becoming the universal language of the world, much to the disgust of the French: American advertising boards were already starting to intrude on the landscape as Sony, Datsun, Hyundai, Polaroid cameras (what a rage at that time) and some, more focussed such as 'The Oriental Trading Company' (original) and poster after poster of the face of the Ruler of Abu Dhabi, Sheikh Zayed, another remarkable man. There was clearly a competition between the two States for dominance which tended to keep the other five members in the background. These were almost village sized compared with their big brothers, but having, in some compensation, romantic sounding titles such as *Fujairah, Sharjah* and *Ras-al-Khaima*, the smallest *Ajman* and *Umm al Qaiwain*. They were quite eclipsed by their two major brothers, but this did not prevent them from believing in the necessity of having duplicate facilities such as International Airports and major hospitals.

Creating a city from scratch has its advantages. Like Washington in the United States, the Planners are able to map out wide avenues and dual carriageways, get the parking right and remove the light industrial units out to parks on the perimeter for such activities. This was a modern-day Haussmann just as he had set out Paris in the 1860's. Doha, in contrast, remained a bit behind these modern states; it still had the mix of industry whether it was heavy or light and it was not uncommon to see welding and grinding sparking away in the middle of the road as there was insufficient space inside the building. Abu Dhabi's square grid was a considerable improvement upon the idea of Doha's spider's web, a hangover from the past where rapid growth was creating continuous rush hour conditions.

The airport was busy despite Dubai being only sixty miles away. It was a comfortable feeling seeing my aircraft ready and waiting as my brain was churning over a thousand ideas. It was as if I was trying to get off a speeding carousel to collect a particularly nice candy floss only to glimpse an even bigger one on the opposite side. (*green and grass* could be considered suitable substitute words coming to mind).

The BAC I-II tail, poking over the fence in the distance made me happy to get back to the less frenzied town where my family had set up house. What this part of Arabia would be like in twenty years' time was easy to imagine for there could only be a continuation of the race for supremacy of these two oil-rich cities in the future.

The day was too short an experience to allow me to come to terms with doing business in other Arab States. It was clear that with the relaxed view on alcohol for Westerners and the modernist views of both the Rulers of Dubai and Abu Dhabi, these two countries within the U.A.E. would accelerate away from their Gulf brothers particularly when they got around to thinking about tourism. In every Arab mind was what to do when the oil ran out.

Both Qatar and the Emirates had a predominance of Sunni Muslims but in Qatar there was a tighter hold on religious, Sharia law due to Qatar's very close proximity to Saudi Arabia. This is not to say one could drink alcohol in the street in Dubai or for women to walk around half naked as they might have done on the Promenade de la Croisette in Cannes. There was a line which you did not cross, and you learnt about that line very quickly which ever Arab State you were in. Of course, if a State was to develop its tourism, then higher provision was *de rigeur.* A beer on the beach would be almost as important as Piz Buin.

I am reminded of this when recalling the looks and stares of the older locals. Just as in England, we seek a modicum of respect in our religion despite making a cartoon out of the Archbishop of Canterbury from time to time. Our Press also knew this line existed, where attempting to step across would be a foolish thing to do. For Doha, there would be exciting times to come and exceptional architecture to conjure with, but we needed to advance cerebral attitudes in the Emirates, not just to make a case for flooding money into the system. The last few years have proved my case. The world has now recovered from the traumas of 2008 and Dubai and Abu Dhabi once again have returned to the big build though, perhaps most are more cautious in how they proceed. Qatar generally, Doha particularly, began to pick up speed until, very soon, its waterfront looked like a reflection of its neighbours.

It really was not many years after I left the Middle East, fifteen to be precise, when Shaikh Hamad, the son of the Emir took over from his father in a bloodless palace coup and van-guarded a new, and modernist road forward, away from the old mediaeval state.

A few days after my first visit out of the country, Shaikh Khalifa's birthday came up on my diary. A party of us agreed to go together as none of us had had the honour before of wishing His Highness a Happy Birthday. This time, despite the heat, Jay pulled out my light suit and tie and four of us headed down to the Corniche. Everywhere there were cars, none parked in a bay or a space by the side of the kerb: abandoned might be a safer term. It was a scene reminiscent of 'The Highway of Death,' Highway 80 at the end of the first Iraq War... though without the death bit.

Eventually we were obliged to do the same, leaving the car wedged into a narrow gap. Peter, a civil engineer being the driver climbed out through the roof, understanding and then admiration following disbelief, appearing on the faces of other drivers close by who had wondered how our driver would get out of the mess he was in. We left the roof open as it was not going to rain; besides, any alternative would mean pushing the car out of its slot, with the brake on!

We presented our paste board invitations to the security heavies who patted us down with their hands as they did not have metal detectors despite being the Emir's bodyguards, and joined a queue stretching along the main corridor and out of sight. Cardamom coffee was brought to us, giving me time to catch up with business and news from the many other Engineers and Architects. Even our English Dentist was in the queue talking about a new material called 'floss'. We all seemed as busy as each other and the dentist reminded me I was due in a week's time for my first inspection. Bless him. How kind.

The wait was interminable. Finally, we rounded the door to see His Highness was standing on a low dais surrounded by tassels and guards in equal quantities. The scene was engrossing as we watched the tribal leaders come to pay their respects and, no doubt to remind His Highness of the favour which had not yet been paid back. Perhaps there might be a discussion from one Sheikh Jabor about payment for his land?

Along the walls were massive chairs with gilded scroll arms. Red and gold brocade upholstery lined up in a magnificent military array below mirrors on both sides. They reflected the queue of men of all ages, some with gold threaded *thobes* placing them a step or two higher, in our opinion, than the others with plain white cotton. As they shuffled forward in line – no queue jumping here I noticed - their robes swayed together back and forward: kelp beds in the Sargasso Sea. Shaving was not de rigeur even for a Royal birthday party and many a wizened face sprouted white whiskers. It was left to the younger, worldlier men to show off their freshly barbered chins, for remember, this was before designer stubble became fashionable.

The idea of what to say to His Highness began to pick away at my brain, words that would not have already been said after seven hundred and forty-five brothers and businessmen had wished him well. Variations on a theme no doubt.

In due course, we arrived at the head of the queue where the poor man stood, bemused, his arm visibly tired. He showed no recognition in seeing either me, or the others and as I was about to say something inane, he mumbled something that sounded like: 'Nice to see you,' but was probably 'thank you for coming' in Arabic so I could have been mistaken. At that moment, our batch of well-wishers was pushed forwards and onwards by a security guard. We retreated from the Majlis, looking for a cold anything at all, but none in view. Walking back up the corridor I saw the

Ambassador. He was kind enough to walk over and greet me like a long-lost uncle.

'Glad to see you here, Richard. You may not think there is any point in all this, but it is not the Emir you need to think about, it is his Ministers. They like to do business with those ex-pats who recognise the way they conduct their personal affairs. They will have noticed you. Now, you three. Drinks tonight? Six o'clock? Richard, bring that lovely wife of yours.'

The other two were bachelors as were so many Engineers in those days. Drinks at the Ambassador's Residence was always a good place to do business and explore the pulse of the country.

We all accepted and walked back up the deep pile carpet past the alert, security guards and stepped out into the brilliant daylight. As the roof of the car had been left open it meant that the temperature inside was the same as that outside. There had been no shade and dust had descended onto the fascia like a silken glove. Removing the car from the wedge proved successful though it took about quarter of an hour to cool the car sufficiently to get in and eight locks of the wheel to negotiate enough space to ease out of the slot. We motored off home to see how the lads were progressing.

Rhona handed me my new business cards which now proclaimed Partner below the name, new map on the back. They were printed in gold with a black Times Roman address the sort of thing we all tended to collect in plastic envelope books, much better than ploughing through the telephone book which had so many errors it was not worth using. Jay returned from the school and we decided to have dinner at the Gulf Hotel after the Ambassador's soiree and make an evening of it as we no longer had to worry about finding a 'baby-sitter'.

We had finally achieved the level whereby we were able to pay for an Iraqi girl. She was always very polite, quiet but strong enough to stand up to our boys. For some reason, the Iraqis made very good child sitters; this is not to denigrate them in any way, it was just a fact of life like so many other surprising statistics about these people.

The Iraqi men were often very competent Engineers and worked widely throughout the country including our own office. They consistently showed skill and understanding, particularly in the knowledge of how buildings reacted with, and weathered in the desert. The wars which followed were a tragedy to this warm, friendly nation with, often its great sense of humour.

That night, we attended upon our Ambassador's invitation. We all stood in a small, tight circle with our drinks held defensively in our hands. One erudite individual was, as usual holding forth on some complex subject connected vaguely with politics. The discussion led on to the awful way in which Great Britain was being governed, a subject which could safely be acknowledged as not changing over hundreds of years. The Ambassador stood behind the speaker, listening carefully. In the end, he interrupted.

'Gentlemen, you have all roundly condemned our Government as being little more than a swindler, a deceiver, and an incompetent organiser of anything larger than the making of a rice pudding and even that is, according to you, open to doubt. You almost all suggested you would live anywhere than Britain. So, I will make you an offer. Give me your passport and I will exchange it for you, so you may take any other nationality in the world. I can arrange it, believe me. Who is on for it? Come on,' he added, 'who would like a French passport?'

He had probably done this party piece many times before. It was said with a smile but the exactness of what he had said struck home to all of us grouped like herons waiting for a frog, around his lofty presence. If he had been serious, which one of us would have given up his right to be British, despite her faults – none of us I believe? These were the years of Harold Wilson, of the auto-motive industry strikes, the era when the country watched the nightly television scenes of Union officials walking in through the front door of No.10, and where nothing seemed to be going forward. We looked at each other and studied the floor, none wanting to be the first to respond and thus make a fool of himself. I stared up into those cool, calculating eyes with their slight glimmer of a grin and shook my head.

'I rest my case, gentlemen,' he ended with a wave of his gin over our heads.

It was a neat trick. He had managed, in his loyalty to his Queen to remind us all that Britain was, in fact, a bloody good place to live, despite the problems we, or rather they, were going through. It was an appropriate time to leave. Jay caught my eye and we departed with handshakes.

'Try the flat-tailed lobster,' the Ambassador's wife called through the door as we made our leave. How old-fashioned it all seems now, how admirable and appealing it is today in a world of badly brought up children, universal rudeness, and where the absence of manners abounds. Chivalry? Honour? How about the resignation or non-resignation of a Government

Minister when he or she has clearly done wrong? Our world isn't any better these days than those we lived in thirty years before, though, with some reflection on that statement there is the sole exception of better dentistry perhaps.

It was a week later when a call came through notifying me to attend the Ministry of Defence office for an official signing of a contract. This was not the main work as it had yet to be designed and approved but the lesser one of carrying out the research brief into what would be needed in the future. It was for us to fill in the hundreds of blanks in the document; it was important for one piece of work should lead to the next. We needed to have this agreement with some wet ink attached at the bottom.

With considerable trepidation, I walked into a building where, hitherto no-one from my office had even been allowed to walk further than the perimeter gate. Like many of the constancies in the Arab mind, they felt they had to be continuously on the alert for a coup (a comment that was to be underlined forcefully some years later).

In any revolution, the first tasks for disaffected officers is the occupation of the radio station and the Ministry of Defence. Both were therefore, rigorously protected by better trained guards and more secure examination of passes.

Today, after a minute examination of my document and a check on a list in the guard house, I was allowed into a luxurious lobby with a high, airy ceiling. The marble floor was polished and there was a definable sense of power and gravitas lacking in the other Ministry buildings. Here were papers, notes, science magazines and journals on desks, files stacked in piles; filing cabinets appeared to be well-used by secretaries who knew where things should be.

It was nice to believe they understood exactly what they were doing! Beckoned forward again, after a wait of half an hour, I entered a large, airy room, this time with metal grilles attached on the outside of the windows built as sun screens, but simultaneously preventing any views, into or out of the room. No long range telescopes here to see what lay on unguarded desks.

The Minister was a man I had met before at a cocktail party at the British Embassy, a man well aware of his own authority which was reflected also in the size of his stomach. While the other Minister I had dealt with was going to build the base this rather large gentleman would operate the finished structures. He welcomed me in traditional fashion and waved the contract in front of my face, either to cool himself or to tantalise me. An ink pen by Schaeffer, rested on an ivory stand, a pot to the side, Quink, black. It was all there.

We exchanged comments on the research for he wanted to know how this first part of the works was proceeding. We had, naturally, started the work before the contract was signed. He had to report to His Highness in due course and he was careful to make sure he knew what he was talking about. The pen disappeared into the ink at last and hovered, nay quivered, in anticipation of validating the sheet of paper when, the door opened and his brother walked in unannounced carrying a long box.

For a moment, the Minister frowned, having been interrupted, until he gathered it was a present for him. The parcel had appeared from behind the back of his brother and was laid almost reverently on the desk. It was made of cardboard with a cheap piece of string tied loosely into a bow. It must be flowers, I thought.

Eagerly the Minister opened the lid and took out a high velocity hunting rifle, the type you use to shoot seals. It was quite beautiful, if such a machine for killing could ever be so described, with an imaginatively tooled breech, a polished, carved stock and a blued barrel. The telescopic sight was also tinted, wide angled and deadly. His eyes lit up at the sight.

'*Bukkrah! Bukkrah*!' he addressed me apologetically.' 'Tomorrow, please.'

'*Yallah*,' he said as he turned with his brother, speaking now in high-speed Arabic no doubt translated as: 'Let's go shoot some seagulls, bro.'

The ink dried on the nib until only a tiny black globule remained on the pristine gold. The lid of the ink pot remained lying open and for a minute there was the temptation to tip it on its side but, no doubt, there were hidden cameras in every room. The contract remained where it was and I walked out swinging my hands at my sides like a disgruntled boy.

'*Bukkrah...Insha'Allah*.' I mouthed miserably to myself.

It was a true and object lesson in how to do business. The Will of Allah transcended every aspect of life. It was fruitless to try and change the system and dangerous to challenge the statement. Tomorrow was another day. *Carpe diem*!

The Minister would be reminded he had to report to the Emir of a satisfactory outcome to the meeting and Rhona would be at the end of a telephone ready for me to return to the town. I thought of everything that rhymed with duck but gave up after finding only one word which fitted the mood.

Rhona reminded me to collect a cheque from the Ministry of Economy and Finance. Tired and frustrated, the sum was, however, large and the Guildford office could do with

a transfer back of much needed funds to their own coffers.
I got in the car and headed down to the Corniche where the
four storey cream-painted building of unimaginative design
looked like so many others and belied the fact it housed the
men who paid us our hard earned fees.

It is now absolutely essential (well, hilarious) to relate
to you, verbatim, the manner in which we went about what
might have been a simple task: namely to pick up a cheque.

- Park in a cool place. The car will be a long time in
  this position.
- Enter the Security Area and be told, in Arabic, to go to
  the fourth floor. I recognised the word *Ar'ba meaning*
  four.
- Walk up four floors in un-cooled staircase and present
  documents. These are scrutinised over a period of
  ten minutes, no, sorry, fourteen minutes, because of
  a re-think. Am told to go down to second floor for
  validation.
- Walk down un-cooled staircase and present my
  documentation at the *Validation Department.*
- Am told this is not the correct floor for Projects under
  two hundred million riyals and to go to the fourth
  (Ar'ba) floor (again) and see *Minor Projects.*
- Walk up un-cooled staircase, now very hot and
  eventually find *Minor Projects* which is achieved by
  chance as there is no sign either on the door or in
  the corridor. Have to knock, and open six doors in
  turn and shout out 'Minor Projects?' to the Indian
  scribes who also had mountains of paperwork which

cascaded across the floor. Heart drops wondering if my cheque is under the pile.

- Extraordinary surprise as I am shown a piece of paper taken from a pink file - time taken about half an hour – and told to place my signature at the bottom of a receipt book.

- This man then goes away for half an hour to photocopy the document four times. He returns just as I was considering bursting into tears. He smiles, considerably pleased he has taken the English bastard down a peg or two and tells me to go to the ground floor. I ask why. He says, 'to collect the cheque.'

- I walk quickly down the un-cooled staircase to the ground floor and find the correct room. It is huge and filled with a queue almost as long as the Emir's birthday party. Thinking, 'Sod this,' I walk up to the front of the queue wishing for long leather polished boots to crack my whip against and clack loudly along the floor. I explain that the Ministry has told me to collect my cheque immediately as it has been delayed quite long enough. I attach a beady stare, which was returned, suspicious almost, but I stand my ground. Eventually the cheque is retrieved, already signed by two signatures and handed to me. There is much disgruntlement from the remaining members in the queue although there is not a single white face in the line-up.

Understanding dawns. There is no need for me to go at all. I could have sent our gardener for all they cared, and he could have cut their nice grassy patch while he waited.

Jay commiserated with me and brought out drinks, as we sat around the pool. Team Doha listened with hardly a smile on its collective face until the afternoon's laborious event had been fully narrated. Then, the bastards brayed…loudly.

As we were laughing, including myself, there came a loud shout in the street followed by a fairly substantial sigh, one drawn out with the frustration of someone having screwed up somewhere in his day. All five of us rushed around the side of the house to find Mr Andersen, a Danish neighbour from across the road clutching his car door handle tightly. He did not let go as we approached in some alarm and was quite pale in the face. When he saw us, something seemed to depart from his eyes, a sort of tired resignation as if giving up the ghost and life itself, (the sort of resignation when you step in your pet's mess in bare feet) then slowly opened the car door.

In so doing, five hundred gallons of water emerged, sparkling in the sunlight and cleaning the immediate area of the street. The tarmac turned black again and the gutter gurgled for the first time in its life.

'I told him to clean the car-'

'Inside and out,' we all chorused. It was a repeat of the *Wakkrah* painters. We might call it Wakkrah syndrome? The law of literality had struck again. The literal meaning of every word has to be seriously reviewed prior to action when dealing with Yemenis', Baluchis', Afghanis, Indians and Pakistanis'. Andersen's Mercedes, pride and joy of the street would dry out in due course. His embarrassment at being caught out despite five years in the Gulf would not.

'Come and have a drink,' said Jay.

CHAPTER TEN

Big House, Little House

Au s the new team settled in, the workload began to increase proportionately. My three staff settled in and began to form what I would like to describe as a team. We were all dedicated by now to becoming better at our jobs, vastly different as they were from those in England.

It was then we were approached by Ali bin Ali himself, the supermarket owner, to design him a new house. His old one was *'pre oil-war,'* sitting on a dusty radial road connecting the 'C' Ring and the 'B' Ring probably an embarrassment to his son (who I grew to know very well) though he never commented upon it himself in a negative way. It did not reflect his new found financial status when I called on him as a courtesy, but he explained to me he had been comfortable with his house until the Emir had suggested he build a better one.

One of the most difficult issues an Architect has to deal with, particularly, but not only, in the Gulf, is to extract a brief from the Client that has any sensible meaning. One also has to understand that putting in a great deal of time and effort into a design out here did not necessarily mean one would be commissioned with the work at the end. Typical comments from Ali, who was a gentleman and a decent family man, were: 'It is too small Mr. Richard. Sheikh Jassim has a bigger front door than this whole house.' The idea of where the kitchen was to go was not even discussed. His wife was not involved, so the idea of a *Smallbone* kitchen did not raise itself above the horizon. Curiously, the bathrooms did. What details we were able to extract were his ideas for his own private bathroom. This was to be special as, having been a summer visitor to London for many years he had seen the *Bonsack* bathrooms in Harrods. After an entire sketchbook of jumbled ideas (rather like one of Beethoven's conversation books) a result finally bubbled up to the surface with the following brief.

The master bathroom should be large (naturally) with the bath itself to be carved out of a solid block of Carrara marble to be obtained from the whitest bed possible (therefore Carrara C). Over the bath is to be a convex plaster canopy gilded entirely in gold leaf, each of the four corners to be supported by the beaks of four cranes (storks) carved in the whitest of alabaster with their heads pointing up towards heaven to support the canopy. From the centre of the canopy, temperature controlled water will flow down suspended fibre optic cables illuminated in an alternating array of colours. The whole to be set on a dais with steps leading up to it on four sides. Two basins will be carved also out of solid marble with solid (naturally) gold taps.

I also gleaned that:

The main staircase should be in two separate flights each curving up either side of an enormous hall (he had seen these often on Hollywood musical films of the Thirties, usually with Fred Astaire or Ginger Rodgers prancing down the treads). At the top, they would meet where a river (sic) would pour over the landing edge down to the Hall where it would enter a pool and be re-circulated.

Imagine what he wanted for his bedroom!

Because of the difficulties I had been warned about by the Shell engineer in *Umm Sa'id*, the Partnership had agreed to release their model-maker and he was well on the way. We needed him badly. it was now he was needed most.

Harvard arrived one evening as we were having a post-work relax all together around the pool. There was a honking outside and, on investigation we saw a dark-green stretched Land Rover, covered in dust, and studded with flies long departed from this world. It was parked in the road with a black, curly-haired, slightly wild-eyed man emerging from his seat. He looked remarkably like David Essex in his youth, an intensely likeable man though vague and pre-occupied in his approach to life. His ability to find our house had been astonishing. Crossing the Empty Quarter was one thing. Finding our house without an address when he was new to Doha was something else.

He had made excellent time from Guildford, stopping only to sleep and wait while his documents were carefully checked at every frontier post. Having had no-one with him, it had to be an achievement of considerable merit. The car was filled, not only with all of Harvard's model-making equipment, lathes and power tools, all in miniature of course, but there were jars of Tomato ketchup, Marmite, salad cream, H.P. sauce and a dozen other simple goodies which could not be bought in the shops. The boys, who only had another two weeks before they went to boarding school in England, were ecstatic, licking the ends of knives which had been plunged straight into a jar of Marmite.

We had a workshop set up for Harvard at the main office and Henry took him off to *Wakkrah* to get settled into his room. With Harvard installed we could get on with building a model of Ali's house.

Jay decided we should have a barbeque for the expanded *Family on* a local island that Friday to celebrate Harvard's safe arrival and to give the boys a last swim and sail. The island, *Al Safliya*, off the east coast, more a whale hump of sand, had become a favourite place to go at the weekend where many ex-pats met to discuss work as well as to water-ski together. It was not a far drive. At the beach we unloaded, not only our mini-sail but three well-filled cold boxes, brollies, towels, books, sun creams and the typical gear that accompanies any beach party anywhere in the world. This we ferried over the twenty minute distance by the simple expedient of allowing ourselves to be transported by one of the local Arab's in their flashy speedboats.

I had a need to talk to one of the engineers who worked for the Ministry of Public Works. Paul was a bachelor Englishman who was also involved in Doha Radio, a new venture that went out live in English. We decided to go water-skiing: there was always a boat on the island manned by an Engineer or an Architect. We sat in the water side by side waiting to be pulled up, chatting away as if we were a couple of house wives discussing the price of goats' tongues.

At this juncture, my readers should be enlightened to the fact I am not the best water skier in the world, standing upright being just possible while moving at half-speed through the briny. Curves, jumps and cross-overs are complete no-noes. Thus, it was just as my hand was about to be raised signalling to the distant boat to get going, when Paul said in an unnaturally high voice: 'Richard, I don't think you should do that.'

I looked towards where he was pointing with a wavering finger. Ahead, directly in line with the boat, and thus in the direction we were soon to head off to, was a fin. It was a black fin, a shiny and a rather pointy fin. It was cruising slowly in front of our skis as though inviting us to come on over for lunch - with some fava beans and a nice bottle of Chianti. The two men in the boat stared at us impatiently, waiting for the signal, not seeing our problem and lack of desire to have the engine fired up. At last, seeing none, they assumed we had given one and we rose out of the water before both letting go with an alacrity not seen by me since gym at school when we were *teased* by 'Mary,' a silver topped cane which the gym master used as a cattle prod.

The bloody Dolphin decided to emerge at that moment, giving one of those watery gurgles and probably inventing the phrase: *taking the piss.*

Harold, white and under cover of a large brolly was not too impressed with our antics having heard the spun version of my water skiing efforts earlier that morning. We were right to be careful, however, as there were hammerhead sharks and manta rays off the island, both of which we saw from time to time. While a Manta Ray might just kill us with a slap of its wings in an unknowing fashion, the sharks were a real danger where *quandary, jam* and *pickle* came to mind in one big rush, *hungry* was probably another, oh, and sharp teeth of course.

The water skiing was useful in that the noise and vibrations of the engines tended to keep the larger animals away, especially those with large mouths and larger appetites. We made an executive decision to abandon the ride and returned to sit on the beach in the full sun discussing work and relationships with other ex-pats.

'You need to meet David,' he said. 'David is setting up a quiz programme for Doha Radio and wants to know if you would like to put forward a team.'

He threw a hand at the beach towards a man who was frowning in concentration as he listened to some music on his radio. Occasionally he would spread some imaginary marmalade in the air, which we found out was called conducting.

David was a delightful and highly erudite bachelor, steeped in the vagaries of the later Beethoven quartets, classical in every respect, who proved over many years to be a very good friend. In those days he was a bit of a wild boy, liked the lager and joined in with our House Parties with considerable energy. The proposal for us to put forward a team appealed, for if it was geared around the practice, we might become better known on the circuit.

Thus was born *The Christopher Wrens*, one of the competing teams of the Brains Trust and composed of all Architects.

Back in the office, Ali's model progressed as had the time for the boys to leave for England dwindling down to a few days. We took the Land Rover and headed out one evening into the desert, up to the dunes. It really was the ideal machine for the desert, kicking off the sharp rocks and soft spots as it trundled along in low gear. The boys enjoyed the ease of jumping into the open back with the bench seats either side. It was already cooler as we arrived and Jay selected a spot away from the prospect of scorpions finding us and made a sort of camp.

An idea dawned; something to let the boys talk about at their new school. I pulled the driver's seat as close to the wheel as possible and packed my eldest in with a couple of cushions.

'Now, we learn to drive.' He was eleven at the time so his feet were within a smidgen of reaching the pedals and he picked up the idea in a short while. Without the worry of traffic, other than his mother sitting on a large rock, which was significant, I must admit, he roared off in low gear locked in a tight circle. Sand spiralled out from the rear wheels, jagged rocks flew in all directions making Jay and my youngest decide discretion was the better part of valour. They ran for a higher part of the dune where, having climbed up ten feet they were able to watch the antics below from the Dress Circle. After a sweaty quarter of an hour, my youngest had a go but the only way he could reach the pedals was to lie almost horizontally, which was fine for the engagement of gears but visibility was considerably reduced...in fact he was unable to see anything at all. In the end, he was given remote instructions (as blind Olympic skiers) such as: 'Right, right... *Right!*! Straight on... no!! *Straight on, for God's sake! Sorry Mummy. Say sorry to Mummy.*'

'Don't swear dear', Jay said, dusting the spray of sand off her skirt as if they were sandwich crumbs. But she was pleased with my effort. She was going to lose her two sons in just a few days.

We drank 7Up as the stars came out and I gave the boys a lesson in Astronomy. They would never have such a good view as this when at school. The Plough looked like a squashed parallelogram upended over a barbeque fire of stars and the Milky Way was as though I had emptied a bottle of Absinthe into an aquarium.

Those last few days were special. We tried to memorise every idiosyncrasy of our two sons, realising how quickly they had left their summer childhood behind them. They had grown taller out here, browner and healthier. They could say '*Salaam Alaikhum*' without embarrassment and mix and talk with the local Arabs with no awkwardness. Now they were flying out of our lives into the regime of a Public School with dorms, lights out and tuck boxes.

It became time to take the boys to the airport. Jay was to go as well and see them into the school. I had made it a bit easier for her, suggesting that at the end of the term they could come out with her mother. It was, nonetheless, a heart-wrenching moment as I kissed all of them goodbye. All of a sudden, the two boys looked small and defenceless. They were trying to be brave but their lives were to change dramatically and there was a big unknown at the end of the flight despite the fact Jay was going all the way with them. We kept up the banter as we queued to check-in, telling them the driving lessons would continue in the holidays.

This time when the plane took off, the silence was even more pressing: it hung like a noose from a Judas tree as I blamed myself for having let them go. It was the first time in my life that the boys had been out of my sight for more than day with the exception of Scout Camp and sleep-overs. Returning to the office, Rhona, intelligent and sensitive to the situation brought a large cup of coffee to my desk and gave me a surreptitious hug.

There was a reminder of this gentle event a few weeks later when instructions to return to England to discuss new policies with my Partners gave me a week-end alone in Suffolk. I rang the House Master up at the school, a lovely old building in the countryside of East Anglia and managed to get my sons on the phone. After all the 'how-are-you's' I told them the Sunday was free for me and would they like to go out for the day. There was a long silence.

'Well, Dad. That would be nice, but I'm going hot-air ballooning.'

'And I'm going canoeing,' came another disembodied voice.

It had only taken five weeks but I was able to report back there was no need for concern over home-sickness.

When Jay came back and had got over the initial emptiness of the third bedroom, her life began to expand as she found she was not tied to school runs. We were able to go out of an evening – frequently – without having to use a sitter and we could stay out later giving me particularly, much more flexibility in setting my own timetable. On the first occasion of being *a deux* we took ourselves off to the opening of the new Doha Cinema. Multiplex had not been thought of over here, but it was a modern auditorium with excellent air-conditioning and a screen as wide as a Montana sky. We sat in a special reserved area, quite Raj-like in fact, within a wooden barrier set slightly above the main seating rows, as if we were pashas reviewing our troops. The film was 'GOLD', you may remember it starred Roger Moore and Susannah York. As it started we saw that every seat was taken. Seats were filled with brown and grey shifts and short-sleeved shirts; there was a twittering as if a murmuration of starlings were coming in to roost. The noise continued for five minutes until an usher, no usherettes in fishnet stockings yet, told them to pack it up or *Yallah!* They calmed down, putting their heads in their knees and looking sideways at everyone else's knees as if they were naughty children, missing some of the adverts for soft drinks and perfumes.

And then the main film started.

Those who are old enough to remember the film about gold mining in South Africa might recall the Jacuzzi scene. All had been well as Susannah and Roger canoodled and flew about the veldt. When they arrived at the house tucked away in the back of beyond they made up their minds to have a bath, that is, both to slip into a Jacuzzi together without a lot of clothes on. Well, actually, none at all. As this happened, the cinema, below our seats erupted with fury, the wrath of the crowd issuing threats accompanied by whistles. In came the ushers, but it was too much for them as they could also see what was being portrayed on the silver screen, and a couple of policemen had to be called. No doubt, the cinema projectionist was sacked for not censoring the film beforehand. The next film was called *Footprints on the moon* and the auditorium settled to peace and calm.

~

It was finished. Harvard lifted the huge model of Ali's house into the Land Rover ready for a presentation. His son, Hassan, was there to make comment also, for his English was perfect. It took two of us to lift the model out of the car as it was almost three feet long, being set in landscaped palm trees, and perfect in every miniature detail.

But, Ali was not impressed. His rotund figure dressed in a simple striped *jallabiyah*, shook with disappointment as he looked down on his house. He tried to wave the model away with the fingers of one hand 'It's too small, Mr Richard and I can't see what is inside.'

But Harvard was used to such comment. From a pocket, he pulled out a tiny replica of the man himself dressed right down to his *keffiyeh* (Cadmium red) and immaculate *thawb* (Dulux brilliant white) and the stomach accurately depicted in scale. (Rotund). Carefully he placed it in the main doorway. As if by magic, the house was transported into full size, the palm trees soaring above his head and the driveway providing access for ten cars. Each window became a vision onto another world and his front door now stood ten foot high. Ali beamed.

'*Zain! Zain! Zain!* But-'

Harvard was still in motion. He held his hand up for attention.

He lifted the roof off the house as if removing a silver cloche from a presentation dish of nouvelle cuisine. Thankfully, he did not say 'Voila!' Below was every one of the rooms on the first floor Even his bed was in place with painted tassels on the walls, but again, Ali's face failed to light up. This time, Harold was not to blame.

'What is the problem, Papa?' his son asked in not a little frustration. 'The first floor also lifts off.'

He had everything he had asked for. They exchanged words in Arabic before going on to explain.

'My father has, er, certain needs at night. Needs that do not require him to be seen in the corridors.'

'Oh, like going to the lavatory in the middle of the n-'

'Possibly, possibly, Mr Richard. My father has the need sometimes.' The penny clicked. 'Ah, I understand. I have not shown the second, parallel corridor here in case your father did not wish for him to be seen. The second corridor leads from here,' I was guessing wildly while Harvard was making surreptitious notes, 'to the lavatories.'

Ali's son translated my words. He began to beam again. 'Zain- no, Good! Good! Good!'

It was yet another learning lesson in psychology which, although it had its lighter moment was an important message all the same. The sensitivities of the Arab had to be respected and he might have lost face if we had not picked up with his son on the design requirement. It was the same as the night when the table decided to drop its top on our knees. We had to think on our feet when these events occurred and hoped to

God we had made the right decision. In fact, we were able to introduce a second parallel corridor into the house, though the design difficulties were sorted out in Doha. Guildford would never have believed our requests.

Ali led us into his dining room; he spent a good part of his life in London and was accustomed to western ways, where we had a celebratory drink and snacks. Levant food was always very good. *Hummus*, something you find in all supermarkets in England but with disgusting additives, was made by hand of course, in those times, but so fresh it was delicious. It is prepared from mashed chick peas and tahini, which is sesame paste, olive oil, salt and garlic. Here it was set in a ring with pine nuts sitting in the centre with the oil. It is probably the oldest prepared food in the world and might put Marks and Spencer to shame if they learned it had been made for centuries. *Tabbouleh*, where his maids had chopped up Bulgur wheat, tomatoes, parsley, scallions and mint with oil, cinnamon and fresh lemons was another traditional dish. It's a labour of love for the chopping, was and must be, very fine and he was obviously proud of his maids' recipe. It was outstanding, and so refreshing, especially after the way our bodies had heated up in the presentation. Flanking these dishes was *halloumi* the Levant cheese, this time pan-fried and mouth-watering, being toasted to a light-brown. The sweetmeats were as good as anywhere in Lebanon; *Baklava,* layers of filo pastry with chopped nuts, syrup and honey, fattening as hell itself (Is hell fattening?) though that had no issues with us in the Gulf because of our relative fitness. *Baklava* used to be made in the Imperial kitchens of the Topkapi Palace and was now a commonly found sweetmeat in Turkey. (If this reads like one of the plethora of TV cookery programmes I apologise, but these recipes were straight from the Qataris' tables).

The heat tended to make us sweat off any of these excesses but we also sailed and swam and now it was time to take up squash as we had two courts in town near the Corniche. These were built of concrete and in the fine tradition of the wind towers were cooled by the simple expedient of having a gap between the top of the walls and the roof. It managed to reduce the temperature by ten degrees or so. There was nothing like a fancy glass back wall and the floor was lino paint on trowelled concrete though to a pretty high standard.

My usual partner was a giant of a man with a reach seemingly from one side of the court to the other. I consequently didn't win much, well... on reflection, never, but it was good exercise for us both. He ran a Travel Agency in town for an Arab owner and had all of the ex-pat business. Although he was always much better than me, his patience was justified in bringing me to a level where we could have a reasonable game. Waiting for the ball to be served to me, an ever-increasing dark ring would form on the concrete entirely encircling my tensed body. The stain would magically move with me, turning the circle into the gender symbol for a male. If I fell back (often) the ring was transformed into a female.

It was astonishing how I had acclimatised to the weather, after all my fears. Here I was, playing in forty degrees of heat with no cooling whatsoever, in a sport that, traditionally, has always managed to raise one's temperature anyway. It produced a six pack and a degree of fitness I had not had since the days of the Newquay Hornets, despite the fact like so many in those days, we all smoked Ali bin Ali's

(Rothmans) as if there was no tomorrow. At three shillings a pack it was not exactly a concern. Those were the days; you may remember when you were never alone with a Strand. For those who have never smoked - and I have not smoked for the last twenty years - try one after an Australian steak with a large gin and tonic.

Squash led me to an exciting new facility in Doha. A group of enterprising locals had grouped together and built a Club close to the water. It was ostensibly for anyone but in reality the ex-pats used it more than any others. It was luxurious, with a magnificent outdoor pool, food served to the poolside, squash courts, a marina and comfortable lounges and changing rooms. Members were able to buy fresh crushed orange juice from oranges ripened on the vine which mitigated the dangers of sunstroke. We were able to receive early membership to the Doha Club and the daily visit became our *raison d'être* for lunch time existence.

Time has now passed but I recall the Club Owners quaint idea of issuing a plastic card which we could use as a key to the Club and as a charge card! Whatever next, wondered Jay.

As we always took the afternoons off, being too hot to work, a siesta in other words, we would drive down to the Club and claim a favourite sun bed by the pool. We would order a club sandwich and a juice and flop in and out of the water like walruses whenever our skin temperature reached a critical level. Lying full out in the midday sun became a normal event. This was an activity that I could not have envisaged six months earlier but by now the sunburn had coloured between my toes and under my arms, places where no sun had gone before. In fact, I looked quite comical, well, usually, when, on

removing my clothes at night there was a vivid scar of white,
I mean pure white, encircling my body somewhere between
my navel and my upper knee area. We never forgot however,
just what the sun could do, just as a seaman is considerate and
respectful of the sea, but we no longer thought of burning as
we used to do when we arrived. We were reminded of this later
on when the boys returned for Christmas holidays, pale and
white after a term in England in the autumn.

With a pool to swim in at any time we were away from
the house, a Club to meet friends in, two Squash courts,
butter in the supermarket and Minisails, our worldly needs
were satisfied, despite no television to speak of, no radio,
theatre, pubs and no newspapers.

Minisails and the Gulf made a terrific cocktail as it didn't
matter if you could sail well or not at all, whether you were
the right side up or upside down it was all the same fun. The
warm water made it a delight to fall in to or to capsize, as
the immediate and often expected immersion was cooling
without a shock and enabled one to climb on board again
and have another go. In a very short time we had mastery
of these single sailed craft which could be rigged in under
a minute yet sliced through the water off the island with
considerable speed. Women, and men, who had never sailed,
five-year olds, those afraid of the water, all fell for the spell
of the Minisail and within a short while there was a small
fleet of them. Later on, some of the better sailors migrated
up to Lasers but the afternoons became magical, sailing on
my own, leaving the pressures of the office for a few hours.

Reading this through again it would appear, dear reader,
as if we did nothing but wallow in water of one degree of

salinity or another...or sit in the sun, but really it wasn't like that; it merely replaced the time I might have spent if I had been in the UK watching television.

Because of the expansion in business, Rhona always had to keep an eye on available houses and their rents. These were soaring and were making the cost of ex-pats in the Gulf an expensive element. Each time a villa became available I would go and see it even though there was no demand for it at the time. We were never going to be a large office, as might Dubai and Abu Dhabi; the country was too small, but we needed to keep up to date to see what was available if our own rents went too high. Thus, it was the week after the boys had gone back to school that I called to see a house, single storey, but on the 'C' Ring road, which had just been completed and handed over to its owner. He did not want to live there, preferring to rent it out to the highest bidder.

At first sight, it appeared reasonably built. It was vertical, that is, in plumb, and the walls relatively square. It was when I went inside that matters began to become slightly schizophrenic. Every house in the Gulf has some terrazzo flooring; it makes sense with the heat of the summer. However, the "Builder" had laid his electrical conduits along and across the floor to reach the multitude of power points. As it was all to be covered up, the conduit was not exactly laid in straight lines as was easily determined by the fact the tiler had laid his terrazzo tiles straight to the concrete base, in other words, now levelled with the top of the conduit piping. He had found, of course, this would not do, causing him to cut the tiles around the piping. The result was a very different crazy paving effect dividing the floor up into segments, each different in size and shape and of course, the black lines each ran to a different power point. The same builder, who had obviously allowed this to happen, (he had probably shot himself having seen the result) was also the plumber or at least I assumed so. When we went into the three bathrooms, each in turn confirmed there was a rather nice Italian W.C. suite butted against the outer wall. When I took a gander through the window, the *swan necks* of the toilet outfalls appeared on the outer face of the building where they stopped, ready to discharge anything we might try…onto the garden thus providing instant manuring to the hollyhocks.

When I enquired, in a strangled voice, to the Agent, why had the builder not connected the toilets to the sewage system he was lost for words of any significance. The previous paragraph began by using a capital 'B' for Builder, but it was found by the end of the visit, to be valuable to discard the upper-case letter for something more akin to lower case. Needless to say, this house was passed over in preference to sleeping on the beach.

With the departure of the boys came the advent of autumn. Temperatures in July and August had climbed to the mid-forties falling to twenty-five at night. Now the temperatures were coming down to the eighties and we were told by the 'oldies' to expect the days could fall to below ten. Jerseys and light sweaters were pulled out of a moth-balled drawer and hung up to air. The water heater had to be reversed so it would do the job it had originally been designed for and Jay pulled out rugs from a chest. We also spent an evening at the Suq where we found cheap, Japanese fan heaters and bought some for all our houses. It was as if we were preparing for a siege rather than weather which would have been classed as *delightful* in the U.K. We were led to believe that we could expect about an inch of rain both in November and December but when the first one came, we experienced a cloud burst, an almost solid sheet of water crashing down through a black sky where it roared into the dry, filled up gulleys by the sides of the roads. Because maintenance is not a word which existed at that time in the Arab dictionary, the drains were filled immediately, causing the storm water to overflow and run down the roads just as it had been that remarkable day with Henry on an even more memorable dinner table a few months earlier.

Unsurprisingly the water entered the office where it washed the terrazzo floors and emptied mud into the swimming pool. Meanwhile, upstairs in our house, the roof was patently incapable of allowing the rain to run off, perhaps because of the large cracks in the roofing material, they, having widened out during the summer. Jay was not sure which section to tackle first as we watched the cascade travel down the stairs, three at a time to join the water already waiting for it in the main office where it had arrived a little earlier.

Rhona was found, standing on a stool as if a mouse had entered the room, bewailing the fact there were three Architects in the building and '…not bloody one of you know how to deal with it.'

The others had to go back to their own properties to see what damage had been caused but, in fact, they were able to report back that the older houses never did let the rain in, as they relied on an old-fashioned cement screed rather than any new-fangled water-proofing materials. Rubber sweeps worked best of all and we always kept one in the office as we never knew when the rain would come.

~

As autumn drew on and our name became better known to the Ministry of Public Works we began to get knocks on the door during the evening. As no-one knocked on the door normally we soon learned what it was for. On the doorstep, there would always be a small parcel with a business card but without a name personalising it. Inside would be a watch, always a watch, always in gold, some so heavy one's wrist might have been permanently sprained. It was this builder, or that contractor, making his mark for the next job, a sort of memory jogger, an aide memoire, a note in a diary even, the alternative to bidding under supervised competition, a standard method of attracting one's attention.

Always the next day, either I or one of the lads would drive down to the particular jewellery shop in front of the Suq where we handed the watch in to the shop owner. He would study the ceiling as he recognised the 'idiot English' but he was able to tell you who had bought it in the first place, where upon we were able to return it to its rightful owner apologising for the fact he must have dropped it on the way home. It was not the way to do business in Arabia, and there were many English companies who took whatever was offered, but I wanted our practice to be above *baksheesh* so we could make the often-difficult decisions needed without compromising our standards. But, of course, the donor had managed to get his company name in front of me anyway.

October brought the start of the construction of the accommodation buildings for the Japanese Steel company. There were three separate units of four-storey concrete block with reinforced columns, nothing special, and nothing unknown in the way of engineering. We did, however, carry out regular crushing tests on sample blocks to ensure they came up to the standards of our specification. One cold day Henry came into the office with a glum face holding a piece of paper in his hand.

'Not good news boss. All the tests have failed.'

'All?'

'Well ninety-two percent of them.'

'That *is* serious Henners. Get Huxley in here. We need to plan what we are going to do. Rhona let Guildford know. Contact John, say we will send him details later.'

We chewed the fat for half an hour, but there was no going around the problem. Either we accepted the failures on the assumption they were not load-bearing and thus did not matter or we would have to order them to be pulled to the ground: neither was a good solution to the problem and there were massive issues looming rather too close on a troubled horizon.

Henry was emphatic. 'We knock 'em down Boss.'

'That might mean we lose future work with the Japanese. Mr Fukida is stressed enough as it is-'

'But, it's not our fault. We are carrying out our checks as we are paid to do. If we leave this go what else do we leave?'

'And we will get a reputation for letting things slide,' agreed Huxley.

They were right, of course. They both made absolute sense despite the fact that we could have a major delay on our hands but I was also very proud of them. Most of the angst surely to rise would fall on their heads when they walked out on site. To my knowledge knocking a building down or, in this case, buildings, had never been done before in the Gulf and we would be watched very carefully by everyone from the Ministry of Public Works up to the Emir, who would see an inexcusable delay in the opening of his Rolling Mill, beginning to materialise on his horizon.

I made up my mind. Whatever the Partners said in reply, we on the ground always had the final say. Based in England, they would see nothing wrong in condemning such tests anyway.

'Take the walls down, Henry but advise everyone in writing of what we are about to do first. Everything must be written down and copied in to everyone connected with this job. We can expect a visit from whoever is installing and supplying the blocks. Who is it by the way?'

'Sheikh Jassim.'

'Buggar, I thought it was. And he is thinking of commissioning us on his new factory. It's a big one.'

'I know Boss, but what else can we do?'

'Nothing Henry. My problem. Start the ball rolling by advising the Ministry of Public Works first thing tomorrow.'

CHAPTER ELEVEN

Baghdad, Baksheesh and Burnt Sesame

The situation was quite serious. Saving face here in Qatar was almost as important as in Japan. And our client *was* Japanese to make it worse. I rang John in Guildford and had a long talk with him over the problem. He commiserated with me but, as expected, he had to leave the final decision in Doha. My next task was to go and see Hitoshi and wondered if we would be still on first-name bases at the end of the day.

He was, as usual, on the telephone and he waved me into a seat. In his mind, there was no time for coffee and it certainly did not extend to granting me a special favour either. A long time passed while the Japanese parroted back and forth. Hitoshi was clearly speaking to someone in higher authority as he kept making slight, apologetic bows to the window. Eventually he ended the call and shook hands. He sat down, plucked eyebrows raised, wondering why my unexpected call at the office.

'Ahh, ever'thin' okay?'

'No. Big ploblem Mr. Hitoshi.

The other's face visibly lined, possibly permanently, the sallow cheeks taking on a pallor of definitely non-Eastern appearance. It was not a good start to a difficult explanation. I explained in detail that the block tests had failed, the reasons why they had failed and what we had to do.

'If we do not, Mr. Hitoshi, both of us will have a reputation for weakness and, before the end of the contract, many others will take up the same advantage.'

We were, as some American once said in 1921, 'between a rock and a hard place', but, to Hitoshi it was more of standing between Hell and Hades.

'What can we do?'

'First, we keep calm and we plan how to sort this out. We *have* to knock the walls down but not the frames; by the way although they are already up to third floor height, the floors are not yet in, so the blocks can be knocked into the central openings; and then we will try and catch up with the programme. If we can do that no-one will have any plob… problems at all. In fact we could be shown to be knights in shining armour.' I felt Hitoshi was not too good at translating that last phrase but he got the gist. Words such as *Samurai, rolling heads* and *Hara Kiri (Seppuku)* were suitable in the current climate but the image of us as leather-clad warriors from the past evaded me.

'How we do this?'

I was inclined to say 'f**k knows' but his sensitivity level for these Anglo-Saxon crudities was fairly low, and the Japanese do not have any swear words of their own, annoyingly.

'We need to speak with Sheikh Jassim. It is his blocks which have failed.' I was warming to an idea. 'If it gets around the country, as it will, he is going to lose face and the Emir might well be displeased if he learns the delays are due to his blocks. We, I, need to speak with him and see what he can do.'

I left an unsettled oriental pinning his hopes on what could be done to save the day. Hitoshi was an administrator, and a good one, but not a strategist. His loss of face could be considerable if this were not sorted out, but as far as I could see he levelled no blame at me. Thus, sorted so far, Rhona was asked to ring Sheikh Jassim and say I was coming to see him on an important matter. Shown in straight away it was obvious he had had the news.

We had, nonetheless, to go through the ritual of the coffee but a single cup was enough for me that day. 'Now, Mr Richard, you have a problem?'

'*We* have a problem Jassim. Your blocks have failed.'

He held up a beautifully manicured hand. 'My blocks are very strong. The tests are wrong.'

'They were tested by an American Company, Jassim. They do not make mistakes on this scale. I have to knock down all the walls we have built so far to the ground. If not, I will lose work in the future as no-one will believe we are a strong and professional company. You must see my point of view.'

His face said he understood exactly. He might have an Arab's mind for the desert but it was also a highly intelligent one.

'And my reputation? As a builder of fine blocks?'

'That is why I am here. We need to resolve this problem here and now and then I will go back to the Japanese to tell them how we go forward.' There was a fear that on my return Hitoshi might be found with a ceremonial sword in his stomach.

'Well…Mr. Richard?' The inflection was as clear as the reflection of Mount St. Helen's in its lake on a still day. It was for me to get him out of his hole.

'Well, what we say to the public is that we have now found out the ground is unstable in the area of the buildings. Sink holes and the like. We have to knock the walls down so we can check the foundations and then rebuild using your excellent blocks, which we hope will not fail the next time. But, and here is where we need you. You will need to double the supply of labour to the contract to catch up with the programme. Even if we can convince the Emir and the Ministry of the need to knock the blocks down we still cannot fall behind the end-date.'

Jassim was silent for a long time. He turned to the window, perhaps hoping for a sight of a line of camels to soften the harsh realities of business. A minute passed and I was beginning to think he was going to dismiss my suggestion.

Eventually he turned back to me. 'This is an elegant solution to the problem. I will give instructions to my men to knock the walls down themselves. This way it will be known that I am taking my responsibilities seriously. There will be no cost to the Contract and they will continue to make blocks and lay them.' He smiled and shook my hand. 'And, we will catch up the time. I think you and I, Mr Richard had better spend a day in the desert. We will go riding on camels and forget the trials with which Allah tests us. I will need to look at the crushing strengths of my blocks and see if you have a problem in your specifications. It may well be that they are too high.'

I dismissed that one from my mind. It could wait for another day. The idea of being Lawrence for a day appealed.

'That seems like a very good idea Jassim.'

On automatic pilot, the car drove itself back the same route as I mulled over the way that Jassim had come to terms with his problem. Here was an Englishman, living in his country on a temporary basis, who would one day go back to his own home. But he, Jassim, would have to remain with his block-making factory saddled to a specification which was almost certainly way too high for this small country at present.

Hitoshi wrung both my hands with his own as if they were wet sheets going through a mangle. 'This is good. Vel... very good. I can tell my superiors in Kobe that we are still on... tlack?'

'Back on tlack, Hitoshi, back on tlack."

As I drove up the 'C' Ring road to the office, two good relationships had been forged out of fire, friends even, who would remember me and the practice next time contractual difficulties arose. The world was becoming more multi-hued each day dealing with Japanese and Qataris and soon we would be conferring with Koreans and Americans.

The lads were briefed on how we were to get out of the mess of *Umm Sa'id*. We decided that we would always try and have a fall-back solution on hand for emergencies, what is known these days as Plan B.

Rhona came in holding a telex which had been waiting for me on my return.

'Going places, I see.' It was a Head Office memo from John.

It was to be Baghdad this time. That was Iraq. At least, my school geography at which I had passed 'O' level with a reasonable margin was proving useful. In those far off days, Baghdad in my mind was a place for men who flew around on carpets, jumped out of giant sized brass jars and conjured up genies.

While trying to find an atlas, as often is the case, not ten minutes after receiving the telex, we received a rare visitor, for we usually went out to the client rather than the other way around. This time, however, a small, slight Chinaman bowed his way into my office. Rhona dusted the spare chair with the back of her hand and flipped it forward into place.

'Hsien.'

'Excuse me! I beg your pardon?'

'*Mr* Hsien, it is my name. And you are Mr Richard-?'

'Richard Newman, Mr er... Hsien.'

Rhona's cheeks gave a slight pucker behind our client's back, at my confusion. 'Would you like some coffee, Mr Hsien?' She asked sweetly.

'Ah, tea please.'

And so we both sat down, me to listen, Hsien to deliver a message. The additional activity of the morning had drained me. Now I had to sit and learn what was wanted as Hsien, knees folded tightly together, valise perched atop the knees waited patiently for the tea to arrive. Rhona, with the sensitivity for which she became famous, knew instinctively that it was important the door should be closed for this meeting. It was the first time it had ever been shut, a fact underlined by the squeal of the hinges as the sand ground itself out of the butts.

Mr Hsien represented a massive government construction company from Taiwan. They had made an application to be placed on the bidding list for the Naval Base and we had replied that we knew nothing about them and were unable to see any of their work in progress as they had no buildings to show us in the Middle East. It had always been an absolute necessity to check these companies out carefully, for their brochures and statistics often belied the actualité.

We all know about spin and self-aggrandisement as they had always been world-wide and I did not count Britain out in these matters. We were as full of bullshit as anyone else. We thus had to scratch around and look under the surface. As a result, we had had no alternative but to reject their wishes simply as there was no evidence to go on either way. (Today, we would go on-line and read all we needed to know and study photographs of their work via their website.)

It was Mr Hsien's idea that I come to Taiwan to see for myself how well they could build. He explained that his government, often hard-pressed by mainland China, had to earn its own foreign currency. It was achieved in two ways. Either, Taiwanese who had become eligible by way of age could work overseas in Chinese restaurants – hence the expansion of these all over the world, or they could work in the construction industry. It was all *National Service.*

Either way they chose to work, funds were then repatriated to Taiwan to support the country.

The other side of this giant operation was to produce the food for the thousands of restaurants worldwide, so authentic menus could be reproduced at the drop of a tin, or two. It did not paint a convincing picture to learn that a building operation worked side by side with a food production company. There was, anyway, a difficulty. If I were to be seen feeding off the hospitality of a Contractor on a bidding list, our practice could be accused, rightly so, of collusion, of having been in that Company's pocket especially if he then went on to win the job. I explained this to Mr Hsien.

'But, you ask that we demonstrate our ability to build. How else do you expect us to get on the list?' This was all said with a great deal more politeness than written down here but you get the drift and he had a point.

'If I were to come, there would have to be conditions, and you would have to keep to them.'

'Yes Sir. And what are these.'

'One. I must not be put up in a hotel that is anything better than four-star rating; similarly, the air flight must not be anything more than standard economy. These will match what we are permitted to do as a practice.'

Mr Hsien gave what I have always read about but never seen before: the *inscrutable* look of a Chinaman. 'Of course. This can be arranged easily.'

'Two. There must be no entertainment in the evenings. I will spend time in the day visiting your new buildings, but I am to be left alone after work.'

'Of course. No entertainment. What about eating Sir?'

'Naturally, I will eat! Three. I will need a translator, but not one from your own company. I need an unbiased view.'

'All our translators come from an independent company.'

'Good, good. Four. No presents. Definitely no presents.'

'Presents? My dear Sir. We can assure you that there will be no presents.' At this juncture, Mr Hsien sensed victory but the slight smile on his rotund cheeks was short.

'And that includes no girls or discreet knocks at my hotel door. That is Item Five by the way. Is this clearly understood?'

'Certainly, no girls.'

What was worrying me slightly was that Mr Hsien was taking no notes. 'I understand Mr Newman. But, you will come?'

'I will need permission from my Partners for such a trip. We've not done this before.' It did not seem necessary to mention that most things we did out here were not done in Guildford.

We parted with the promise to meet again in the next few days. A visit to see one of the great building contractors' operations in the Far East was a good opportunity, for they were far in advance of us in building technology. They also ran their sites on a military basis, which was why they ran up the ladders on site at the blow of a whistle. The workmen were, in fact, under National Service orders and had to obey, what were in effect Sergeant-Majors. These people would be seen on our sites in future years, lined up in the early morning for roll-call. They all had neat, washed overalls and blue helmets, (like a regiment of UN soldiers) the man with the whistle on a lanyard waiting for his watch to strike seven. At the tickle on his pea, instead of a football being kicked, seventy men would run up the ladders shouting out what seemed closely to mimic the word *banzai* but was probably only 'let's go boys.' Anyway, banzai is Japanese and not Chinese. (Banzai means 'ten thousand years' - of long life!).

All this was for the future but only just, for the world was accelerating at a mad, unchecked pace with a focus on the Gulf and I, seemingly, was one of those at the centre of the storm.

Iraq and Baghdad had been temporarily erased from my thoughts pondering on how to get to Taipei but a reply arrived to my telex the same day from Guildford, detailing who I was to meet and suggesting Taipei could be included at the same time. Providing I watched my back carefully to see there were no Contractor's presents in my bank account on my return, it was felt that being involved with such a successful company might be beneficial to us.

On his second visit, Mr Hsien beamed like a moon, shedding its light upon me. We agreed that after one night in Baghdad, and on my return the next day, a de-brief to the lads and Rhona, I would be free to go on to Taipei. Dates were agreed and Rhona booked me on the flight to Iraq. Where Taiwan was concerned everything was to be left to Mr Hsien.

With the benefit of hindsight and the tumultuous years covering two Gulf Wars, weapons of mass destruction and Saddam himself taking centre stage, Iraq would be a focal point of my thinking thirty years later. For the moment, it was with a pair of rose-tinted glasses that I took off for Bagdad on a November morning.

One has to remember that in 1975 Saddam Hussein had not yet come to power. The Ba'ath Party was still being run by

Al-Bakr, but, following several upheavals with Saddam, the current leader was soon to disappear from the scene and he died four years later. It is not often known that Al-Bakr was Saddam Hussein's maternal cousin.

At the time of my arrival, there was relative peace, certainly nothing to make me want to check with the Foreign Office before leaving, and there was no problem in hiring a taxi which took me to the Hotel. The hotel's name, Sinbad, a childhood book of mine, should have sent me some sort of warning but it was only for one night. Nonetheless when the porter took me to my room, I felt, as a bare minimum there should have been a door. A splintered doorframe told the story of a riotous night.

I returned to the Reception.

'Sorry, Sir. We have had a problem.'

'Problem? Giant cockroaches, giant rats, giant-er dry rot?' Perhaps to start with a room with a door might be a good idea; and a lock possibly?'

The Receptionist, an educated man explained ruefully that there had been a fight with a number of oil men rousting up the city on their bonuses. He would upgrade me to a Suite which turned out to be the same standard as a Spanish three-star hotel, right down to the room overlooking a building site.

Everywhere there was building going on. It was just like Dubai or Abu Dhabi...or Doha for that matter. For all the world was fighting to be lodged along the Tigris which drifted by my window, filled with milky-green water; palm trees framed the banks.

The Iraqis were, to a man, or woman, charming, polite, well-mannered and helpful, especially when they learned I was there representing investors from the United Kingdom interested in building hotels.

The chink of ice in my glass, a tonsil touch of lime wafting in front of my face, allowed me, at the same time, to study the mass of people coming and going through the lobby. The atmosphere was quite different from the Gulf States, much more professional in mood and culture and recognisably western in style. It was, one supposed, cutting edge Arabia?

My man duly arrived, not too impressed by the hotel but we had a reasonable terrace looking out over the water. I carefully explained that because of business, all other hotels were full, which pleased him as he was looking to build four hundred quality bedrooms of international five-star category in Baghdad. The locations of two sites were both outstanding, in contact with the river, the airport road and the business quarter which was being planned. But there were political overtones I had sensed even in this short time and these needed to be bottomed before I went any further.

'What is going to happen to the government here, say in five years' time?'

'Mr Newman. Now we have the Ba'ath Party, well, two at the moment but that will soon sort itself out. We will have stability.'

I was not sure what he meant by two parties, but he went on to explain there had been a split in the original Michel Aflaq Party which had been formed to bring all of the Arab States together to oust the incumbent Western Powers. Aflaq had gone and Saddam was still four years away from power, pacing himself just below the political surface. Western sources were telling me he was stirring up pressures that had every chance of breaking out within a short while and almost certainly before any of the proposed hotels were built.

I could see that by the time we began to cut the foundation trenches there might be a very real possibility of a coup and all the disruption that could mean. My client dismissed any suggestion there could be a revolution saying the men behind the Presidency were far too strong to allow this to happen. The words, *arrogance* and *misjudgement* come to mind... with the benefit of hindsight.

It is easy, with this observation to look back on my decision then to inform my Partners that any work in Iraq would have to be treated very carefully, by getting fees up front. A number of my colleagues did carry on and got their fingers very burnt. We talked around the issues but the project was slipping away from my grasp even as we talked and my lack of enthusiasm must have shown. In the end, we shook hands and agreed to remain in contact by telex. The abiding image of my visit was of an energetic and intelligent people who, twenty years later, repeated ten years after that, did not deserve the anguish and terror they received from both sides of the fighting forces.

The plane lifted off on my return journey having had fifty percent of my hotel bill deducted, and a further apology. On arrival back home I handed in a report for onward telex transmission by Rhona. The suspension from contact with anyone during an air flight, immediately after a meeting had been an excellent way in which to marshal my thoughts and commit them to paper, ever mindful of my Partners searching questions as they followed up my initial findings.

Upstairs, finally with Jay, we had supper together. We discussed the coming Christmas not far away, and her mother's arrival with the boys. There was the decision to make on who we would invite for a meal on Christmas Day. This would not be a day for business in any way, despite being a Muslim country and there were bachelors out there who would otherwise be at their homes having a quiet day on their own. There would be no Morecombe and Wise show in the evening or a James Bond film to follow, but we could all play PIT, a form of cheating as my mother-in-law was so adept at doing, and the lads could wash up for us.

The next morning saw me at Doha Airport, with its usual complicated bustle. The same immigration officer nodded at me with familiar condescension. As I had been so busy up until my departure there had not been time to check my tickets. Rhona would have done so and had provided me with a small pile of documents needed for the journey, held together with an elastic band and a typed note telling me who was meeting me and where. Inside was a briefing note on the company researched in Guildford.

Damn!

My ticket was first-class return for the flight via Hong Kong to Taipei! The Contractor had won the first round without a shot being fired. Don't get me wrong. I would enjoy flying first-class as much as anyone but it could be used in the future as a lever; as John had said to me, 'cover your backside on this one, Richard.'

'Mr Nooman? Champagne Sir.' The stewardess was Chinese and willing to be at my service. A fragrance wafted over me as if I had plunged my head into a flower shop. Her yellow silk cheongsam managed to follow the profile of a delightful figure so that as she bent towards me her bottom rose like Aphrodite from a Cyprian sea, to the gentleman sitting opposite me.

My seat was the first in the aircraft and there was no-one beside me despite the fact the plane was very full. Newspapers including the Telegraph (heaven preserve us, there was the crossword,) compounded my problems; Time Magazine and a brochure from the Contractor were included. Strange his brochure was spread out on the adjacent seat along with the other goodies, though it had no connection with China Air.

The flight was uneventful, Needless to say, no-one sat down alongside my chair. There was a calm, allowing me to think over whether I had made the right decision on Iraq. This bridged the gap until we touched down briefly in Hong Kong having flown through the dark canyon of the high-rise buildings on its approach to the airport. People were clearly going about their domestic chores on the fourteenth floor quite oblivious or, if so, unconcerned, as a rather intent Englishman peered into their living rooms as he studied their canaries.

Comfortable in my decision to advise my Partners to put Iraq on a back-burner for the time being, we took off again with more champagne and space to spread. Taiwan rose above the horizon with a formidable mountain range running down its spine. Any guide book will tell you the island, Taiwan, formally Formosa, is 245 miles long and almost 90 miles wide. The land manages to span from a tropical climate on one side to a sub-tropical climate with a number of micro-climates nestling on the other. Since the exodus of many frightened people from The Republic of China who had fled to the island in 1949, it was able to demonstrate to the world how much more effective a democracy could be at work than the Communist way of mass use of labour. Unfortunately for the mainland, direct and very close comparisons could be made with the Taiwanese at work and play. It was quite an embarrassment to Mao's nation, as if it were a permanent whitlow on the end of a very red finger.

Below me, dual carriageways swung across my view, squid arms in a trawl net; large factories vied for the shortage of available flat building sites and clearly coming into conflict with adjacent mechanised farms. Only the houses showed some sort of relationship with the original country. From the air it was impressive and had correctly earned itself the right to be a member of one of the *Asian Tiger* countries.

We landed with quite a thump but no-one seemed to notice and there were no Americans to boo the pilot. The same yellow clad stewardess came up to me and invited me forward holding up a hand to other passengers some of whom were pushing to get off the plane as soon as possible. The door opened and there was no-one else in front of me at the landing steps. It was still rare in those days to have loading bridges.

This was where the problems *really* began, I mean *Really*.

At the bottom of the steps was a large black car with a Taiwanese flag flying from a miniature chrome flagstaff on its front wheel arch. Standing awkwardly in line were two men, Little and Large seemed best as a way to sum them up quickly. Behind them stood a Chinese girl with a clipboard tucked under her stiffly held arm and what I took, correctly to be a driver. Drivers all over the world, even she-drivers, have an attitude of being slightly military in posture and indifferent to their passengers' well-being, never mind where one stood on the social ladder of importance.

Two photographers walked up the first three treads and flashed off…at me! Being the retiring type I stepped back quickly to allow the important V.I.P. to receive the attention he undoubtedly deserved.

Damn! Again! It was for me.

Unsure whether to hold a hand out to wave to my public or shield myself with my valise, I arrived uncertainly on the tarmac of Taiwan. The two Chinese gentlemen stepped forward in unison with the right foot first of course and came to quite a neat halt some two feet from my face. There was the smell of toasted sesame seed on the big one's breath. Their smiles were calculated to knock me off my feet, the big one rotund, so rotund in fact that every crease in his face had been ironed out, seemingly with a steam iron, but then, the Chinese had always been associated with efficient laundries. This did cause his eyes to disappear into deep pockets of flesh puffed up as if he were going to disappear into himself. He, bless him, seemed unaware of the fact. He was as wide as he was tall and, no doubt, he had often been mistaken for a dirigible. The other was his opposite: lined, tiny, built like a jockey and only coming up to the lower part of my shoulder.

The fat one held his hand out. 'Dung.'

'I beg your pardon?'

'Dung… my name. How do you do Sir. This is Pei. Pei, this is Mr Richard. Mr Richard, this is Alice. Alice is your interpreter and this is your driver.' The last un-named was a delightful girl even in her tight uniform and cap. She nodded briefly; probably this was as much as she was permitted to do.

'Mr Dung. These photographers. I do not want pictures of me.'

'Now, now, kind Sir. All we wish to do is to make an album of your visit and this will be placed in our Hall of honoured guests who have visited our famous factories. Please, this is the way we do things in Taiwan.'

'Welcome to Taipei,' said Pei (the two words rhyme) as he signified his wish for me to get into the car, the marque of which I had not seen before. It was later recognised to be a Cadillac – silly me for not knowing - but I was not impressed with the big lump of tin: more flash than durable I felt, and an absence of anything tasteful in its design. But, it was big!

Alice sprang to the door and would have helped me into the back seat if it had been my wish but did manage to wrap a tartan rug around my legs noticing the chill of twenty-two degrees of median temperature. One photographer took a final shot of my backside sliding into the leather upholstery and we were off to town. Chromium-capped cut-glass decanters sat snugly in leather saddles built into the back of the driver's seat. There was after shave if you wanted it and magazines were carefully placed in a rack. There was a pair of binoculars to study any bombers flying over from the main land.

You will have noticed I make no mention of Customs, Immigration or collection of luggage. The reason for this is because my luggage had come off the plane straight away and as the car had been on the apron of the airfield, it simply bypassed any and all buildings it encountered. Mr Hsien was in deep sh** ...trouble. No wonder he had taken no notes during our meeting.

Alice smiled intently at me seeking any word for translation as we drove past well-tended fields on a road the Americans would not have been ashamed of claiming to have built. (well, they did, in fact). Ahead I could see towers of the city rising up, mostly new ugly blocks. The smog lay low over the buildings and was a reminder of the traffic problem, exacerbated by the fact the island is bisected by the Tropic of Capricorn with all its humidity and monsoonal weather.

Alice and Dung pulled out a beautifully printed – and personalised - itinerary for me and began to read off the various events spread out before me. Luckily, this seemed reasonable. A visit to Head Office to meet the important people, visits also to see new buildings including naval stores and a quay and a trip to Taroko, an entire mountain of 200-million-year old marble to see how they cut the grey veined stone out of the quarries. This seemed more like it. Professional, allowing me to ask any questions I liked and ensuring it was me and me alone to make up my own mind on the Company. There would be a 25-minute flight to Hualien and the gorge, needing me to impress upon Dung that there was to be no repeat of the farce at the airport. Dung smiled behind his eyelids and nodded in complete compliance.

'Damn!'

The bloody hotel was one of the tallest buildings in Taipei. It was built like an enormous pagoda, quite out of scale with the original, ancient design, with bright red balconies framing each floor and cantilevered over the city of concrete blocks and neon signs. It is often a problem, when attempting to maintain national architectural characteristics in one's designs, to maintain the scale of its original source. Pagodas may be large in scale, but not thirty stories high and the hotel thus failed its primary test despite being located in a miniature treed parkland.

Its rating was luxury. This could be seen easily as we purred to a halt below a porte-cochere of pale grey Taroko marble with five gold stars incised into the polished stone face. Alice explained that as there was so much marble in Taiwan it was as cheap to use as any other building material and we would be seeing its production in two days' time.

Outside my room, my rather small bag materialised from nowhere. Beside the door of Burmese teak beautifully carved with rather rude men entwined with rather rude ladies, was a very high stool, (by high, I mean about five feet tall) off which a small boy leapt down as we hailed into view. Having left my three minders for an hour, so I could get cleaned up, (strange phrase, is it not?) the porter and the boy were my new companions and proceeded to conduct me into a gargantuan (my synonym finder could only come up with this comparable description, so I had to settle for it) room with a view of the rooftops of modern China. It was explained to me by the porter that the boy was mine and he would do whatever was my wish. Unsure how far this offer should be taken, we both decided that, as there was only one thing I needed to know right now, being the local time…I would ask what the local time was. Well…I couldn't think of anything else. So I did…. ask the time, that is.

My case was opened in front of me and my knickers were held up before being displayed to the world before being folded away in a drawer with my socks.

'That's fine, that's really good…. but now I would like you to go away for a while…goodbye, shoo,' my hand flailed like a combine harvester. It was time for me to be alone, to take stock, to address the porcelain and such things as businessmen do on arrival in a new country. The boy did not like being attributed to a goat but eventually got the message, having the last say as he snatched up my pyjamas and two shirts and pirouetted through the door, humming.

How would I be able to make an uncompromised report of the pros and cons of this Contractor? Imagine having to tell my Partners about the rent boy sitting outside my bedroom all night waiting for a call? Or the hotel; what about the first-class ticket?

Carefully, using both hands pressed to the frame, I opened the door a soupçon of a crack and took a peak out, then stopped breathing. The boy had brought up an ironing board and was busy placing immaculate, guard-like creases down my pyjamas. I retreated quietly and made myself take a shower, cautiously and quietly locking the door in case the boy decided he wanted to wash me. I did feel better with a clean shirt on my back having taken control of my thoughts. So it was a new, determined man who exited Room Eleven hundred and three with a determined look on my face.

An hour later my three support staff were standing almost where I left them as if they had just stood there all the while waiting for their most valuable client to emerge into the lobby. They were in earnest conversation, which halted the moment they saw me.

'We have late lunch, and then we go to Head Office.' This sounded better.

'Very good,' as confidence built in my voice. I would take control and show these Chinese, well, Taiwanese, what we are made of in Britain.

The car was waiting outside, blocking the entrance for any other cars, its flag slightly forlorn in the heat of the day while the driver made moues with her lips in the mirror. I climbed in, making room for Dung who took up most of the available space in the back seat. Pei took the front seat and Alice was next to me. I rejected the offer of a blanket.

We drove into the city, as familiar to anyone who knew Hong Kong which Jay and I had visited the previous year, with its tangle of narrow streets and neon signs hanging from every available space, filling the airspace above our heads. The coloured plastic panels stained the street level in reds and greens causing pedestrians to change colour from one to another at the same time.

The Taiwanese were well-dressed and had a purposeful air about them, performing a quick sidestep as we approached before accelerating away again on their essential tasks. The idea of eye-contact was unknown, preferring to have their internal radar working, to remove an otherwise embarrassing collision.

There were strong aromas of the same toasted sesame oil and soya in the air which tickled my nose, teasing my appetite. It had been some time since the champagne and smoked salmon 'bits' had been enjoyed on the plane; and the rare roast beef…and the mille-feuilles… though, I had to admit, the Roquefort had been a trifle salty, but was tempered by the home-made Belgian truffles….

Our car rolled to a halt outside a bland block fringed with a run of large plate glass windows. Through them I could see most of the population of Taiwan, sixteen million people, (currently 23 million in 2018) eating quantities of food. Jay had always told me to eat in a restaurant where the Chinese ate. Some logic in that, except here, everyone in this city *was* Chinese.

We entered what could only be described as a vast temple, close to the size of Ripon cathedral, well, quite big. The room echoed to the chomp of hundreds of mouths all speaking with their mouths full at the same time. There was very little in the way of sound-absorption except bodies, so the resonances were quite pronounced and brought an uncomfortable feeling of exposure and nakedness as we entered. Each table hosted at least fifteen diners with tiny children using their chopsticks with a dexterity I would never be able to match. As we approached a table at the far end of the room, a dozen men and women rose as if one, each holding their hand out in turn. I had no idea, after the first Chinese equivalents of 'Tom Dick and Harry, whose name was whose, following which they all sat down but only having made sure I was firmly in my seat. Alice sat next to me as this was going to be a meal in Mandarin (they also have their own language Taiwanese, although Mandarin is the official tongue), and explained that my new neighbours were all very high up in the company.

As we ate an outstanding meal of eleven courses, where soup came in the middle, I was studied throughout on the basis that if I had made the slightest twitch of an elbow in the direction of, say the lavatory, the entire table would have risen to attention to allow me space to achieve my need. This can be particularly difficult in this country where you are charged by the sheet when you go to a public loo and what on earth would one do if one had caught a touch of Montezuma's revenge? You can hear it, can't you? ('...two please...no... rolls please, no, no, no, <u>rolls</u>, ah, buggar, lohls.'). An early executive decision was made, not to go, and to eat carefully.

The die was cast; the balance was there, the table, thirteen to one. Although this boiled down to the fact I was king for the day they were as equally determined they would win the job.

We finished the meal, so delicious it needed someone to write it all down. There was the obligatory Peking duck but with pancakes so light and tasty that the English equivalents do not even mention a merit in my book; prawns wrapped in filo pastry and dipped in chilli sauce; mushrooms of every variety stewed in rice wine; bamboo shoots in oyster sauce; fish-flavoured eggplant; sour fish; sweet and sour fish; and crispy butterfish, octopus, pork of every variety. It went on but I would bore you with my extreme gluttony.

Sated, we left the hundreds of others still eating, as if there was no tomorrow and drove off in convoy to the Head Office buildings. The corridors were interminable, with rooms shooting off on both sides, packed with clerks sitting, spines upright – no-one slouched here - at metal tables, adding up columns of figures with these new calculators.

Phones purred and chortled continuously as a thousand staff in this one building engaged themselves in winning over the world.

There were lectures on the company's assets, profits and abilities through the translation of Alice who worked tirelessly at her job. I had a sneaking suspicion she worked for the company, despite having been told by Hsien she would be an independent. The tentacles of this enormous operation spread out throughout the world pulling in Dollars, Sterling and Deutschmarks in its rapacious and never-ending appetite for foreign currency. It had become clear they needed to be represented in that area of the world which had so much work.

For me it was rather like being invited to examine a vineyard where one vine looks exactly the same as the next, for after ten vines they all begin to merge into one giant grape-stalk.

It was all reinforced with a tour of *every* single department. *Ad* and *nauseam* spring to one's wits quite easily, having received a classical education, and learned how problems were dealt with, materials exported to sites and personnel were trained. By seven in the evening we were all beginning to wilt (well, I was), and I longed for my boy on his stool to unlock my door.

God smiled. 'Mr Richard' said Alice at last. 'We believe you may be tired. We take you back hotel now and tonight you like eat alone? Have rest so tomorrow we can leave early.'

This was what I wanted to hear. 'I like, Alice.' She smiled.

As I got to my room, my boy was still there idly swinging his legs on his stool. As soon as he saw me, his eyes lit up and he opened the door, letting me in first. He slipped in like frogspawn through your fingers despite my protestations. Laid out on the bed were my ironed pyjamas – the first time there had been any need of them since my arrival in Doha; they had been shaped into the form of a man sending semaphore! The arms were spread out as in a crucifixion scene and disappeared into the bottoms in a swirl of Chinese folds. The boy disappeared into the bathroom and I heard him rummaging about.

'Good night sir. Sweet dreams.' His training, I must say was immaculate. It was even better that he had gone for the night. In the bathroom my toothbrush had received a signal stripe along its full length and balanced on the side of the basin, only awaiting my mouth. Full, tired and evaluating just what the morning would bring I slipped between down pillows and soft sheets, ignoring supper with the air-conditioning hardly a whisper compared with my units back on the 'C' Ring Road. The first part of the night was expended in dreaming of Alice arguing with a large rabbit in a keffiyeh.

Breakfast was brought to my room by my boy, (well, what else could I call him?) Intercontinental in standard, the coffee excellent, orange juice pressed half an hour before. I showered alone and dressed in a freshly ironed shirt concerned that the material which constituted my pyjamas would not stand up to another energetic ironing. (luckily, they did…stand up to another iron that is, not standing up by themselves).

Dung, Pei, Alice and driver were in the lobby waiting for me, making me glad I was on time. One would not like to think what might happen if one were late and messed up their printed itinerary.

'Today, we go see some buildings, and, we have a surplise for you,' said Dung his raincoat wrapped rather too tightly around him. As we cleared the Porte-Cochere the reason became clear. There was fog and drizzle hanging in a leaden sky, quite normal for this time of the year, my guide book had informed me, though Alice had said the night before it would be gone by lunch.

'I do not like surprises, Mr Dung. Buildings I like, surprises are for children.' Was I to lose control so early in the morning? My words sounded like a Dickensian novel. 'The work house for you Dung, if you don't shape up.'

'Good sur-plyse,' said Pei enigmatically as if he were about to announce a new planet had been discovered on the far side of Neptune. 'We have been invited to take you to a school by the Government. Special honour for you, Sir.'

As I could not conceive of how this might implicate me in some plot, the offer was accepted.

Through the car window people hurried to work along the wet, greasy streets swarming across the crossings like swarms of ants in the Belgian Congo. The city was large, approaching three million in the down-town area, but this rose to eight million in the metropolitan ring, something akin to London. The architecture was depressingly familiar, with almost no national style to the designs at all. I could understand that the Taiwanese had needed to equip themselves in this new island of theirs and change and adapt it quickly. Panache and élan could come later when everyone had a home and a shop. It had been repeated a year earlier in Cyprus when the Turks invaded the north of the island. Following the arrival of U.N. troops, the Cypriots, south of the Nicosia line, had thrown up hotel after bad hotel, tight to the back of the beaches to bring in currency with almost no town planning to control the rampant awfulness. In time it would change as their town planners stood back from what they had created and realised modifications, well, total demolition, would be needed. One fully understood the desperate need for the Greeks to develop new income streams quickly but it was a great shame to see this lovely island smothered in bad planning.

In the meantime, our car departed from the city roads and drove south with brightening weather until we reached a new industrial site. There were several factories, all very new, all beautifully landscaped with lush tropical planting and all built by Dung's bosses. We discussed the merits of large span construction and meeting deadlines. It was this last point that surprised me. They were way ahead of anything we could achieve at the same time. 'It was all a matter of applying oneself to the ploblem', they said, 'then following up with well-trained manpower.'

I did not agree with this entirely, for concrete had to cure; sites had to be set out carefully. Pei though, was quite scathing in his attitude towards English Builders who worked to rule and unions. It stung me into reply.

'Maybe, Mr Pei, but our country does not have the reputation for collapsed buildings as yours has. If you had the regulations we have to perform to, your buildings would not fall down and your programmes would also then have to be extended.'

Seeing me slightly miffed, Dung said something in Mandarin. Pei shrank back like a cur from his master's hand

and studied the attractive variations in ground level. I smiled inwardly. Rhona would have been proud of me.

After six buildings, we repaired for lunch up in the foothills of the mountain range which ran the length of the island. The sun came out as the clouds sloped off towards mainland China. We were able to look out on an exquisite landscape of deeply rolling hills, the slopes divided into terraces, much shallower than, say those in The Oman, perhaps five metres in depth, the crops of growing rice bright, vivid green, especially where the sun caught the young plants. Small villages nestled in the hollows attached as if they had grown out of the ground. Hot sunshine and a substantial amount of rain (2,000 mm p.a.) give rise to two or three crops a year.(that is 2 metres of rain or over six feet in old money).

Abruptly, here was the real beauty of the island, well removed from the dreadful city. I could imagine what the terraces would look like when they were flooded with water for the planting season and glinting in the bright light. The hills appeared to go on forever, sustaining the ever increasing population. Taiwan was clearly a good place to live, far removed from the slog and drudge of the mainland. Yet, they were the same people with the same geological earth and the same intelligence.

We drove into a large village, more a small town, though it maintained its feel of a rural atmosphere with chickens and extremely fat sows wallowing in mud? They animated the landscape as we swung into a courtyard surrounded by a series of low concrete block buildings.

A tall gentleman with a wispy beard had heard the arrival of the car and came out to meet us. He bowed quite low, jabbering delightedly to Alice who had taken command again. He was dressed in a silk chemise of brilliant blue and a pair of baggy trousers also in silk. This was obviously the school and Dung and Pei without delay lost interest in such a thing as education. They pulled out cigarettes and leaned against the car for all the world like a couple of spivs waiting for a tip on the three-thirty.

The Head Master, for that is who he was, greeted me warmly, it felt genuine and probably he didn't have many visitors from the big city. He took me through the main door and entered a room filled with children of nine or ten years old. They were dressed in blue and white uniforms and sprang to attention as we entered, respectful yes, but curious as well. Huge brown eyes with only a slight hint of a puffed eyelid followed my passage through the room. They had been warned of my arrival and explained to them who this Englishman was; important to Taiwan. A geography lesson was in progress and there was a map of the eastern part of the globe. It showed China in all its looming bulk covering most of the oiled paper coloured in green. Most surprisingly, Taiwan was shown in the same tint. This made no sense at all. As the children sat down I asked Alice for an explanation.

'Confucius said, a long time ago, that everything goes around in circles. So, we believe that China will one day come back to us.' It was a simple but telling explanation of their belief and their hopes and aspirations bound up in their desire to be reunited one day with the mainland.

The expectant faces of the children sitting upright at their desks gazed in genuine fascination at me, images of faith and happiness. Discipline apparently was very important and morning reveille was sounded, just like the Taiwanese Contractor's men on their ladders. They had been taught not to slouch, so they remained with their backs against the seat rests, eager now to sing the song for me they had practised. It was their National Anthem, shrill perhaps, but believed in, definitely.

I stood like Henry before Agincourt (well, perhaps not quite at that level) amazed at the strengths around me, slightly humbled and wondering if we had gone wrong with our own education. Like all great powers, our time as a world power had been finite, each succeeding nation having less time to carve a niche than its predecessor. I became maudlin, not like me at all, and had to clear an annoying tickle at the back of my throat as we passed through the building and out into the blazing sunshine.

We walked for a while in the park, along a grassy lane with the mountains as a backdrop, some rearing up to seven thousand feet, approving of the view which fell away before us in rounded folds, one mounting the back of the next. Even the twitchy Pei was enchanted by the peace of the place while behind us floated the chanting of the children as they continued their geography lesson.

When it happened, it was one of those seminal moments in life one would never forget, slight as it turned out to be, an everyday occurrence to the rest. It gave a whole new meaning to 'did the ground move for you dear?'

The ground shook, noticeably.

'Earthquake,' said Alice. 'We have many here.'

There is no way that one can describe the disorientation of the mind when the one fixed, unalterable element in all of life, the stability of the ground, begins to disintegrate in a series of spasms just as if a child were being sick. Fine cracks and dust rose from the ground in front of us and two water buffalo waved their necks in disarray, their lunch of grass forgotten in their mouths,. With a shuffle and a murmur, the ground returned to its usual state of inertia and we walked back to the car. I have to admit, my heart was beating faster than normal although, out in the open we were comparatively safe, unless, of course, the ground had opened up and swallowed us whole!

That evening we met in the lobby, eight employees this time, all having agreed we had done enough building inspection. Time to eat and see Taipei. We took taxis down to a bar full of Americans. This was a rich panelled emporium but with cheap neon lighting, the two elements in direct contrast with each other though not a sign of chewing gum on the floor. We drank gins and tonic and whisky while I recounted to them, through Alice, what life would be like if they were to win a contract in the Gulf. After a second drink, Dung stretched mysteriously over to me, putting on the air of a second-hand car salesman. He was whispering.

'You like monkey brain?'

I was quite ready for this one. The barbarous habit, now banned, of placing a live monkey in a cage under a dining table which had a hole cut out for the animal's head, had been relayed to me by an ex-pat a couple of weeks before. During preparation, the chef would force the head up through the hole and slice off the brain cap like a boiled egg to expose the warm, living brain to the tender mercies of a long spoon. It is scant comfort that the monkey is fed with rice wine to make it drunk before the feast.

'No!' This time my voice cut the air in front of my host. I did not need to say any more. Dung knew it was illegal to go to such restaurants hidden out in the countryside, a dying trade which the authorities were anxious to stamp out. The brain is like tofu, I am told, not even special in taste. Why is it that China demands sharks fin, elephant ivory, rhino horn and, live monkey brain? Until these disappear from this country it cannot call itself civilised.

'Ahh, so,' he replied. 'Then we go into town, special restaurant.'

It was another outstanding meal. The Chinese, as you are well aware, eat almost anything that grows or moves, in fact, come to think of it, one cannot imagine any meat, fish, vegetable, plant or insect they are unable to convert into food. The simplest dish is made into a banquet by the addition of sesame oil, fish sauces and soya. Ginger root, garlic and fresh herbs play a large part. One can't recall (again) all of the dishes we consumed that night, brought in turn to the revolving central section but we did have kidneys in a sauce of bean thread, shredded gherkins and ginger root, fresh scallop slices with oyster sauce; cashew nuts deep-fried in honey; butterfly shrimps in rice wine; Szechuan gherkins in red hot peppers; jellyfish – I cannot remember how they were cooked), cold tossed seaweed – the list was endless. It took us almost three hours to get through the food. There was one item on the agenda to be politely by-passed: Chinese wine which turned out to be very comparable to that made by Jacques having left his Beaujolais Nouveau out in the sun for a week… without the Nouveau of course…and also the Beaujolais.

I stuck to Coca Cola.

At last we sat back, stomachs distended, without a care for the future. There was much belching to which we all contributed with considerable gusto. Nice because Jay would not let me do it at home.

Dung leaned over again. More monkeying about?

'You like girls?'

'Well, I like my wife.' She was still a girl to me. 'And, no thank you. Just bed.'

The idea of attempting to have clandestine sex with any girl even if she had been Brigitte Bardot, with my belly in its current state was laughable. Looking up I noticed the rest of the party had all craned their necks towards me, the better to hear my reply and were watching me with more than a touch of amusement. Ironic amusement, that is. This was part of the itinerary not shown on the itinerary… nor, for that matter, was the monkey brain. As Dung returned to an upright position with a rather resigned look on his face, they all smiled and turned to each other saying, in Mandarin: 'Told you so, the Blitish are so, so…. Blitish.'

Another night of ironed pyjamas preceded a fine dawn. We were up very early and taken to the local airport where we were booked onto a plane, an old DC3, redolent of the Berlin Airlift. The airport served the people of Taipei with domestic flights although on the opposite side of the runway were a number of military jets. Looking down, much of the island could be seen with its mountain range and lush, sub-tropical vegetation crawling up its backside. The flight to the east side of the island culminated in a quite disturbing situation generated by the pilot as he came over the intercom with a speech which, roughly translated was: 'Fasten your seat belts.'

The twenty-seven other passengers, at a stroke, began to stand up, holding on to each other with wobbly legs, reminding me of a London Tube coming into Oxford Circus Station at speed. The two stewardesses were obviously used to this mad scene and pushed their respected travellers back into their seats in quite a forceful manner. Like an octopus attempting to climb out of its basket, as one sat down another arose, so I was given a personal Chinese display of heads bobbing up and down from behind the seat backs, inscrutable eyes focussed and determined to be the first off the plane.

Needless to say, at least ten were still standing as we touched down, precipitating them into the nearest lap. This spectacle might have been performed also by Dung and Pei but Alice, remaining loyally with me, perhaps out of politeness, and allowed them to pantomime back into their seats.

When we landed there was no chance of me, (if it had been arranged, which it had not,) to be first off the plane. With a concerted gathering of wicker baskets, bundles and *implements* (I had no idea what any of them were so I just mention them *en passant)* they made for the only door, the dogs of war let slip, snarling at their heels. In less than a minute the cabin was empty save our own party. A solitary sweet paper drifted down in the disturbed air. It was quite evident Dung and Pei had had to constrain themselves from getting up ahead of me; Alice, more westernised, merely smiled and looked up to Buddha. I acknowledged the Captain with one of my 'friendly' nods, who too, was shaking his head at the uncontrolled departure. I smiled as though I was an expert in air safety and as if to say: 'wasn't that the most disgraceful display…ever, Captain?'

The same black car was waiting close by, evidently driven overnight to meet us. We took a two-lane road that curled up into the mountains. It dived through tunnels cut through the rock with precipitous cliffs swooping down to the *Liwu* River vertically below the car window. It was, by any modern comparisons in the world a considerable engineering feat. There were, said Alice with some pride in her voice, thirty-eight tunnels as the road climbed up to a plateau.

'This whole mountain is marble,' said Pei, 'and some granite. But we have enough marble for all the building we will ever need.

Arriving at a factory where the stone was converted into objects as diverse as chess sets and boot mud scrapers, an official came out and shook all of our hands and pulled me gently by my sleeve to where a sheet covered a block. Underneath, now exposed by a rather flamboyant movement of his arm as the sheet was plucked away, a table was revealed made entirely of polished marble. It must have weighed a ton.

'This is for you,' said Dung. Who else? I managed to ignore him completely and turned to Pei and said: 'I would like to buy one of those chess sets. Can you arrange it for me?'

'I gather, Sir, you are not pleased with the table. We have arranged to fly it to Doha for you.'

'If you do, Mr Dung, you will be obliged to tell Mr Pei and your Directors that they will never work in Qatar and

I will do my best to see you do not work in the Gulf, at least with any British Consultants.'

Long, or very long silence.

An even longer silence followed the long silence. (Dung's mind was probably churning over the word: *bluggar!).*

My chess set arrived and I paid for it, feeling rather like Tony Hancock in the scene where he buys a newspaper from a news-stand, holding up coins for the world to see. It wasn't too heavy and was going to make a good souvenir. Dung was definitely depressed and quite out of sorts. He was failing his Company.

That night I ate in the hotel and managed to read a copy of the Wall Street Times. Not such a good paper as our English equivalents but it was news. There was an article on page four about a company called Microsoft using terms such as 'Hardware and Software'. What it was all about would be for later reading but it was to be the new way forward in business. I made a note for Rhona to find out more on my return.

The next day we all stood at the airport, the photographers having finally left. I turned to Dung and Pei and thanked them for their courtesies.

'Mr Dung. You may tell your Directors that they will be invited to bid for work in Qatar. Not,' I held up my hand as it seemed as if they were going to kiss me on the lips, 'because of your hard work here in Taiwan but because, quite simply, you have a very impressive organisation and you are perfectly capable of building anything, anywhere. Tell them, please, there is no need to curry favour, (I wasn't sure of how Alice would translate that one) with British Consultants as they will always make up their own minds and decide on the merits of the case. And, if you do try, it is the quickest way to lose a contract before you even win one.'

Two very low bows followed. Alice received a kiss on the cheek from me, followed by my present to her which had been kept back in my pocket. She looked at the ground, slightly embarrassed, but was very pleased.

Doha looked good from the air. This was my home. Rather like the Great Wall of China which can be seen from space, the blue of my pool surely could be seen from a few thousand feet. And there it was, someone looking up as we came into our approach. Home for Christmas.

CHAPTER TWELVE

Bedroom Eyes and
Seven Dwarfs

It took me a while to find my bearings again. Jay had been organising Christmas, wanting to get ahead with the planning. This holiday was an important time for her and the Family and it was no less so because we were three thousand four hundred and ten miles away from Guildford. The boys were coming home after their first term away, smashing news, for despite the letters which were sent out to us regularly, it was not the same as having them here. Phone contact was not as easy as it is today, what with mobiles and Skype. Telex would be obsolete in a few years and its successor, fax, in turn would become old-fashioned. Until then we had to dial International.

Work had settled into an efficient rhythm. Harvard was being asked to build more and more complicated models led by the design teams in the U.K. spurred on by the fantastic and fanciful ideas from our prospective clients searching for even more extravagant Offices and offices.

While I had been away, the Ministry of Public Works had rung to ask me to a meeting on a new venture for them and for the country, but only after Christmas: they wanted to enjoy the holiday as well. Rhona had set up a time and date but there was no other clue as to what it might be about.

The weather had cooled while on my jaunt to the Orient and the rain – that strangest of elements - came the day after my return. It appeared from nowhere, not with a light touch to the face, but an indication of winter coming this time as it fell in a torrent while walking towards the Suq from my car. Although we had experienced that other flood, this time it felt different. One moment it was a clear road, the next it was lashing down. Falling rain is not a phrase which came to mind in Doha: perhaps God had tripped over one of his buckets? With such speed did it arrive that it set the sand on the ground in motion as the water struck the particles which leapt up; they rose so high off the kerbs they resembled a cornfield in the wind. The locals' laughed, pleased to see the rain. After the first fall, they held out their hands as if in supplication, letting it run down their faces in delight at the advent of cooler times. The heat was just as intense for them as well as us and those traders in the Suq could not afford to spend the summer months in a cool London.

As the rain eased off, the humidity turned up, demonstrating a rancid humour with a vengeance, equally forming instant sweat on my face and an oil slick under my arms; but, winter was coming; it was on the way. For the next few months we would need to turn our attention to keeping the water out of our buildings rather than the heat. I wondered if Rhona had had to climb up on a stool again?

The Suq was bustling with people, locals and ex-pats. They were stocking up for Christmas, Muslims and Christians alike, and it reminded me of school when my Jewish pals always took advantage of the holiday.

So why not enjoy the festival? The *Eid* holiday after the Ramadan fast which had finished early October this year was an excellent excuse to stuff oneself with food; this was just an extension of their holiday: all brothers together.

Jay had also organised a camping holiday in the desert once her mother returned to England. As Edna was in business she could not give up too much time gallivanting around the Middle East and ten days out at the frontier were going to be a real tester for her anyway.

I went home, wetter than a cloth that has dried a hundred glasses, but content with the anticipated cooler weather. We all needed a break from the energy-sapping heat: Taiwan had been particularly trying and Doha had had extreme temperatures this year. Time to pull out unfamiliar clothes, shoes as well, now mildewed and needing polish; even ties didn't seem so silly. And, it was almost fun trying them all on, to the expected comments such as: 'you've put on weight dear.'

During the time we had installed ourselves in the new house and office, we had had a gardener in to work on the soil which had been delivered for the front which was then seeded. With watering every day and an Englishman's attention to the green stuff we had grown a green sward by the time mother-in-law arrived. In a hardware shop we found a second-hand Atco push lawn mower the type we had lugged up and down the lawn 'being nice for mummy'. Mummy, of course, had been under a shaded tree smoking

Du Maurier and taking occasional sips at a Whisky Collins with a careful eye on the spinning blades as they removed grass like a grim reaper of corn. To find such an implement out here was extraordinary but it could have been left by some British council worker twenty years earlier. It was mine for ten bob. We hired a gardener but, being a Baluch, we could not understand his name, even when we had asked him to speak s-l-o-w-l-y. Jay had the bright (?) idea of naming him Alfred and Alfred seemed to adopt his new name with considerable ease. We introduced him to the Atco which he eyed with suspicion, sufficiently to make his red beard bristle and his even redder hair shake sideways. He had never seen anything like it in his life, for cutting grass to him was with a pair of shears and the back breaking task of shuffling forward on his haunches. He had no idea what to do so we gave him a demonstration. I stood, back straight, looking forward, chin in and gave it a push. Grass flipped up in front of me and he could see the neat swathe of shorter grass behind the machine. Carefully he approached; carefully because he had no shoes and, calloused though they might have been, he was not trusting losing ten toes to this infernal machine. He pushed the tail of his turban behind him and stood erect like I had done and hitched up his ballooning trousers. Chin was pulled in as was stomach. Gripping the handle with a slight tremor of his hands he stabbed at it tentatively like a child testing a newly set jelly with a forefinger.

Nothing happened.

He pushed again and a small amount of grass spewed forth scattering it over his legs – we had no grass box. A huge grin spread across his cracked features as his mouth opened to display at least four worn down teeth, well... three and a bit of one, whereupon he accelerated towards the far wall. On that day, Alfred fell in love with our machine and kept it beautifully oiled and clean in a shed where no-one but he was allowed to touch it, let alone use it.

The lawn was sorted and the Bougainvillea scrambled towards the light over the walls. The Oleander meanwhile decorated the approach to the front door filling the air with its perfume. Edna would be pleased with that.

Time came to be at the airport again. It was late at night, the stars hard and fast in the sky where we picked out another, the belly light of the Tri-Star dropping down towards the runway. Jay was jumping up and down with excitement, holding my hand a trifle too tightly, always a sign of exhilaration, unspoken of course, as we had both been brought up (nicely) not to show too much emotion. It just wasn't done in those days.

We watched the two boys and my mother-in-law walk across the apron, she '...*a bit stiff dears*' after the seven-hour trip. My eldest looked up and saw us waving. None of the old-fashioned modesty with them. They yelled out excitedly and Edna smiled up at her daughter with a crinkly sort of grin, slightly embarrassed at being stared at by over a thousand people.

We sorted out Customs and Immigration; there were hugs, a few tears of relief and we were into the taxi as my Datsun could not take us all with bags and Christmas presents.

'Well, here we are,' Edna said, studying everything carefully, as she would be asked for all the detail on her return to England. She planned a diary of every event so she could eventually read it out to PROBUS and the W.I., the church magazine and her mates at '*The One Bull*' on her return, so we needed to give her at least one experience a day worth writing up. This would not be too difficult.

In fact, it started about one and a half minutes after we got to the house, as she was looking out of our lounge windows on the first floor.

'Why are those men crouching down by those palm trees dear?'

'Cra-,' I was about to say but changed it to 'defecating, mother-in-law' as Jay's face moved from icy to hard.

'Quite so!' Edna decided that was not worth recording for PROBUS posterity, even if it might have been acceptable to some of the more adventurous of the Women's Institute, coming from the faith that this country was perhaps a little bit different from Bury St. Edmunds. Hers was a world of the Cathedral on Sunday, Cancer Shop on Wednesday and Guinness most days. Public lavatories were places you did not talk about except in hushed tones to one's sisters, there were four of them – 'do you want to…er…go dear? Take the opportunity?'. It was called 'spending a penny,' a hangover from the good old days of pre-decimalisation. Her son-in-law had almost used a word not to be found in Fowler's Modern English Usage, and with such aplomb, as if it were a commonplace hereabouts. The Middle East had gone to his head. No doubt it was the sun.

But it was good to see her. She had been an exceptional mother-in-law since we had been introduced to each other, me as a star-struck twenty-three-year-old, twelve years earlier, and she suspicious of this new man in her daughter's life.

'He's got bedroom eyes, dear. You had better watch him,' she had remonstrated with her daughter having been introduced to me. 'Make sure he gets you home in good time.' Good time - for what?

Thank God Jay had not taken too much of the imparted wisdom on board. Bedroom eyes. Whatever next?

The boys were in the pool five minutes after they got into the house, exclaiming it was cooler than when they had left. It was also over-flowing from the rain we had been having. Edna was taken to the guest room, almost three times the size of her own back in Bury, where she studied the air-conditioning unit with interest.

'What is that thing for?'

'That's for your cool air, dear. Not that you will need it at this time of the year. It's cold now.'

Edna had been delighting in the temperature, now one o'clock in the morning, where it would not fall below sixty-eight or so. She pressed the button lightly and the machine roared into life. She skipped back two steps as the full volume of the cooled air hit her in her perm. 'Quite so,' she repeated, turning the thing off again. Jay smiled and brought her a glass of water. 'It's been filtered Mum. Be sure to drink it.'

'Oh, I don't think I need that dear.'

'Just drink it Mum. If you get sun-stroke tomorrow, we will send you back to your Sisters.'

Edna had seen the cockroach also but pretended it did not exist. I, nevertheless, flipped it out of the room. 'Don't kill them in here mother-in-law because their sisters will come and eat it up.' She shuddered at the thought as she said goodnight.

Christmas arrived in a rush. We even had a tree, admittedly made of silver foil and green plastic but everyone was happy with the final effect. The boys had pasted coloured strips of paper together and we bought balloons from Ali bin Ali's.

Jay had been incredibly active buying a turkey shipped in, courtesy of Qantas Airlines. She had made a plum pudding and mince pies. She had to cater for quite a large party as well as my family as there would also be most of the bachelors we knew.

Christmas morning stirred itself alive without the normal accompaniment of church bells or the crunch of tyres on compressed snow. There were no fields edged by frost rime on leaf bare elms, nor a vicar resplendent in white robes with his hands crossed in front of him smiling benevolently at his flock as he anticipated a good Collection.

But we did have... the Seven Dwarfs.

We had already declared this a non-work day along with most of Qatar. Unknown to us, six bachelors and Huxley had got together, the seven of them planning a small surprise for lunch. We were upstairs putting final touches to the extended table, telling the boys to leave the crackers alone. Edna sampled the sherry, worried if it had gone off in the heat, when we heard the sound of music, or rather, singing, from below stairs from one of the offices.

In the crassness of today's political correctness, those people who prefer to be acknowledged as being p.c. would have then described the arrival of seven vertically challenged people. To me, to us all, it was the arrival of the Seven Dwarfs. (Most p.c. public may not be aware of the delightful, very old story, far older than them, centred on a girl known as Snow White).

Our bachelors plus one, tromped up the stairs, left arms holding onto the shoulder of the one ahead singing 'Heigh-Ho'. Green paper elf hats flopped over their foreheads. They brought with them, fun and a lot of laughter, as they devoured Jay's cooking and a chance to be in a Family atmosphere at Christmas. There was no snow, not even a sparkle of frost though, maybe, the glitter of the sun on the water of our pool brought a familiar brightness to our table. Having races with the Hornby Double-O made up for it all. Edna fell asleep as usual after the meal and the boys managed to place a sink plunger on her head without her knowing, which was captured on film and made immortal in an album as a fond reminder of a very good day. We felt quite ready to go back to work in the morning content we had celebrated our main Festival as well as we might have done in Plymouth.

A week later Edna had to fly back to work. She had managed to pick up a bit of a tan, with which she was delighted, and written in her diary that her daughter and son-in-law were now alcoholics by law. As she had drunk us out of whisky, the statement was a trifle rich but she had entered a world she would never have considered visiting otherwise, living, as she did, in the cloistered life in the shadow of Bury St. Edmunds Cathedral. She had been astonished that people on the same planet as her could be so different, could be so strange in their dress and use the central reservation of the main highway as a potty, seemingly the only place in the world to go for a chat.

'It makes a nice change from the Cancer shop dears.'

I told her the Romans had communal loos on Hadrian's Wall, explaining this was only an extension of the same idea. She nodded understandingly. It was amazing what ten days could do for one magnificent mother-in-law.

The boys had another week of holiday and we had arranged to camp with ten other friends at Dukkan, the location, you will remember, being the residence of the sea snake. We had borrowed a large tent from the Ministry of Public Works and one of the couples had decided they would camp in their car with their dog, a stray saluki.

When we left the house it had turned hot again, unseasonal heat which, nonetheless was welcome for the holiday, and we drove due west to an arranged site on the beach we had chosen near Dukkan. The tent was huge, an army one, and with the phalanx of Engineers and Architects we had available it only took four hours or so to put it up! (Rather too many Admirals and definitely not enough ordinary seamen). The couple who had thought that staying in their car would be a good idea now reassured each other of the sense of their judgment.

Our groundsheet was attached permanently to the walls of the tent fabricated in this way to keep any nasties at bay. Five campers were able to sleep either side with their toes facing into a narrow corridor for access.

As I loathed camping with every ventricle in my heart, I made the early decision to be at the entrance of the tent where escape could be achieved at a moment's notice to freer airs... it was all so...so up close...and personal.

The sun went down taking a deal of its heat with it and we lit a fire from drift wood off the beach. The orange and red flickers highlighted the ring of faces mesmerised by the light and the primeval mood, where the sirloins hissed and spat fat; beef sausages browned; (no, we had not got to the state of having pork sausages in Doha yet, though it was to come), and the talk settled to a murmur. Eventually the youngest members decided it was time for bed, if not for sleep, and they disappeared down to the bottom of the tent. Five minutes later most of the rest of us thought this was quite a good decision whereupon it fell to calling it in turns for the shovel. We only had one between us; this is one of the reasons why camping is not for me. I am not a prude but the thought of having to use a shovel which had been applied a few minutes earlier somewhere else, somehow diluted the memory of the Sirloin steak. When I trudged off to the merriment of my family, (horrid people), feeling like Oates going off into the wilderness: "I may be some time," was my quip before going firmly in the opposite direction to those who had boldly gone before me.

Ten people trying to undress in one tent proved impossible so it was generally accepted we sleep in our swimming costumes. Small alarums were raised, as the scorpions now began to move under the ground sheet and at least one member of the group anxiously enquired if a scorpion could sting through the sheet and thus into our unprotected flesh. Not having a clue on that point Jay provided some comfort by saying '...no not a chance.'

We settled down, each listening to nine other people turning over on unfamiliar and hard bedding. Comments such as: 'bloody pillow' were fairly common but at last, one after the other, they began to drop off, lulled by the break of waves only yards from the tent flap and the exertions of erecting the tent. It took a long time for me to nod off but, finally, all ten of us succumbed to sleep.

Although I have always slept lightly, a strange dream rose up in my mind about a man shaving me with a huge dollop of foam applied by a very hairy brush. The man's breath smelt of an armadillo's armpit which, eventually caused me to wake up if only to prevent him from spreading his halitosis through the tent.

The camel, for such it was, had wandered freely, unfettered from the Bedou's camp, finding interest in the new object on its beach. Enquiringly, it had stretched its long neck inside the flap and found a face to lick. As I opened an eye to see this enormous creature about to eat me whole, this caused me to levitate horizontally (for the second time in my life) this time to the ridge of the tent, and, in so doing, naturally, it woke my fellow campers. We shushed the animal away, (have you ever attempted doing that? –shushing a camel away at midnight that is?) and re-settled everyone with a pillow. Sand was removed from beds and Jay fixed me with one of her stares. Crushed, I fell into a dreamless sleep until we were all awoken by the second crisis of the night. Our young couple sleeping out in their car had decided that their dog could spend the night with them, albeit not in the same space they had created at the back by folding down the seat backs.

It was not their dog which caused the next trauma. It was a species of silver fox, attracted by the smell of cooked meat bones, who had conned itself below the car where it proceeded to reconnoitre the site. This woke the dog, who then attempted to get out of the locked car at a fairly frantic pace. In the darkness and chaos, the couple could not find the handle, the dog continued to bark, the fox bolted and we all woke up. At the beginning to all this I told you that camping was quite definitely not for me. Now you know why.

Winnebago's with ice machines? Yes.

But, the sun coming up on the sea, the gentle lap of the water and the chilled orange juice, 'with real bits', allowed us to return to the world with a gentle slide into Friday. Two Bedouins wandered over saying, in sign language they had lost a camel, but no-one was in the mood to help them look. We gave them a cup of tea and they left with the usual 'Go with God' attachments. The couple from the car managed to find enough sticking plaster to dress their wounds caused by their dog's claws and we removed a ton of sand from the tent.

That day was spent skin diving, floating in the limpid (good word) water and reading under canopies rigged up by the male folk. I yawned incessantly until we made off home across the desert, tanned and relaxed.

～

So many ex-pats had now decided to make this country their home, that the strength of interest in a single card placed in the window of Ali bin Ali's which asked for support for the 'Doha Players', was enormous. Never having had any experience at all of Amateur Dramatics but knowing only that they were often stricken by torment and tortured tears and yes, even tantrums, it was surprising how much interest was engendered.

Being in the Middle East was no different. *Someone* had volunteered me to be a set designer, which turned out to be a set painter as well. There was no turning back once my name had been written down on vellum or some such materiel of worth. I had been accepted into the fold.

There was amazing talent, so rich in ideas and so lateral in thought that the BBC flew out a team to film one of our productions of *Mother Goose.* When this was performed, with its ultra violet lighting in the magic wood, the Qataris, who were packing the seats, hooted in delight and joined in fully with the '*he's behind you, mate*' routine. I would have enjoyed hearing Mr Fukida shouting out with the rest of them. 'Ahhh, he behind you, ahh mate.'

So successful were these pantomimes that we were approached by the Doha Players to convert our back garden for a production of a drama, as the Players had lost their building after Christmas, to a planned development. As we did not use this portion of our land we could see no reason why we could not let them have the space for as long as they wished. Once again, all of our staff were involved in getting the borrowed seats set up in rows, Huxley took charge of building a stage (it took two days to take down so securely did he build it), changing rooms were installed behind blankets hung at a prim height from poles and the Producer, a terrifying woman but of considerable skill and experience in handling such artistic matters, strode about with a megaphone haranguing us if we stood about looking un-busy. We sold out the first eighty tickets for the first performance and the seats that night filled up early. Bottles were passed surreptitiously from ex-pat to ex-pat as there were a number of Qataris placed strategically in the front rows so they were unable to see what was going on behind them. The noise levels were high as almost everyone there knew everyone else and the evening became one of the essentials within the *Qatar season*.

There was only one flaw. As with all the best laid plans having the potential to go awry, our agenda had omitted the consideration of a single issue. Rats. As everywhere in this country, the rats had, like the ex-pats, multiplied verily, attracted to the theatre that night by the noise and crackle of crisp papers. Even as bottoms began to be placed on seats they began to scamper along the aisles between the rows of legs, squeaking in fright as they encountered a particularly large foot. The ladies spent the entire play with their legs extended in what Architects would describe as 'cantilever mode' that is, they were held out level with the waist while tucking their skirts in tightly under the thighs. It did not make the evening a relaxing one but a number of the younger women were rather pleased with the 'firm stomach lines' which developed as a result.

The time arrived all too soon for the departure of the boys again repeating the pain of separation. Jay wondered if we would ever get used to the temporary emptiness as their plane took off. The trouble with my Family was, I am told on good authority, that we had taught them to express their opinions fully and loudly, so when they were not there the house echoed forlornly to Jay's solo call of 'Dinner!' We made up for it by having friends or work colleagues over to fill the quiet spaces and to take our minds off our sons and within a week we had managed to slip back into our routines.

Like all good stories, my eyes were then opened towards another new horizon.

CHAPTER THIRTEEN

Khanjars and Martini Henrys

I was to be on the move again. The progress of the Naval Base design had got to a stage where we needed to have feedback from other Gulf States on what they were planning themselves, what boats and ships they already had and what facilities the men received. We had no idea, so my Partners felt some time put in by me in The Oman, would be very helpful for the Architects back in London and Guildford. It would enable me to send back the sort of briefs which could provide the future needs of the Qatar Navy.

The Practice arranged for access to the Omani Navy through the Royal Navy and once again it was back to work in another country, one that had always been a land of legend and fable enlarged by tales from my father who had often docked there with the Royal Navy during the war.

In some ways it was easier to come to terms with The Oman than say, Dubai, for the Ruler, His Majesty Sultan Qaboos ibn Said al-Said had had a private schooling in England followed by Sandhurst. The effect it had on him was to transform his nation, right down to the application of black and white chequered hat-bands to his police force caps.

The BAC I-II touched down in *Muttrah* having flown in directly from the sea. As we approached, an incredible range of mountains, the *Jebel Akhtar*, reared up into the sky. The Green Mountain, a sheer cliff of rock which was totally barren, rust red and dark umber, and not green at all, was forbidding and quite alien. There was not a single sign of life anywhere, not even a bird in the sky. In front of this stone shield the scenery changed dramatically. There was a lush greenness, a colour contrast to take any painter's eye into custody. It was almost a pencil line to separate the two. Just down the coast, *Muscat* is the eye of a Rhino with its horn hooking into the backside of Iran. The town lay like a pearl earring, with its two sixteenth century Portuguese forts, one either side of the entrance to the harbour. Between them, like another pearl in one of their oysters for which they were rightly famous, was the Palace of His Majesty Sultan Qaboos.

Far to its south suspended in a brown haze, the rim of the real desert could be made out where very few, other than the Bedouin, ever ventured. So vacant of life is it that it is aptly named the *Rub Al-Khali* which translates quite aptly into the Empty Quarter.

I had no appointments there.

At the smart, clean airport, there was an urgency in the air and staff were smartly dressed in recognisable uniforms not found further north. I was met by Muhammad, a man with a white curling beard and a pair of eyes stolen from a hawk. They managed to look right through me so it felt as though we were in communication by telepathy.

He wore a white full length *thawb* with a pale coffee-coloured cloak edged in gold thread. His belt of polished leather and silver thread held a magnificent, curved dagger thrust nonchalantly under the band in front of his stomach. It was a *khanjar* with its near right-angled bend in the blade and seven silver rings, all of which I felt was a bit over the top for lunch time. He was followed by a good-looking boy, a nice lad called Hussein. As a driver, he could barely reach the pedals but managed the old Buick surprisingly well, driving with considerable care. It was a far cry from some of the driving witnessed, for example, in Baghdad. Whether this was for my comfort, following an instruction from Muhammad or whether he always drove like this I don't know, but it made a change from the normal will of God attitude of so many drivers in this part of the world.

The sweep of the Corniche along the waterfront of Muttrah was an older version of the one in Doha, confirmed by the rusted state of the railings. Immediately behind the road was a line of white-painted three storey houses, each one sporting dark stained wooden balconies with fretted screens, projecting over the pavement at first floor and sometimes the second storey as well.

We passed many Omanis, all distinguishable by their beauty and I do not mean just the women. The men were tall with clipped and trimmed beards, many displayed old rifles some inlaid with silver. The rifle was a symbol of manhood showing their courage and determination. Compare this against the Health and Safety Executive in Britain today, and one gets a feel for the contrasts of the two countries.

We stopped to take *qahwa* (coffee) with a friend of Mohammed's. As our small party approached the house, we found the air full of the smell of sandalwood. Entering, a tall man in an adjoining office now rose and came through, walking quite majestically with a stick though it was not for medical reasons but a wand of office. His beard was trimmed close to his cheeks dressed in clothes similar to Muhammad. He also had a khanjar in tooled silver which definitely clashed with the modern Rolex on his wrist. He was the local *Wali*, the local senior Governor who had asked to meet me so he could get up to date with our own plans. His people would come to him with written requests for help or advice and it was his role to provide answers. He turned to me with similar hawk eyes, putting my own grey lenses to shame. The inevitable, but welcome coffee arrived brought in by a girl with henna on her hands, her dress cut in the style of a western costume woven into black and red vertical stripes.

'Mr Richard,' he stated in Oxford English, 'we have arranged, while you are here to go into the interior a small way so you can see part of our life. The Oman is old and was the richest part of the Gulf in its time and will be again. A good brother of mine, Sheikh Jassim, over in Doha has suggested you would like to do this. Muhammad will provide you with camels and the proper clothes.' This last statement was offered with a slight glimmer of a smile to his cheeks.

The kindness of my friend Jassim was overwhelming. This was a good man, a man I would like to think could be called my friend. The cardamom coffee was the best yet experienced in the Gulf and barely allowing for my three cups to run down my throat the *Wali* turned, without delay, to matters of business, running through our plans in Doha.

'We would like to do business here Sir, as well. We believe the Gulf is a good place to work.'

The man inclined his head in a half-nod. 'Here it is good but in the south, we still have many problems.'

'In *Dhofar*?'

'Yes. His Highness is gradually overcoming the rebels' issues because he likes to meet his people rather than remain sitting like a peacock in his palace all of the time. It brings him very strong support for what he needs to do in that part of our own world, but, until the land is quieter, I suggest you plan any work here in Muscat or Muttrah. You will have seen good hotels on the road from Muttrah: we need more.'

Two other Omanis who did not speak English arrived from a side door. They, like my hosts, transferred themselves to mats in the characteristic fashion of one knee crooked underneath the body, the other knee raised to support an arm. It became apparent that the only male in the room without a khanjar was me, so I guessed this dagger was part of everyday clothing, just like a tie to us. They held slim sticks which all the men in the street had been carrying. On enquiry one of the newcomers held it out.

'It's a camel-prodder,' explained Muhammad. 'They have been to the camel market.'

Of course. Ridiculous of me to have asked. Why didn't I think of that?

The *Wali* was speaking again. 'Our country is planning to build a very big naval base at *As Sib* not far north of Muscat. It will be the largest building contract ever made in the Sultanate of Oman. We will have frigates and fast patrol boats.'

My ears waggled obscenely. Work was like that. We went on to discuss Doha's requirements. Muhammad said, rather scornfully: 'Qataris do not have the same traditions of the sea as we do. Their men become seasick in these fast motor torpedo boats because they bounce across the water rather than cut through the waves.'

'I understand Muscat used to have one hundred dhows at any one time in its small port.'

'Not Dhows, Mr Richard. In The Oman, they are known as Launches.' This was a curious term for what normally described a fishing or cargo boat. A launch to me was much more like a Cutter or a motor torpedo boat.

'Our launches took trade to all parts of the known world. In the south, we produced Frankincense; we have copper in the hills, and salt. Without salt in the desert you die.'

We were getting off the point but our hosts seemed immensely proud of their traditions. In just a few hours I had become aware there was an important culture reflected in their housing, their dress and way of life. It was far more colourful than the northern Arabs with the contrary Qatari view of sweeping everything old into the sea. Here it was clear the people wanted to hang onto all of their culture and to preserve it for future generations. They might be more savvy about future tourists who would want to see such houses.

Gazing up in this house with its airy ceilings and inscriptions from the *Qur'an* cut into the wood beams, there was a philosophy, an ethos here entirely different from my home. Qatar had found oil and gas much later in life and had

fewer traditions with its people: it was soon to overtake The
Oman in its wealth and forge a new existence for itself, but,
without being too disloyal what I had seen of The Oman made
me comfortable, as if I had visited this place in another life.

The girl arrived back bringing incense and rose water
for our hands and it was clear my allotted time was up. Time
to go.

We dined that night in the Al Bustan hotel, an
Intercontinental block of clichéd Arabia but excellent food.
There were few places for businessmen to go to; the ones that
might later be described as 'boutique hotels' with a stronger
flavour of the Arab world were a few years away from being
built. We ate lamb and couscous with very fresh salads and
a fish starter of King Mackerel. I ignored the sardines which
were a speciality of the coast or so the menu declared, where
they are caught in the south in huge numbers; the left-overs
are used for fertiliser on the farms.

A smart waiter implored me to try the customary sweetmeat, one that is served in almost every house for guests.
Halva is made from ghee, brown sugar, cardamom and
honey mixed with starch. It is incredibly sweet, what mother-
in-law would have described as '…too sickly for me dear.' One
knew exactly what she meant. I tried a piece for my host's
benefit and said: '*Zain!*' (well, what else could I say?). The
bitter coffee helped to cancel the sweetness.

Muhammad explained that the tweezer-like tongs
hanging alongside some khanjars were, in fact… a pair of
tweezers. The countryside was full of thorns, and many feet
in earlier days were bare, so by carrying these tools with you
the offending splinter could be extracted before sepsis set in.

The next day we began preliminary talks with the naval representative bringing me rapidly up-to-date with their own massive plans. It dove-tailed with our own thinking in many ways, but there was a lot to learn about how the ratings would live. A ship is a ship, especially when a frigate might well end up being sold to The Oman by the Royal Navy. But these crews were very different and they had other needs.

The Mosque was a pre-requisite and a focus for life; the halal kitchens would be much simpler and the Heads (lavatories) as modest as we could make them. My notebook was almost full to overflowing ready to be turned into tape as our designers needed as much information as soon as possible.

At five in the afternoon, having missed the afternoon rest and following a fuller day than anyone around me had expected, I was offered a chance to go to the Suq, a wish which had been expressed earlier.

In the leafy square, broken pieces of limestone, ready to trip the unwary, lay scattered about the dusty ground, under very welcome shady flame trees. No-one had thought to remove these rocks to one side to keep a clear path. The sun was fretting this floor with amazing patterns running back up and across stone walls as the beams forced their way through the over-hanging palm fronds. It also settled like newly-emerged butterflies upon the gnarled brows of the old men who leant against a wall in line abreast, chatting about the past and watching the women go to shop. The same sticks as I had made comment upon, were clutched in their grimy hands though whether they had any camels to tend anymore was in doubt. More women arrived, seated on donkeys led by their men folk. The scene was biblical, reminding me of all those religious stories we had read aloud in R.I. at school. Any Victorian water-colourist traveller could have painted such a scene in absolute assurance that nothing would have changed for two thousand years, give or take the gold wrist watches.

Behind the wall was a very old Mosque with its tower only two storeys in height, the tops of its walls were crudely crenelated to declare its age and Moorish past. It was a very simple structure but this did not detract from its rightness to be here in the old city. There was no sign of any loud speakers so I had to assume the *muezzin* would mount the worn steps five times every day of his life to call the faithful to prayer using his own voice. As age grew upon him his voice must have become more and more croaky.

With the arrival of the shoppers, the colourful scenery became more intense. Orange predominated in the many cashmere shawls, filigree gold earrings with tassels also in gold were fashionable and the reds, browns and yellow weaves merged one into the next as a background to the white thawbs and embroidered caps of the men.

I studied the rifles carried by so many of the males, as fashionable, yet ordinary as the manner in which we stick an I-phone into our hand today. Looking closer, many of these rifles were Martini-Henrys', production of which ended, according to my information, in 1889. No doubt those of you who have expert information on such things as guns will advise me otherwise if I am wrong. They were well oiled, as if they were capable of firing and had been fired, and it was enough to say about their age that these were similar rifles as used in the Zulu Wars with Lt. Gonville Bromhead and Lt. John Chard aka Michael Caine and Stanley Baker.

Time for bed. It had been a full day, so I slumbered right through until my early morning call at five. The sun was orange, the sky dusty blue as if raw umber had been added to cerulean, a good enough backdrop for the camel ride scheduled for the day.

Muhammad was downstairs with two youths, each in bright orange and red chequered turbans with a free end hanging down by their ears. They shook hands and indicated a pile of clothes and pointed to the Gents cloakroom. My heart sank a trifle...well, plummeted quite a lot. Pantomime time again but this was not the Doha Players. I locked myself carefully in a cubicle and removed my clothes. The long chemise, called a *wazara*, was pulled on over my head, just like a shirt. Its colour managed to match the rustiness of my face though this could just as well have been the first stages of embarrassment. A cloak, the *bisht,* but without gold trimmings followed and a pair of flip-flops, the latter rather letting the side down. Exiting the lavatory, an ex-pat looked sideways at me, his mouth twitching in amusement – the bastard – and, in full view of the hundred odd locals in the lobby, had my turban attached with its tail, placed firmly on my head.

'Zain! Zain! Zain!'

The expression, flogged to death by now, had been borne on the wind from the north like thistledown. We walked from the lobby with all its grandeur and climbed into a Chevy truck with a plastic tank of water and two spare wheels, four rifles and a cold box of food, taking the road north to Muttrah and beyond. Eventually we turned west and headed towards the *Jebel Akhdar* where the truck moved slowly through a jumble of buildings forming a rag-taggle village.

Almost floating in the heat, the mountains reared up like bad bats' teeth with a glittering band of light in front reflected off what had to be sand. I was in the front of the truck with Muhammad, protected by air-conditioning and a sort of sand filter from the worst of the dust outside. In the back of the truck were our two companions who, assuredly knew a great deal about camels.

We must have been near to Nizwa, the wonderful and original capital. The Friday market which takes place around an ancient tree is still held each week though today we were not to see it. A few miles on we stopped at a house with a few sheds. Spare tyres lay scattered about and clay pots were piled in a heap, the sort of thing you see by the dozen in any garden centre today, the clay pots that is, not the tyres. Camels gaped at me as if I had come badly dressed to a posh party, which could easily be reciprocated, but they lost interest, preferring their meal as they chomped sideways on some awful thing they had found in the ground.

My belief, that the two lads did know a whole lot about camels was borne out by the way they went about saddling up our mounts, or were they steeds? Oman does not use the wooden camel stool as was common in the north. Here they used a frame looking like a double-vice placed on fibre pads with tight girths forward of the hump. To this they fitted a crescent-shaped pad to circle around this cradle, followed by a thick goat's wool blanket and finally on top of this a black sheepskin. I was instructed, on mounting my animal to ride it like a horse, that is with legs either side.

There was the need, however, of course, first to climb up the mountainside of smooth hair.

'And you? How do you ride it?'

They both smiled. 'You may try the Bedou fashion if you wish. We kneel on the top and keep our balance.' Muhammad translated for me.

I had ridden in England from an early stage, borrowing my sister's pony more often than not as she did not like her steed even though it was called 'Happy'. Riding a camel was certainly different, but I felt it was far safer when only five feet off the ground, rather than eight, especially as the ground here was rock hard and not like the soft green grass of home.

I felt reasonably assured that mounting such a beast (a horrid name for such a gentle looking creature: have you seen the length of their eyelashes?) would fall within my ability but balancing on top of a pile of rugs using only your knees, with much further to fall than a horse reminded me that Omar Sharif and Peter O'Toole had both been strapped onto their camels in the charge on Aquaba. Admittedly they were three sheets to the wind when they did it, but I needed some reassurance after being embarrassed in the hotel lobby.

Our mounts were in place, the camels groaned as they knelt on the ground: they knew they were off somewhere as soon as this white man prepared himself, ready to climb up with the others.

It was explained to me that I must stand behind the tail and grab hold of the wooden tree. As the camel starts to rise I had merely to swing my leg over and sit astride: naturally, this is difficult for someone dressed in a turban which was threatening to come loose. If it fell off once in the saddle, how in God's name would I stop the animal, climb down, pick it up and get back on? And put it on?

The three Omanis waited and watched. I stood by the tail (can camels kick backwards?) and took hold of the frame. My right leg swung up and over, surprising the other men and…. but the bloody camel was already rising up from somewhere behind me. It had felt my weight and that was all it needed to start getting to its feet. As I clamped my other leg to the frame, being projected simultaneously in a forward motion, the reverse happened as the front legs rose. It could have been a nasty case of whiplash if the boys had not forewarned me to hang on tight.

Triumphantly, though my turban had by now dropped over my right eye making me look like one of the local Somali pirates, I was on, and up. Clapping came from behind me, but it was not from the men but two beautiful women who, shyly, had come out to watch the fun. This was better than *The Flintstones* to them, with not a lot to do other than watch the Englishman disport himself in the many weird and wonderful means that only they, western people, are capable of. Though dressing the part had been painful there was a very real reason for doing so, attired as I was for a small part in *'Sinbad – The Production'* - it would have been much more problematic if I had tried to mount the camel in western clothes.

My camel was a female; most of them are for riding purposes in this part of Arabia: it looked round at me thoughtfully and eyed my stick even more considerately as if trying to decide if I was going to hit it hard…or just a tap. It had stopped chomping and was waiting for me to engage first gear when… Lo! We began to move in a general forward direction. I would have given a king's ransom for someone to have taken a photograph of me looking uncannily like Lawrence of Arabia although he, unlike me, had a gold wire *Agal*, in his famous picture. All it wanted was for that music to start off in the background.

The most ridiculous item I was carrying was a single shot Martini-Henry loaned to me by the uncle of Muhammad, safely tucked away in a long leather holster unlike the others who had theirs shouldered ready to shoot anything which had the temerity to pop its head over a sand dune. As there was nothing bigger than a scorpion for one hundred miles, it was going to be difficult for anyone to bring dinner back that night.

We set off up the side of an almost sheer wadi, my beast treading with exquisite skill as it made careful steps around the sharp shards of rock. To my left was a tier of terraces; I counted thirty before they blurred in my vision, each perhaps running five to six metres back to the next, though quite a few were much smaller, supported by stone walls. Crops overflowed the edges, all of it healthy looking with some terraces given over to fruit orchards of apricots. These were deeper than those in the Taroko Gorge in Taiwan. The toil to have created these crop fields must have taken centuries to create but now they provided a whole Waitrose basket of fresh vegetables and fruits to the farmer and his family..

The crops were irrigated by the *falajes,* an ancient waterway scheme of channels either cut into the side of the sheer rock or built up in stone, receiving water falling from higher underground streams which never dry up.

Through gesticulation and pidgin English, I gleaned the *falaj* was a water distribution system in which the locals have established rights over hundreds of years with the whole community responsible for their maintenance. When one passed through a village there would come the murmur and chuckle of a water course in the open, curving its way past the houses, bringing a feeling of coolness to the baking ground. In other places, the watercourse went underground, this being marked by lines of wells, cut as much as sixty feet deep, located over the waterway.

We passed a string of camels going down the slope and from each driver we received the mantra of 'Peace be upon you' to which we would reply 'And on you be peace.' (Just like my church back in Britain at half past eleven on a Sunday morning. Having, as I said earlier, read the Koran, I am aware of the many similarities between the two faiths).

My camel uttered groans stemming from the bottom of its stomach as it climbed up to the steeper levels. Eventually, we eased off as we crested a ridge and saw a considerable proportion of the Sultanate spread out below us. Out to sea were dozens of oil tankers and naval craft. Dhows or rather Launches, pottered and puttered about inshore, leaving wakes as fine as white cotton thread from this height. The heat had cooked up the air to broil the atmosphere into a milk brown colour. I had seen the effects of pollution in Mexico City and this was similar, though this time not created by the internal combustion engine. It was just wind-borne dust lifted by the sun's rays.

Muhammad directed an urgent finger towards a patch of camel thorn in flower after the rain which had fallen a few days earlier. It appears that the camel thorn grabs life as soon as it senses any moisture and does not wait for some almanac to determine when it should flower. Muhammad went on to explain there were very few areas of the thorn bush left locally, with so many people living near the terraces. In the south, whole carpets of flowers could be seen after prolonged rain: children eat the leaves, *nabag*, as sweets. I maintained a preference for a Mars Bar to chewing some dusty leaves, but the children of the village will hold them up in glee as if they were in a tuckshop.

Still on my mount, the motion of my camel had become mesmeric as we plodded in single file along the ridge. Below, small villages alongside the terraces fell away below us. Wherever the water did not fall or flow there was desiccation and parched plants. Here and there the recent rain had pooled before seeping back into the rock. This in turn produced small green shoots coiling tremulously, ready to burst into flower.

It was all so extraordinary, so hassle-free with the camels, as my companions were content to keep their own peace and pace until we reached an area where there had been a picnic before. Burnt sticks lay in a circle and sheep bones were scattered on the rock. It was surprising that the local foxes had not removed these the night after the picnic but perhaps someone else had come this way earlier.

I ordered my mount to sit down. It did not. One of the lads said something unintelligible in Arabic and it did, sit down, that is, reversing the order of the whiplash. Parking (?) my rifle against a rock I was rather conscious of the situation whereby I had no idea whether it was loaded or not but felt it would be silly to ask, so I adjusted my head gear instead to a suitably rakish angle drawing my *wazara* around me as if I had just been affected by that ice-cold bar in Alex. I felt good with life and The Oman provided everything one had come to think was 'Arab' or 'Arabian. Contrary to some hurtful 'friends' comments, I have not been paid by The Omani Tourist Board to promote their country but willing, anytime to do so. When I returned, 37 years later to a much-changed country, these elements were still there reflected in the people and the countryside.

We sat, leaning up against a cliff of shattered rock. The lads tethered our camels in a more conventional way than that of the *Agal*. This time, a rope sufficed and the animals showed no inclination to stand up and move about. I would have liked to have seen how the Arabs cobbled their mounts but any enquiry might have resulted in me being obliged to pick up the hoofs, one by one at the front end and would have had a realistic chance of green foam arriving on my neck. Being only a few feet distant I felt it politic to leave it as a study for the future.

There was a cold box with us. It now disgorged hummus, tabbouleh, lumps of cooked pink lamb and mint, buttermilk to drink and a pile of unleavened bread pouches which we warmed up on a fire. The smoke flavoured the bread with a delicious essence making this simple meal one of the most memorable of my life. I did not even fancy a beer, feeling that acting in the same manner as a Muslim out here was quite the proper thing to do. How had Lawrence felt the first time he had ridden out into the desert? It made me want to read his journals on my return to Qatar.

An ox lurched across on a lower path driven by a farmer in a pale orange shift and a dirty white turban. They were still used for ploughing in those days as the farmers found it easier to work their way through the palms which gave shade to the ground rather than resort to modern equipment which was not suited to this type of farming. I have no idea why the ox and the farmer were so high up the slopes but perhaps he was going to provide transport for a local village.

I popped a date in my mouth aware the two lads had not yet eaten but were preparing themselves for their lunch time prayers. They set their rugs up on the crest with a view all the way to Mecca and went through their ritual without any feeling of discomfort or embarrassment in front of the Westerner. I felt accepted and at peace myself: such a long way away from work and the pressures which the contracts brought each day. Not that I was complaining of my lot, but there was more than a touch of guilt at enjoying this day's holiday.

We set off down the hill, following the speeding water channels, taking in the sweet smell of the dates as they wafted up from the valley below, seeing the evidence of where the force of flash floods had swept away trees, bushes, a young goat and large boulders. Over the centuries they had cut through the igneous rocks of serpentine and basalt to create a divide which separated the west of the country from its eastern neighbour.

As we reached level ground we saw a group of men sitting in a circle on mats, all carrying out the same task of making kebabs of skewered lamb. As one man speared the cubes of meat it was passed across to the next to dip it into crushed spices. I counted about fifty of the kebabs so assumed they were being made for the market unless there was going to be a very large party here later on. Looking around at the emptiness it did not seem as if there were too many neighbours to be invited.

It all came to an end at last: *magical*, *breath-taking* and *heart-warming* were words that came to mind that day. When I strode into the hotel later on that day covered in dust, the eyes of the doorman followed me all the way to the gents' cloakrooms, uncertain as he was who the white itinerant smelling of female camel yet who boldly came from the Jebel as if he owned the place. He was reassured ten minutes later when I had replaced my thawb with western but significantly more uncomfortable clothes. They felt restricting and hot, so much so that on my return to Doha one of the first things I did was to visit the Suq to buy two cotton shifts of my own. Turning native? Well, maybe so, but only in the evening when we did not have guests to dinner.

I collected my notes and agreed to return to Muscat in three weeks' time to follow up ideas which had been sent back to Guildford. They would throw up queries in turn and these would have to be answered as soon as possible if we were to keep on track with the programme. As my plane took off for Doha and banked over *Muttrah* I could see camel tracks wending up into the hills, the terraces full of salads and the stone houses clinging to the rock faces as if they grew there.

It was an exquisite country, one that could develop a tourist market of highly profitable proportions for the country. I said goodbye sadly to my friends though reassured we would all meet again very soon.

CHAPTER FOURTEEN

A Bedouin Tent

You will recall, dear traveller, that Rhona had set up a meeting for me on my return from Taiwan. It had been arranged to have a conference with the Ministry of Public Works as soon as I returned from the Oman, anxious to get back into the saddle (no pun intended) and searching for clues, because none of the other consultants invited to the meeting had any idea what it was about either.

Looking around the room there was a representative from each of the professions but there was another man, a whiter shade of pale and just out from England. He sat slightly apart, aware he was not part of the group gathered in front of the Minister until we barged in as all ex-pats tend to do.

'Brian Newton.' The smartly dressed man shook hands rather formally. 'I work alongside the B.B.C. from time to time but I'm an independent.'

That really confused our bunch with our built-in village mentality. He was not an advance guard for next year's pantomime and he held himself somewhat remote as if he would like to be in control of whatever we were asked to do. We had earlier trooped into the large office and said our salaams. Coffee was brought and we were able to relax as I brought the Minister up to speed with what was going on in The Oman. All Arabs have a passionate interest in their neighbours: what height towers they are building; which roads are going to connect with whose; what was the Emir doing today? As always, soon after the allotted time for politeness, we turned to listen to our Paymaster.

'I have called you here today, because the Government, especially His Highness, God bless him, wants to enter upon the world stage. He wants to do this by building a Radio Station and sending out long range transmissions, messages that will proclaim Qatar is a country which can hold its own anywhere in the world. We want *Radio Qatar* to beam its message to America and the world in general.' (Although I did not know it at the time, this was to become *Al Jazeera* which would eventually channel the messages from *Al Qaeda* to the western world).

'We realise that building a radio station has its problems not least of which is the issue of security. We already have a radio transmitter as you English know all about, but this is to be something on a much more powerful scale. We want to build this out in the desert with an army barracks attached, surrounded by a fence and filled with the most modern transmitting equipment there is. We have an advisor here for that purpose,' he indicated towards Brian Newton who inclined his head towards the Minister.

'Mr Richard, we want an exciting design, the most exciting your company can provide, perhaps one that could win a competition or two. This would bring attention to the Radio Station like nothing else could.'

I was half inclined to copy the B.B.C. man in my inclination, but I had formed an early respect for this man so felt obliged to remain on my normal wavelength, (sorry).

'We have an Engineer Architect, Minister. He is what we call a lateral thinker. He links engineering to architecture so that the two are inseparable.

We did have such a man, a Pole, whose recent designs were breath-taking in their arrogance, ignoring gravity and tradition in his drive for a new form of architecture, one where architecture and engineering were indissolubly fused. Having worked with him on the Nuclear Submarine Base in Devonport – a long time ago it seemed now – I had complete confidence in the man.

This Minister sitting in front of us was known for his ability to drive things forward at an unseemly pace for conventional Arabian minds. He did not understand why marks on paper should take such a long time. I had suggested to the Partnership he be invited down for a day to Guildford in the summer which he spent in London, where he could be shown our offices before a day of eating and entertainment at the Partners' expense. They had countered with the idea that when I came over for my next holiday all Partners including myself would give him a special day with the others as the backup crew, so to speak. This could be difficult, as Jay and I had decided to take the opportunity, while overseas, to see the world, and my trip to Taiwan had excited my taste buds, literally, for further visits to the East. There was no reason to go back to Guildford where the country, surprisingly, was going through its own drought. At half the price, we could enjoy Hong Kong, Bangkok and Sri Lanka with only a few hours' travel.

We talked around the project with the Minister taking an inordinate amount of interest in the project. Apparently, our team had been appointed without a bid and we were now charged with getting on with the work. Radio Stations were not a type of building anyone at home had tried before, but I assumed the equipment would arrive in packages, be connected to a rather high aerial and the military housed in air-cooled comfort.

The site was vaguely known to me: sand dunes shrugged their way across this landscape and we could not afford for one of those to move towards our new buildings. We had to assume that the experts allocating land to this project would give us a piece of land considerably better than the sandy waste for the Steel project. While a steel rolling mill was important to the future economy of Qatar it did not have the ultimate prestige of a radio station and there could be no question of any face-saving action on such a project. It had to work and work all the time.

That evening, Rhona sent off a long telex which I followed up with a phone call. It was important to get over to John the vital need for a design of real flair yet one that would work! This was easier said than done, for Architects with panache sometimes forget what the original intention was intended to be. It made me realise that a visit to the U.K. was needed, even if not in the summer holidays, so all of our designers could be briefed on the Arab way of doing things. It could be combined with a visit to the school and I could take the boys out for a meal, hot air balloons notwithstanding.

Langdon was excited. He had always wanted to place the practice on the map with regard to design flair, in addition to answering the brief as it had been written. The two, as I have said, do not necessarily go together and it often took my office to sort out and join the two up in a workable design.

Three weeks later a tube of drawings was received from Special Mail, no delivery to the door, of course, just...special delivery! Today, they could have been sent down a line attached to an E-mail; such are the times we live in. What we did receive was a set of highly professional plans, elevations and a perspective, down to the soldier under his sun canopy guarding the new station.

It was nothing less than brilliant. It was only a draft idea, but our designer had drawn from the raw character of the country and captured the real essence of Arabia while translating this from the brief using the latest buildings materials available. He had extracted three elements: Bedouin life, the camel hair tent and the sand dune. The radio station was to be housed in a very large Bedouin tent, but this one was to be built of ribbed aluminium with an insulated skin and a coating in a dun colour. Tension cables, like ropes, kept the structure live. Almost off stage was a more conventional barracks for the military guards but in Moorish arched balconies ringed with palm trees and an oasis. Around the whole site had been wrapped an artificial sand dune shaped like a Ramadan crescent moon, built of stone. It had a purpose: to protect the site from the *Shamal* which could blow across this part of Qatar in some strength.

'Harvard!' I yelled through the doorway. Harvard ambled in, blinking through his glasses, wondering, what now? He put down a half-carved Arab no more than half an inch high. I showed him the drawings and he bent his head to the task, clearly excited.

'We could make the tent out of metal foil glued to card. Then we could rib the roof, like the real thing. 'Harvard was always quoting the royal 'we' aware nonetheless that there was no-one else in the office who could hope to help him if he were pushed.

'This is good. This is exciting.' He wandered off with the drawings. 'Harvard!' I yelled again. 'You don't know what I want yet.'

'One to fifty scale of the buildings and site, plus, one to ten details perhaps?'

'Yes, maybe. When can you do this?'

'I'll start on it tonight…no, now. Get some ideas together. Say a week to do the main model. A few soldiers loafing about the oasis, a rifle propped up here and there. What about a camel?'

'No thanks. It might detract from the main thrust.'

'Shame,' he replied.

'But what about a lift-off roof with the transmitters to scale inside.'

His eyes gleamed. 'Sure boss.'

～

It was this design which kept us out of being involved in the planning and construction of the Pan-Arab Games. That year we won commissions for a number of government buildings which stemmed from the original concept of our tents. It brought a number of valuable projects which precluded us from taking on any more projects.

Qatar had pledged to put on the next Football tournament, an issue of the most extreme importance to the host nation. The Arab nations play against each other to a background of huge excitement. They love their football no less than anyone in Europe.

The notion in those days for success was for the members of the team to be told they would each be given a rather special car if they scored, strange perhaps but as the years roll on it is odd how things have changed, as massive salaries and bonuses spur on many a European footballer to greater recognition.

A mighty crisis arose because of the shortness of time. There was no proper football stadium in Qatar at the time, no V.I.P. villas for visiting dignitaries. Roads had to be improved, flags stitched together, pavements repaired and cleaned requiring the whole of Doha to be placed on a war footing for a year. One man, I seem to remember he was a Canadian, was given the thankless, if exciting task (thankless if he failed, exciting if he succeeded) of co-ordinating the entire project and was given *carte blanche* to obtain, procure, seize and grab by any means, the wherewithal to get the buildings ready for the games. A Boeing 707 was placed at his disposal which spent many hours in the air as it flew all over the world purchasing gold taps and flag poles, search lights and sound systems. Oh…. and lots of footballs, I expect.

One of the best engineering companies in the world, highly respected in any quarter of our globe was brought in to design the stadium. Site supervisors were paid to see that no chapattis fell into the concrete, a common occurrence elsewhere, and to monitor the programme. If Khalifa Sports City were to rise from the sand in record time they had to ensure the whole shooting match would be closely co-ordinated with the Canadian and Palace advisors. It was a very tight programme which soon became frantic as things went wrong, as they always do with such compressed schedules. Disappointed at first that we had not been asked to be involved, somewhere, anywhere, we now realised we could not have spared any time and could have become harmed as so many other companies and suppliers found to their detriment. We simply did not have any more manpower to take on additional work. We could see that everything else would have had to be dropped, perhaps rightly so, to ensure the Games success.

Today, with the sophistication of computer algorithms, we are able to see the problem pinch points well ahead of when they are due to arrive and overcome the issues before they arose.

The simple structure rose up, rather like a bull ring, with shade and non-shade terraces, and four lighting towers. After a frantic year of mind-numbing expense and mental power, the work was finished, the Games opened on time and the country was able to settle back into its routine, as we deliberated on our plans for Ramadan.

Ramadan, which falls on the ninth month of the Islamic calendar began, that year in the summer bordering on autumn. These thirty days of fasting each year are triggered by the first sighting of the slightest thread of a crescent moon and thus falls earlier each year by about eleven days.. It is calculated for all parts of the world with rules even for situations such as when the moon is seen before or after sunset. Essentially, all of Qatar, with the exception of us Westerners, fast during the hours of daylight, between dawn and sunset neither eating nor drinking. Radios are banned and everything and everybody waits very patiently until the gun at sunset, as if one were in a sailing race in the Solent, to let you know you can start to feast and slake very parched throats.

Each day we would see Qataris, Yemenis, Baluchis, Iraqis and Pakistanis walking along the road as it neared evening, carrying brown paper bags of food, held in sweaty palms. Dates and pomegranates provide an immediate sugar rush before a large meal late into the night. For the more senior members of the Qatari work force, retreat into a shady place to wait out the day was an acceptable method of occupying the time through this very holy period, but for the poorest sector, those working on the roads, for example, they would continue to labour through the hours in the broiling sun with no drink, let alone food, standing in stone trenches covered in dust. It was a hard discipline to honour but it was respected throughout the country, indeed, throughout the Muslim world. The nation did, however, certainly make up for their hunger by the size of the meals they enjoyed during the night.

At the end of month-long fast, everyone rushed home to return to their roots: they felt they must be sharing the holiday with their families, which follows, this one known as *Eid-el-Fitr* (Feast of the breaking of the Fast*), the* first of two holidays. (The other is *Eid-al-Adha,* the Feast of Sacrifice).

It is, essentially a time of communication and togetherness as well as children having presents just as if it were Christmas. Presents in the form of food are given to the needy. The two religions, Islam and Christianity, have so many parallels that it is a comforting reflection on how close we really are, despite those who wish to partition us into distinct and opposing factions.

Goats are slaughtered by the hundred, the same as our turkeys being eaten at Christmas, and the sight of men carrying home a goat in their arms became a familiar sight in the town.

We would spend the day in town, greeting people with 'Eid Mubarak - Happy Eid,' and would shake people's hands and share a date or a piece of halva. For those who could afford it they would take the opportunity to fly home, planes to India and Pakistan packed to the brim for the three-day holiday.

Ramadan and Eid holidays reminded us of the passing of time, so that after three years, Ramadan had become a more important part of our calendar than Christmas or, say, Easter.

We began to work closer alongside these decent, loving people, accepting the far simpler way of life and watched in some dismay as they began to complicate theirs with the volume purchase of material goods. Over the five years, we watched the piles of flotsam and jetsam, of trinkets and trash, which eventually caused the mounds of rubbish outside their homes to grow larger.

Many Qataris would spend the summer in London, or Marbella, being unable to spend the time at their favourite haunt of the past, Beirut, where a particularly brutish war was being fought. Certainly, they kept away from the crippling heat: how sensible they were, remaining cool before bringing back the results of their gargantuan shopping sprees to fill their homes. British Airways and Gulf Air must both have achieved improved profits out of just the excess baggage charges they levied.

As more and more houses were built to satisfy the growing demand, not from the Qataris but for the ex-pats, the ratio swelled to 2 : 1 of expatriates to nationals. So in fact, we ended up building two houses for each Qatari, who then rented both of these out and moved back with his family in a third. It was self-generating madness but, of course, we all wanted a slice of the pie before someone stood back one day and said: 'Stop!'

I had to educate the Partners, Ramadan was important for us to observe. We should not press our clients during this period, for they really were not interested in putting contracts to bed, or even having a meeting. While Ramadan was in the summer it was possible for staff to go home to Guildford for a holiday, or to go east as we did. As the Fast moved back closer to the cold months it was clearly easier for our clients to maintain some sort of link with us but the will was not there and the *Insha'Allah* syndrome remained a recurrent theme. We also had to wait for the three-day holiday to end before being able to make a phone call which, combined with the fast itself made for a loss of contact with our clients of several working weeks in the year.

It was just at this time when one's mental faculties were not nearly as sharp as they were in the winter, deadened by

weeks of enervating heat, that one of our air-conditioning
units caught fire. Three Architects working closely and in
harmony with each other managed to throw water onto an
electrical fitting causing a sensational flash and a bang. For
a moment we thought we had blown the fuse in the sub-
station, but the next door neighbour's units kept humming,
and on later examination we found only one of our own fuses
was in a state of deshabillé. Smoke poured through the house
at a terrifying pace and I ordered everyone outside. It was
Huxley who reminded me that it might be difficult to get
the Fire Brigade to find us or, that by the time they did, our
drawings could be ash. So, we went back inside and tackled it
ourselves. Arab houses are built of concrete block, plaster and
terrazzo floors so apart from one's own possessions there is
only a small source of fuel for any fire. Our drawings, models
and site surveys were essential, however, and we pulled these
out into the sun while Rhona directed a hose pipe...held by
me. The fire went out quickly, leaving drips of water on the
window sills and streaks down the plaster. Within half an
hour, the sun had dried everything in sight with a rather
sorry looking air handling unit lying on Alfred's lawn giving
him some distress when he saw it later that evening. Henry
painted the wall the next day and a new unit was delivered
and fitted, so there were no excuses for the main office being
too hot.

After we cleared up, we all had a game of water polo in
the pool and pondered on just what we would have done if
the fire had got out of control. Jay suggested the Fire Brigade
could have navigated by the column of smoke we were

producing; Huxley similarly but following a line of water tankers all anxious to sell their water.

It was at this moment we realised we had twenty thousand gallons of water about ten feet three inches from the source of the fire which we had not touched during the whole episode, but, what the heck. We were there to design naval bases and Palaces not to fight fires.

CHAPTER FIFTEEN

Second Wind

Work became a massive, whirling pressure boiler. It never eased up and in some ways increased when the Americans arrived.

By this time, we had earned a good reputation for executing contracts and had become knowledgeable in the ways of constructing buildings on sand. Is it not strange to find us building in the desert on a daily basis when one of the biblical verses we learnt sitting in the bath all those years ago was all to do with not building on sand?

The sand in the desert cannot be used for mortar or concrete as it is too round and too smooth, polished by the wind action. *Railways*, *England* and *leaves on the line* gritted my teeth from time to time as I thought of it.

We needed sharp grit so the mortar could bond together and until Qatar built its own crushing plant, we had the bizarre state of affairs where Contractors would ship in coarse building sand from Britain. Desert sand is so dry it lifts in the slightest wind, driving into corners within corners, silting up wadis' and swimming pools and scouring paint and steel until all was bright. There was considerable danger of windborne sand blocking nacelles in aircraft and engines and any externally mounted machine.

And sand when you are having a picnic; now that *is* annoying! Sand on barbequed sausages is particularly off-putting, for having thought the crunch earlier might just be salt: this caused our left...or our right...or both, molars to grind down to a point. And sand in your sandals when your feet are wet! Quite awful.

Over a period of time everyone became canny to the problems and worked out ways in which they could deal with it. This could not be said of the Americans who began to arrive in force. Charming, clever but virginal, they were able to win contracts by the sheer professionalism of their presentations, using money and modern presentation techniques we just did not have. As a result of one such presentation an Architectural practice from Seattle won the competition to design the new Doha International Airport. As we had just won the design for Terminal Four at Heathrow we were naturally disappointed. We invited their team for drinks knowing that we could offer them discounted site supervision with established Architects against the very much higher costs of keeping their own men out in Doha. They needed a travelling shop of American goodies, American style homes, sidewalks clear of sand, and all things to make them feel at home. Only the oil companies were able to support such costs.

As their design progressed, they would bounce ideas off of us in the evening. Conversations would run as follows:

'Dick,' they would call me Dick, (which is not to be copied here if someone asks you who the author of this book is), 'Dick, how many pairs of automatic doors for the main entrance do you think we need?'

'None,' I would reply, enjoying the second beer they brought with them.

'None? What do you mean none? Passengers have to get into the building somehow.'

'But, they won't be able to get into your building, will they if you have automatic doors?'

'Jesus, Dick, why the hell not?'

'Because Moheim, it's Richard by the way, because after the first *Shamal*, the door mechanisms will have jammed up with tons of sand being dumped in the aluminium channels supporting the tracks. Maintenance out here is non-existent so the doors could be stalled for days. No flights, no income, naughty Yankee.'

This was followed by what is called a pregnant silence. Moheim, Jessie and big Hank would confer deeply.

'What would you suggest then, Dick?'

'I would suggest, Moheim, it's Richard by the way, that you install four or even five pairs of ordinary doors, you know, where the passenger has to push the panel and hey, presto, the panel gives way to the pressure.'

The strangest thing was they never clicked on to the fact you might be just a teeny-weeny bit penetrating (no, that is unkind, mordant might be better) which, in turn meant that I always had to extricate myself from the ensuing muddle. In the end they won as they were able to adapt their beautiful drawings to a design which was so simple and so right for its use we wondered how it was we had not thought of it ourselves.

The dialogue with Moheim continued onwards if not upwards. In the Gulf, simplicity is the key. Many locals, for example, might fly for the first time in their lives to go to, say,the *Hajj*. They are not able to read; hence signage is of no use to them, nor can they necessarily understand pictograms. They might have an enormous bundle of clothes done up in a blanket. The result is a circular object, say five feet across carried by this passenger and he is not going to be parted from his possessions, not for anything. No amount of pleading is going to speed up the check-in process. (To this riposte the American gentlemen eventually came up with the idea of having a system of check-ins where one is always moving forward in a straight line. There are no diversions at all at this stage and the traveller feels he is already at the *Hajj* where he is also surrounded, hemmed in and directed without being told what to do.)

I felt obliged to end on a magnanimous note. 'Toilets, Moheim, toilets are another problem for many travellers who are not acquainted with the use of such devices. In America, John Doe goes to the bathroom (where on God's earth did that one come from?), addresses the porcelain, zips his fly and is out in seconds. Here, it is as easy to defecate on the nice clean tiled floor as it is to go inside one of those hot, airless cubicles where you are unable to talk to your neighbour except by kneeling down very low on the floor.'

Moheim, by this time was in mild disarray, he deliberated on how his team would ever get the project off the ground. He could see I hadn't really broken into my second wind.

He also thought my office had gone seriously native. (Good point on reflection). This was the cue for our own team to suggest we meld seamlessly with theirs to sort the whole range of problems out.

We won respect from them because they learned, as did the whole of Qatar, that we had knocked down the walls of three big buildings even though they had not been finished. Henry had stuck to his guns and carried through the demolition despite the Main Contractor going through the Third Act of *La Traviata* at the idea. Our Japanese friends had managed to save face over the whole episode even if the local populace felt we had over-reacted and could have left the buildings up despite the situation where they knew the ground was unsafe. Allah's Will would always triumph: it was not possible to go against His Will so we might as well work together to achieve a solution which satisfied all parties.

∼

There was no doubt we lost work from the Qataris with their private business, such as their Palaces, as they believed their neighbours would laugh at them if they allowed us to knock their new houses into the sand, but with the Ministry of Public Works and the Ministry of Defence we gained brownie points. We were never going to win with everyone, so we might as well stick to what we knew, for at least we had the Ministry which mattered, on our side.

With work arriving from various Ministries, came a new problem. At least, it was not so much a problem as a tiresome episode which repeated itself at regular intervals.

These periods coincided curiously with the announcement of our practice winning a new contract. There would come a knock at the front door, always at night, always when it was dark, but, when we answered it no-one could be seen. The main gate would be closed, the street quiet, but on the doorstep would be a small package, neatly wrapped in the familiar style of the one good jeweller in town. As I told you earlier, it would always be a watch, always gold, always heavy, almost always a Rolex. In those days Rolex had the same cachet as Mercedes, so giving anything else might have been seen as an insult. The Contractor would always manage to make clear who the present had come from without a letter of introduction.

'We did enjoy meeting you on the island last month,' or 'we met at the Games last year and had a drink together,' wink, wink, nudge, nudge, know what I mean?

Both Jay and I each took one present in our time out in the Gulf. Both were gold watches, not the *Oyster Perpetual* currently the fashion rage as they were the size of a ship's chronometer but very nice presents all the same. They were given by a non-Sheikh with no axe to grind, no contracts to win but as a result of us providing support and help to his family when it was needed. The gesture was from the heart and we accepted for, to refuse in these circumstances would have been a serious loss of understanding by him.

There were companies whose consultants lived off the presents they received, posting it all home for future en-cashing. Our practice had a strict policy even to the extent of not taking Scotch and wine at Christmas in England and I was not about to start here just because it was a few thousand miles away. (*Sanctimonious* and *being a prat* are observed daily, here).

The other problem we had was another knock, this time at the back door of the house. This was for an entirely different reason: this would be the request for alcohol. It had to be refused for I could have been sent back home and the callers knew they were in the wrong to try. For all we knew it could have been the religious police trying it on to test our vows when we became alcoholics.

The cry of '*Mufi whisky*' was a common one, as we made sure we declared there was absolutely no Scotch in the house. This would be followed by a lift of the shoulders and much throwing down of hands, just like Colline saying goodbye to his overcoat in *La Bohème*.

We always tried to comply with Qatari law. It was, after all, their country and we needed to respect all their customs, their language where ever possible and obey their Sharia law. I have never understood why, in this country we have to bend so far to accommodate other religions. Yes, we must and should tolerate them, yes we should allow them to worship freely but, those that wish to live in this country alongside us should respect *our* way of life and our law as built up over hundreds of years. To hide behind the shield of multi-culturalism, or worse, using the faulty screen of the Human Rights Convention as an excuse is wrong in my (humble) opinion. Perhaps all Government Ministers would benefit from working overseas to see how it can work without pandering to the politically correct. And, if they had been there, as we were in the 'Seventies' they would have seen Sunni and Shia, Moslem and Jew, Iraqi and Iranian living together in harmony. So, what went wrong?

Now, that's a big one Richard.

~

At last, we came of age, and aged, in every respect of our lives. Life became a tradition and traditional. We had fashioned an annual race for ex-pats involving nationalities from all over the world. Because the sea surrounded us and dominated our lives, not least because the de-salination plant provided our water, we decided we should have an annual raft race, one of those daft, British-based ideas which developed like Topsy into a full Friday's event. As mentioned, there were so many skills between us all, that building two dozen rafts and then racing each other became not only a national honour to win but grew into an international competition where country was pitted against country. It became vital to demonstrate that one's boat, or craft as Henry liked to put it, was sleeker and more beautiful than all the other nationalities on parade.

'Zer Germans,' I remonstrated, 'zer Germans *ver, ver* strong in zer paddling; zer, sorry, les Françaises cheat all *le temps* and the Japanese always lose because they are still bowing to each other when the 'lace has started.'

The imagination which went into the design of each craft was astonishing. The Contractors of course had access to materials and power tools and the ability to build anything… beautifully, which very soon had to be controlled. It became apparent early on in the first year one or two were going to build catamarans capable of very high speeds (all entries had to be man-powered) but this did not stop them coming up with gearing to their pedal chains which drove their propellers of a very sophisticated nature. Cries of 'unfair' and 'shame' and many more insults of a far more inappropriate nature were hurled across from craft to craft. Henry, naively having agreed to be an adjudicator, found himself in the middle of a number of arguments, with one case of a duel at dawn being proposed where each side had three pieces of pitta bread each could throw in turn. I was able to slip in a few comments such as, 'do you really think you will get the next contract from us...now?' diluting down the Head Foreman's potential projects list by three hundred percent, but we were not much better. Henry was a boat builder and understood terms such as *hard chines* and knew what happened to the speed when he increased the overall length at the waterline and was a very fine boat builder in his spare time: however, we saw no reason why anyone should become aware of this fact. Our craft remained hidden until the day of the race in a lean-to built in the garden. (We were afraid our boat might be seen from a passing satellite).

Ours was a sailing craft with sail material garnered from the Suq and stitched together by one of the ladies. We knew how to rig such a craft, built as it was out of oil drums, and had it decked out in boards salvaged from a building site.

At the beginning of the first race we stood alongside our craft, tanned, muscular and handsome, and that was just the boat, ready for the off. We had to launch the boats into the water as they used to do with cars at the Le Mans race track, and take off as fast as we could go, making a circuitous route back to win the prize. Two buoys marked the course. For some reason, the basis of which has been lost conveniently in the mist of time, our boat decided to go around in a circle all by itself, but in the opposite direction to that planned over coffee a week earlier. As we drew away further and further from the other boats I was reminded of the *Bismarck which*, hit in the steering housing navigated itself in circles until finished off by our Royal Navy. We were not so much finished off as late in finishing, i.e. last, but the event was successful and repeated as an annual event. Later that day, we found out our beautiful craft's rudder had been sabotaged!

Such are English traditions created and if one were to go back today maybe someone will have invented a race of egg-rolling or cheese rolling down the sand dunes at Easter.

Maturity also meant we became involved with the Radio, forming a team known as 'The Christopher Wrens'. We thought the name was good, almost good enough, in fact, to be accepted on University Challenge and would show how clever and widely, knowledgeable Architects could be. It was a simple General Knowledge quiz show with questions thought up by an Englishman of terrifyingly high I.Q. It was the same David who had been steeped in the later Beethoven Quartets on the beach. His love of classical music became clear when, for example, at home, I would play one of the arias from *La Bohème* and omit the recitatives.

'You cannot possibly comprehend the depth of the opera, Richard, unless you play the whole thing from one end to the other.'

You get the mood of the match? The mood of the quiz? Yes, *quite* and *difficult* hover over the surface of my mind.

Thus the questions were levelled at contestants having comparable I.Q.s' with no compromise from David down to our level; more a concerted effort to show us up as *prats*. This last word is the second time it has been used but it is not Arabic, but old English, so old in fact it has had to be protected by italics.

In the first round, the team pitted against us was an English Contractor of repute. These were clever people, not the type of builder with a bare bum showing over his jeans. They were intelligent, sharp, yet amiable with it, a difficult combination to match. One was a close neighbour. But they went first and failed to answer a single question at all, remaining mute when asked, 'What happens when you mix sodium hydroxide with naphtha......?' When asked if they understood the question, as nothing being said on radio is quite boring for listeners, the answer was a muffled, 'Nah,' and the next question would then be read out to them with fear and loathing remaining in the eyes of these stalwart men.

It then came to our twirl of the dice. We were lucky in having two questions in turn which we could answer easily. It was rather unfortunate that the sensitive microphones picked up 'bloody fix, that's what it bloody is,' when it wasn't, but we were not going to let it pass.

I, being leader of my team politely said, 'It bloody isn't bloody fixed,' and our Question Master had to settle us down with some firm words. We went through to the next round and sensibly the questions were watered down. We would meet afterwards in one or other of our houses where a smorgasbord of plated food created by our wives would be ready within a very short time. The grub and beer would calm us all down to a point where we would have a good laugh about it all. Wives became used to receiving demands within a half hour of notice for nosh for twenty hungry guests and, like tea ladies for the Cricket Club, never let us down.

~

In between all this we took a holiday in Thailand and, after enjoying the nightlife of Bangkok drove around the country which is a water colourist's dream. The wind powered water mills pumping salt water up to the pans to dry out were mirrored in these fields. It must have done something for us especially, for Jay declared three months later she was pregnant with '...Number Three'. There was no facility to scan in those days and, indeed, we would not have wanted to know the sex, so all she said was: 'This one I am going to enjoy!' It did mean she would have to go home to have the baby as, being British and proud of it, and not knowing what a British Government might do in the future, wanted a full British Passport (remember what H.E. had said to us?) for the new arrival.

She eventually jetted off into the sky six weeks before it was due; the silence which followed was even more impenetrable than previous times. Jay was the kedge anchor in my life, one you never miss until the boat is drifting onto a rocky shore. Then you begin to realise her strength and her plain, practical sense as she interpreted the numerous idiocies of the Gulf into no nonsense answers. Rhona would make sure I was secure, fed and busy but, with Jay gone and the boys in school, the first floor of the house echoed mournfully to the sound of the Carpenters.

My third son was born four days before Christmas. Although I had flown home for the holiday I was not at the bedside when the new member of my family arrived. Edna phoned me, calmly in control, wanting to know a). Where was I? b). As I wasn't there, when would I be there and c). As I wasn't there but would be there...soon... perhaps I could have been there all along.

Digesting this, knowing that Jay did not really like me being around: 'let me just get on with it,' was her usual riposte particularly as I would be giving more concern and trouble to the doctor and midwife than to her. It was as well I was in Guildford and she, one hundred miles away.

The three of us arrived back in Doha together having left the boys, now growing into young men, at their school for the spring term. The land stretched below as familiar now as looking down on Plymouth Sound. Neither did the sand hold the fears of our first landing in Qatar, nor was there any need of a tutor instructing me in how to pronounce the name of the country. The bachelors had had to fend for themselves this year and Alfred was ready for his Christmas present. The aircraft landed with hardly a murmur to the air-frame causing four Americans at the back to start clapping. Why do they do this?

'We're home,' we both said to my youngest but he didn't murmur as he hadn't yet learned to talk.

It was strange getting used to the presence of a young child in the house again, always having to remember we could not leave the house without someone being there. A few weeks after our return Jay came into the house with the shopping and dropped the bags on the kitchen table. Rhona came up the stairs to ask for something and the two started chatting.

'Jesus!' said Jay. 'Daniel's still in the car!' The two women dashed down the stairs and out through the garden where Alfred was digging the flower beds. He stared as the two western ladies disappeared out to the car in a flurry of skirts.

Our son, Daniel was bathed in sweat and very red in the face. Jay picked him up and tore into the house, passing Alfred again this time in the opposite direction. He looked up to the sky, scratched his head, frowned and spat. Jay ran into the kitchen and turned the cold tap on full, thrusting him under the stream of water. Sweat disappeared, unhappy face returned to normal, and he erupted in giggles at seeing our concerned faces.

It was a timely reminder the desert can still kill; the heat of the sun should never be taken without due consideration of its ability to swell the tongue and shrivel the skin at the slightest chance. We had spent the last four years learning how to live in the extreme heat yet, as soon as our way of life was changed we seemed to forget the first precautions. My son was fine and ready to meet the next issue of living in the Middle East as a very young baby but from then on, we were much more careful in his presence. A better illustration of the dangers was a time when a Sheikh, born and bred in the desert, owned a powerful car, specially reinforced against bullets and armoured throughout. One day, driving himself, the Cadillac had a power failure. No-one could get into the car, or out, and he died of heat stroke.

It was about a week later that Jay came down to the office one afternoon saying that Daniel was showing signs of a bug, looking pale, vomiting his lunch over her shoulder and generally not being himself. We had a good Egyptian doctor in town and we took him to his surgery, explaining his symptoms.

'He's got a mild touch of Doha tummy. Probably all that hummus you feed him on.' He was quite a big boy for his age though not fat in any way, I assure you. 'Give him some *lebneh* and mashed banana. That'll fix him up to be sure.'

Jay looked at him queerly. 'What, no pills, no medicine?'

'No. This is nature's best mixture. Nothing is as good as this on the market.'

So we plied Daniel with *lebneh* from Ali bin Ali's, good honest fresh curd, the original goat's curd from Lebanon, and a fresh banana from the Suq. The cure was quite miraculous, almost like the time when our other two sons had caught sunstroke and the doctor's cure then was to administer a large (like a half crown size) pill of concentrated Vitamin C. Nothing else. That time also was a phenomenal cure. It was the same doctor. Jay had a suspicion that he carried the genes from the time when his family had preserved the corpse of Tutankhamen. His simple cures worked: how often does this happen today, being bombarded with advertisements on miracle pills and potions which fail to do what they claim?

When the boys had become slightly delirious from the sun, we were quite worried as they were both very sick from the heat directly on their backs; they were pink and burnt. After the pill, the sunburn did not cause them any discomfort and they did not burn again.

Daniel went from strength to strength as he absorbed the bugs and created the antibodies in his body. By three months he was coming with us to the Doha Club at lunch where his platinum blond hair brought considerable glee and delight to the locals. He would gurgle with pleasure when he was thrown into the pool and then *swim* down towards the bottom at the deep end quite unafraid before striking out for the surface to repeat the process all over again, his eyes always open, to all appearances unaffected by the chlorine.

One thing became more certain than anything else. Before Jay and I had agreed to come out to the Gulf we had been given dire warnings from friends on the dangers of living here. Apart from the 'wild animals' – a badger is wild – we could succumb to the dangers of dirty water, disease, robbers (Hullo? Have you seen York at lunch time on a Saturday?); we would give up everything only to be back in Guildford in a month; oh and burn to death by the sun. In fact, the most certain thing was that our decision to come to Qatar was, without reservation, the best we ever made: the best time in our lives. It strengthened our marriage, brought confidence to our children and kept us healthy. I recommend it to anyone, though perhaps going out now will never be quite the same as when we bought butter in tins and were entertained by the Ambassador on a Friday night.

CHAPTER SIXTEEN

Something Lost

It has been forty years since we came home from the Middle East. In 1980 I flew out to advise the American architectural practice on their continuing work on Doha International Airport and stayed a while. There were many funny moments flying around the world though none more than my times with Alfred and all the others in Qatar. Now in retirement, I have had time to look back and reconsider what we all gained, and lost, from those often mad days in the Seventies when the Qataris could not spend the interest on their oil income and hospitals were built side by side, just for something else to do.

What did we lose from going out there?

While I was away, the Convention on Human Rights 1977 came into being worldwide, causing most, though not all, of the world to shift slightly on its axis. Living in a benign (?) dictatorship those events were not reported to any degree, not a good idea really, so it was only when we came home we really began to understand what was happening.

Regrettably to some, I cannot agree with the way these laws have progressed. Today, Governments and even Local Authorities use the law as a shield rather than as a tool to put something manifestly wrong, to rights. It has meant crass stupidity taking precedence over the sane, rational way these problems were resolved in the past. We need sometimes just to stand back from the brink of lunacy and really ask ourselves if this is the best and only way to go. Is our only choice to place a tick in a box?

There has to be a balance in life. Hiding behind the convention of words, even if they are great words – and they can be stunning in their expression of all we should want out of life – this, maybe, is not a substitute for good governance.

I read the newspapers today and see the world is no better than it was in Doha in 1978. Today, the Emir's son who rules so sensibly has recently granted a piece of land to permit the Anglican Church to build a house of worship right in the centre of Sunni Muslim Doha. Now that is a man who is prepared to try and change the attitude of Muslims in his own country yet has never himself been voted into office. Indeed, he took over in a coup d'état from his father.

I miss the camaraderie of friends, business colleagues and even competitors who worked and played with us daily and nightly when we met at the Club or at our house and always had a good word to say. They did not complain about their lot in life, paid well, yes, but putting in the hours as well.

I miss the light of the fire on the circle of faces as we toasted the Queen for her Jubilee celebrations around a barbeque and I miss the Ambassador putting us in our place with regard to our loyalty to our country.

I miss the desert with its limitless feeling of space, its secrets and its intense loneliness. The night sky is just not the same here in England for it is often drowned out in the light from a million homes. I miss the times when I would sit, cross-legged with a local Qatari talking about his goats rather than business and when will I see again that water the colour of pure turquoise.

As a water colourist today, I try and reproduce this sea water colour with the use of viridian. Sometimes, I manage it and the warmth of the water comes flooding onto the paper. You cannot paint a sea with an exotic heat by using ultramarine or Prussian blue. When I do achieve the mood I want, I put my brush down and think about those wind towers at Wakkrah sitting on the top of the slope and of an Arab in a white thawb standing alongside with his hawk on one muscled arm and a gold Rolex on the other.

You will know by now that I see humour in every walk of life. Life for me without humour has no part to play, however bad luck has played upon one. Humour is all around us, we just have to pluck it out of the air. No matter what the pressures in life are, we must all find time, as did Alfred with his lawn-mower, and Henry with his table, to have a laugh at life. It dispels gremlins, makes children smile and ensures that the 'Next door neighbour comes and cleans the bl**** pool if he wants a bl**** swim.'

Glossary

⌒

I have highlighted certain words in this tale to give prominence to the fact they are terms transliterated straight from their Arabic pronunciation. My own articulation may not match the official intonation.

Dictionaries: they are my own pronunciation but, after five years in the Gulf, they also sound quite like the actual accent. I have listed them here so you can refer to them without searching through this journal.

Why should you want to do this, I ask myself? Perhaps so that you too can describe to someone else in words close to their original, a point I was attempting to get over in a chapter?

⌒

Agal *Ah-ghal* The rope ring placed on the head cloth to keep it in place. It is usually made of black cord wrapped made of black cord around a core of goat's wool. Smart ones can be in gold wire and formally shaped as T.E. Lawrence's picture.

Al Humdillah *Al-hum-dill-ah* Literally, 'Thank God' but used as 'Not so bad' could be better; bit of this, bit of that; you know how it goes?

Alaikum salaam *Ah-lake-um sal-aam* This is the response having had Salaam Alaikum addressed towards yourself. Means thank you nicely and you too.

Bakhsh'eesh *Back-sheesh* (We all know this one). Taking a bribe at its worse, tipping at its best.

Bisht *Bish –t* A light Omani cloak often trimmed in gold wire and light wool worn for ceremonial occasions.

Bukkrah *Book-krah* Tomorrow - *see below.

Burka *Bour –kah* An all-enveloping outer garment for Women.

Dhuhr *Durr* The Muslim call at lunch time.

Eid Mubarrak *Eed Muh-barrack* Happy Eid. Happy holiday.

Falaj *Fa-ladge* The ingenious system of irrigation in Oman.

Halumi *Hal-oomi* A soft Levantine cheese made from goats and cow's milk.

Halwa *Hal-wah* Meaning sweet, it is made from starch, eggs, sugar, ghee, cardamom, nuts and rose water then cooked for at least 2 hours.

Hummus *Huh –mus* Eaten world-wide these days, it is made from mashed chick peas, olive oil, tahini, sesame paste garlic and lemon juice.

Jellabiyah *Jell-a-bee-ah* Casual Clothing worn by men and women and can be striped often simple in its design.

Jebel *Jeh-bel* Meaning mountain but in Qatar's case a raised stony outcrop.

Khanjar *Can-jar* The ornamental Omani dress knife curved into a right-angle and tucked into the waist.

Khe fahlik? *Kay far-lick* How are you? How are you doing?

Keffiyeh *Keff-iyah* The traditional head cloth, worn under an Agal, is a square of cloth, folded and worn on the head. It is often chequered with traditional patterns.

Marhaba *Ma-ha-bah* Can mean hullo or Hi.

Majlis *Madge-lis* Official room for entertaining male guests and listening to plaintiffs.

Mufi *Muh-fy* None.

Muezzin *Moo-etz-zin* The chosen person at the mosque to call the faithful to prayer.

Nabab *Nay-bab* This is the Omani camel thorn plant whose leaves are chewed as a sweet by children.

Qahwr *Kah-wer* Coffee made with cardamom. served to all guests as a greeting.

Qur'an *Koor-an* The central religious text of Islam. The book of divine guidance and direction for man.

Salaam alaikum How are you; nice to see you; how do you do.

Shamal *Sham-ahl* Desert sand storm.

Shukran *Shoo-khran* Thank you.

Suq *Sook* The markets, either open air or enclosed.

Tabbouleh *Ta-boo-lay* Another Levantine dish consists of very finely chopped parsley, bulgar wheat, mint, tomatoes, scallions, lemon juice and seasoning, cinnamon.

Thawb *Th-ough-b* the traditional long one piece dress of the Gulf Arab often also known as a dish- dasha hanging to the ankles. It may be embroidered with a collar.

Wazara *Wah-zara* An Omani chemise which can be brightly coloured and worn under the Bisht.

Yalla! *Yah-lah* Clear off! Go away!

Zain *Zay-ne* Good!

---

* A favourite phrase was: *'Bukkrah, Insha'Allah Mahleesh'* roughly translated as 'Perhaps, maybe, tomorrow, God Willing'. (We say: 'sometime never!' Google puts it at: 'not a hope in hell, mate').

About the Author

Richard Newman is a qualified Architect and a Swiss-trained hotelier now retired twenty years from both. Over a period of 42 years he designed, ran and operated hotels world-wide before ending up as Director of  Development for an Hotel company. He has lived and worked in Qatar, Canada, the United States and Switzerland and developed hotels in many countries.

Richard retired in 2001 to get as far away from hotels as he could and dug out his water colour brushes which had been put away since his time at the Bartlett in London where he learned to draw and paint at the Slade as part of his architectural training.

There is another side to his life: that of writing; writing novels, short stories, anything in fact where pen can be put to paper He has three novels published: *'The Crown of Martyrdom'* based on the life of Ludwig van Beethoven, *'The Horse that Screamed'* following the lives of three people in the lead up to the bombing of Guernica in the Spanish Civil War. The third is *'The Potato Eaters'* and is about madness and post-holocaust trauma on the waterfront of 1950's Amsterdam. His book, *A Nun's Story* reached the Sunday Times Best seller list in paperback and his current book *Veronica's Bird* is currently doing the rounds.

He is amazingly happily married with three sons who all live close-by and three delightful daughters-in-law and five grand-children. Books, music, gardening are his other loves in life and, if you can find a more contented man, he would like to meet him.

Lightning Source UK Ltd.
Milton Keynes UK
UKHW021826080621
385144UK00005B/144